SELECTED CRITICISM

Poetry and Prose

BOOKS BY LOUISE BOGAN

Body of This Death
Dark Summer
The Sleeping Fury
Poems and New Poems
Achievement in American Poetry: 1900–1950
Collected Poems: 1923–53
Selected Criticism: Poetry and Prose

THE NOONDAY PRESS

NEW YORK

Louise Bogan

Selected Criticism

PROSE

POETRY

1 9 5 5

TO MAIDIE ALEXANDER
daughter and friend

§ Contents

In the 1920's, the editors of the weekly journals which flourished at the time encouraged young poets to write book reviews. This encouragement was fortunate in the case of many young writers, including myself. Adherence to journalist rules and standards—a definite point clearly made, a set number of words, and a deadline—helped the apprentice to recognize and beware of the more tiresome attributes of amateur writing; and the young poet soon learned that one of the main requirements of good prose is its lack of "poetic" tone and texture. My first book of poems was published in the autumn of 1923; my first book review appeared in *The New Republic* in the summer of 1924. From that time on I have written criticism with fair regularity, and the present collection is the selected result.

I began contributing verse criticism to *The New Yorker* in 1931, at first in the form of "omnibus" reviews which covered the year's books at six-month intervals. From 1937, my *New Yorker* reviews have appeared as a regular sub-department of "Books," under the heading "Verse," and have run to five or six a year, not including short notices. Here the encouragement of the late Harold Ross, editor of *The New Yorker,* though often tacit, was unfailing; and I have also been able to count on the active help and interest of Katharine S. White and the magazine's present editor, William Shawn. I am happy to acknowledge and to thank other editors who have given me generous opportunity and counsel, over the years: the late Harriet Monroe, founder and editor of *Poetry: A Magazine of Verse;* Morton Dauwen Zabel, who later edited *Poetry* for some years; Margaret Marshall, whose literary editorship of *The Nation* held to high standards; and Edmund Wilson, before, during, and after his association with *The New Republic.*

The arrangement is roughly chronological and material from different sources has sometimes been grouped under one heading. "Modernism in American Literature," which is out of chronological series, I have placed at the beginning to serve as a general introduction.

I wish to thank The Macmillan Company for permission to quote extensively from the poetry and prose of William Butler Yeats.

SELECTED CRITICISM

Poetry and Prose

§ *Modernism in American Literature*

Contemporary sensibilities, if suddenly transported into the physical world of 1900, would experience a sense of oppression and a queer kind of emptiness and freedom. To transport the reader into the full atmosphere of this world was a major concern of Joyce. The action of *Ulysses* takes place during a single day in 1905, in what, in all practical senses, was then a provincial city in a dependency of the British Empire. We receive from the pages of *Ulysses*—from its special combination of naturalism and impressionism—a distilled sense of actuality: a sense of untoward squalor and specialized glitter; a sad and ugly pathos and an outmoded and naive gaiety; a sense of the hidden massiveness of institutions opposed to an extreme particularization of individuals. Newspapers, advertisements, and popular entertainment are at an awkward professional level; a surface gentility coats the basic density of peasant character. Basic decoration and design, from clothes to the façades of buildings and the vehicles in the street, are heavy and pretentious, when not silly and flaccid. Colors are dark or muddied: mustard brown and magenta. There is a pervasive smell of beer, horses, and human sweat. It is a period without outlet; a time when sensitive characters are forced to dream or drink their way out of reality; or indulge in impossible plans of personal ambition and social "rise." It is a period from which one returns oppressed and exhausted, as though released from a trap, to even the contemporary scene and its dangerous machines.

The sense of psychic bafflement and of aesthetic barrenness, at the beginning of the twentieth century, varied in terms of place. It would be felt less definitely in what were once known as "European capitals"; in Paris perhaps least of all; heavily in the British Isles; and heaviest in America. But in the European area, in Britain, and in the United States—three areas which we must keep distinctly separated from the beginning of this discussion—we are faced with the same impression of a provisional, scattered, and shallow culture, as opposed to a culture centered, enlightened, and profound.

In literature "life" has not yet been thoroughly examined on the realistic level; "both sides" have not been clearly seen or dramatically juxtaposed (in spite of the punctual appearance—and prompt suppression—of *Sister Carrie* in 1900). And although the vision of certain poets has already penetrated to the submerged recesses of human consciousness, these findings for the most part have gone unnoticed, or have been only partially understood, when perceived. Hopkins still remains encysted in his generation, as Emily Dickinson in hers. The English aesthetic movement, after the Wilde trial, has been driven underground. Fragmentary insights, broken examples of self-knowledge, are about to surface and to merge; and the time is almost at hand when the true operations of the imagination and of the despised instinctual life of man will be laid bare. The arts' progressive exploration and dissolution of binding reality have already found—in the nineteenth century's latest years—altogether unforeseen support in philosophy (Bergson), in the science of medical psychology (Charcot and Freud), and in "ethnology" (James Frazer, Frobenius, and others). Meanwhile in England, in America, and even in the more enlightened centers of Europe, the weaker members of an entire creative generation have perished from what we now can only consider as a kind of psychic polar cold.

The *fin de siècle* generation of artists was the last forced to live in an almost total psychic darkness, completely deprived of those secular insights which were soon to reinforce the insights of religion at its most spiritual and "mystic" level. The Catholic church had given succor to sensitive natures oppressed by the sense of human imperfectibility, through its doctrine of redemption, from Baudelaire on. And the late nineteenth century was crowded with various reformist techniques, all, however, directed toward institutions and not toward the individual. The sensitive individual was baffled by what seemed to be a complete outer block of thought and opinion, composed of harsh determinist doctrines, bourgeois "optimism" and complacency, as well as by a complete ignorance of the inner reasons for his often compulsive conduct. Instinctively, to ease the burden of talent superimposed upon a base of active suffering, poets and artists shifted their talents over into their lives, thus exteriorizing the symptoms which pointed not only to their own spiritual ills but to the hypocrisy of the society in which they found themselves.

It is now quite evident that this generation—so misunderstood and so generally maligned during and after its lifetime—actually discovered and put into operation the methods by which their successors, with more exact knowledge at their command, made a final and successful breakthrough from minor to major art. These methods were then few, and they remain practically unaugmented after a half-century of "experiment" and "decompression." They are classically oblique methods which have always proved effective when art's frontal attacks have failed. They are the methods of wit—irony, satire, parody, outright ridicule, and caricature; the methods of sensitive naturalism, of "feeling out" the way toward centers of crude but refreshing natural vitality, and of subsequently appreciating them; the methods of assimilation, usually of the features of a foreign culture more aware and "advanced" than one's own; and the methods of dissolution of reality through imaginative means, in the small but usable frames of fantasy and the lyric approach. As we contemplate these methods our understanding of many puzzling conjunctions of talent becomes clear: the side-by-side existence and simultaneous functioning of Max Beerbohm and Thomas Hardy; of E. M. Forster and A. E. Housman; of Samuel Butler and the "late" Henry James; of Ernest Dowson and William Butler Yeats; of Synge and Dreiser; of Francis Thompson and Oscar Wilde.

Thus we see in England, as the twentieth century begins, the minor arts taking up not only the tasks proper to them, but the tasks which the major arts, bloated with the Victorian ethos, had refused. Music comes back to England in the form of the satiric *opéra bouffe* (Gilbert and Sullivan). Caricature tells the truth in posters and book illustration, where the art of the official *salons* is silent. Light (and even nonsense) verse can afford to deal with contemporary matters at a time when the "official" poets are still concerned with their poetic "charades" (Hopkins' word, applied to Browning). And when after a century of "ruling taste" a raft of objects threatened to smother the very public for which they were designed, and when the expression of open eroticism is banned on all sides, Beardsley, with his sinister rococo line, shows up every detail of that taste—basic textures as well as superimposed pattern, plush and ormolu as well as quilting, puff, tassel, and gilded distortion—and fills this surrounding *décor* with creatures openly embodying a fantastic, perverse, and deliquescent eroticism, whose disabused eyes look out on a sort of dressmakers' and upholsterers' hell. This is the terror of the end-of-the-century vision at its highest point; and this sort of vision could not be driven underground, we now realize, entirely, or for long.

Beyond that movement's debacle it is now possible to distinguish its influence on those "modern masters" who were either directly concerned in it or were able to derive from its existence both nutriment and direction: Yeats, co-founder with Lionel Johnson and Arthur Symons of the Rhymers' Club; Joyce, provincial imitator and student of aesthetic attitudes and means not only in England but in Europe as a whole; Rilke, who directly modeled himself on *fin de siècle* lines; Proust, translator of Ruskin; Gide, friend of Wilde before his downfall and his benefactor thereafter; Eliot, who discovered Laforgue through Arthur Symons' *The Symbolist Movement in Literature* (1899); and Ezra Pound. *

Because literature since 1900 is, in fact, only a fantasia

* "[Influences of the '90's] linger in some of Pound's later works more as an emotional attitude than in the technique of versification; the shades of Dowson, Lionel Johnson and Fiona flit about." (T. S. Eliot, Introduction to *Selected Poems of Ezra Pound* [London: Faber and Gwyer, 1928], p. ix.)

on a few themes that nineteenth-century France stated early and, in many instances, actually pushed at once to aesthetic and moral conclusions, it is not entirely paradoxical to linger in the former century while ostensibly dealing with the literature of the latter. Flaubert and Baudelaire, at the nineteenth century's midpoint (1856 and 1857), have already, with *Madame Bovary* and *Les Fleurs du Mal,* charted the direction of modern prose and poetry: toward "innerness," poetic naturalism, the direct examination of the contemporary scene; toward the breaking of frames, "mobility, plasticity, inventiveness." *

The whole tempo and coloring of even the earliest decades of that extraordinary hundred years signals the human and aesthetic drives which we now feel to be our own with such purity and simplicity that it is a pleasure —if we take care to avoid any sentimental nostalgia—to trace our way backward toward certain clearly marked beginnings. Here is our passion for speed, early announcing itself in madcap scherzos, galops, waltzes, and polkas. And here are mankind's ultimate pre-machine record-making and record-breaking means of locomotion: the clipper ship and the thoroughbred horse. Here is our rage for uncanny and tremendous technical virtuosity, showing up in musical performance (Chopin, Liszt, Paganini); our still unassuaged Romantic passion for the ultimate in human feeling—melancholy and rapture (culminating in *Tristan,* finished in 1859). And here is a passion for the all-embracing art structure (the *Gesamtkunstwerk*), the impulse behind which we can recognize; and finally, here is the yearning for the all-embracing Infinite ("l'Azur!").

* Terms applied to the modern novel by Albert Thibaudet, *Histoire de la littérature française* (Paris: Stock, 1936), p. 534.

"Il me semblait que cette musique était *la mienne,* et je la reconnaissais comme tout homme reconnaît les choses qu'il est destiné à aimer." *

It is in these words that Baudelaire expresses his emotion on hearing the first presentation of a complete Wagner opera. And it is at this point that we find the key to Symbolism in the leitmotiv; at this moment when the arts begin to wash over their set boundaries, and to dissolve, even as they begin to mingle. For it is not, as things turn out, to be the logical, the philosophical side of Wagner and his all-embracing musical drama which is to survive as a permanent influence into our day, but the purely musical shimmer and whisper of the Rhine and of the forest which exist at this music's heart. Baudelaire's sensitive instinct at once recognized the importance of both the new sounds and the myth around which they were disposed; the crucially important myth which, in the following century, was to become indeed "cosmopolitan."

This merging of music, poetry, and mythical material took place in the period when French thought, in reaction to the excesses of Romanticism, and in competition with the "successes" of science, was beginning to rigidify into the historical determinism of Taine and Renan. This French determinism was more firmly based historically, more highly organized intellectually, and more emotionally disabused than the amalgam of hope, speculation, despair, and aspiration—replete with sentimental compromises and imperfect logical syntheses—which characterized the intellectual climate of Victorian England. Moreover, its sheer weight of authority was par-

* Quoted from Baudelaire's *Richard Wagner et Tannhäuser à Paris* (1861) in Margaret Gilman, *Baudelaire the Critic* (New York: Columbia University Press, 1943), p. 182.

alyzing, since its dissemination throughout the educated levels of French society was assured by the central and unquestioned authority of the *lycée* and the Sorbonne. The defeat of 1870 intensified determinism's latent pessimism; and it is this gloomy fixity of form and idea against which Rimbaud, Corbière, and Lautréamont reacted with violence; which Laforgue mocked with his irony; to which the Parnassians—in part—succumbed; and which Mallarmé finally resisted with centered calm.

Baudelaire brushes against the living Wagner (the exchanged letters express mutual esteem); Mallarmé touches Wagner through Villiers de l'Isle-Adam, who had known him. The example of Wagnerian music aids Mallarmé to break out from "the cold logic of the page"; and Mallarmé transferred at least the intensity of Wagner's claims for the hegemony of music to his own theory of poetry's transcendent power. The Symbolist revolt brought into French literature, which up to that time had operated more or less *en bloc,* and into modern literature at large from that time on, a permanent *avant-gardism.*

The Romantic and Parnassian revolutions had as their objectives conquest and organization, and a stable condition of poetry—liberty, but liberty within limits. But Symbolism habituated literature to the idea of an indefinite revolution —to an artistic *blanquisme,* to youth's right and duty to jostle the preceding generation while rushing toward an absolute . . . Literature divided itself into normal literature and literature of the advance guard . . . The Symbolist revolution—the last up to now—is perhaps the absolute last, because it incorporated the motif of chronic revolution into literature's normal state.*

* Thibaudet, *op. cit.,* p. 485.

The tenets of this "permanent revolution" have profoundly affected all "new writing," in prose and verse, in our time.

Symbolism ran concurrently in France with the development of Impressionist painting—another breakthrough from formal means to a new refreshment of color and light. The nineteenth century ends with all the arts turned toward the extreme nuance; the actual world is progressively "etherialized" by the arts so that it approaches ever more closely to the outcast world of the ideal and the dream. Poetry has already felt the vitality of the music hall and the popular song through Laforgue, Rimbaud, and Verlaine; the pitch is lowered and becomes more casual and ironic; the neck of rhetoric has been wrung. And now the European nationalist schools of music, themselves strongly infiltrated with folk song, begin to draw together into what will become an "international style." French music itself, under Debussy's mastership, becomes Symbolist and even pre-Raphaelite; Debussy, Mallarmé's close friend, writes a cantata based on "The Blessed Damozel," and a prelude based on "L'Après-midi d'un faune." He will go on to Symbolist opera; and *Pelléas et Mélisande* will entrance Parisian audiences in 1902.

Debussy's music and Symbolist poetry were to widen and deepen immeasurably both form and sensibility. "Causal relationship" in music (the sonata form, harmonic progression) was breaking down, to give way to a music

made up of chords of the 9th, the 11th and 13th—which, incapable of merging, create instead a vibrating, oscillating, glimmering sound complex, trembling and nervous. It was no longer the full chords, the massed sonorities of the full orchestra that interested the impressionist composer, but

the soft muted sonorities produced by handling [the enormous post-Wagnerian orchestra] with the utmost delicacy.
The mighty trombones and stentorian trumpets are muted,
the shrill wood-winds . . . used in their lower registers;
the strings are divided into many parts . . . the ear-shat-
tering trumpets are lightly touched on edge, kettle-drums
and snare-drums . . . discreetly muffled, and the whole is
drenched with a silvery confetti of harp, celesta and Glock-
enspiel, with the tam-tam faintly rumbling in the distance
. . . and this orchestration . . . now takes the place of
thematic construction. We stand here at the frontiers of
logical consciousness. *

This spectacle of the arts breaking through into a
kind of dissolving beauty, at very nearly the same moment, and *in accordance with the same principles,* is
striking enough. The fact that they should soon have
their reinforcing philosophy, history (through anthropology), and psychology, in spite of every determinist
pressure, seems to adumbrate a kind of poetic justice.
Modern twentieth-century literature is so closely allied
to its contingent and sister arts that it can no longer be
detached from them, for separate examination. And not
only is this interpenetration to continue, but it is to be
accented by every new force which enters the situation:
the discovery of African primitives (1905); *Fauvism* in
painting (1905); the Russian ballet under Diaghilev's
direction (Paris and London, 1909); Stravinsky's music;
Post-Impressionism, and so on. These later influences, it
will be noted, are either of a true primitive or a true
"expressionist" nature, either in a pure form or the-
atricalized. After 1918, both in Europe and America,
nineteenth-century Impressionism can collide and be

* Paul H. Lang, *Music in Western Civilization* (New York: Norton,
1941), p. 1019.

strengthened by savage and anarchic, violent and in-
transigent crosscurrents. For the air has been cleared;
truth has been told and insight gained, and by the arts
themselves, on their own ground and according to their
own means, not because of the 1914 war, but well in advance of, and in spite of, it.

It is impossible, here, to indicate in any but the brief-
est way the change-over in America from a largely provincial and repressive climate—social, aesthetic, intellectual, and moral—to a situation of far more buoyancy,
enlightenment, and openness. American culture, in
1900, in the words of Frank Lloyd Wright, was "a life
by imitation . . . spread wide and thin over the vast
surface of a continent." For American writers of the
time, it was not at all a question of dissolving reality,
but one of actually seeing and apprehending; of finding
means directly to grasp and express contemporary life.
The population at large, after the Cuban war, was
openly and naively infatuated with power. New "pub-
lics" were forming. In the suburbs of the cities and in
city "flats" a new skittishness was beginning to be added
to the country's rural and Puritan core. A taste for diversion, for "news," for scandal, was fed by the "yellow
press"; and entertainers were already replacing crowned
heads as idols and objects of interest. The coarser strains
of American humor were dying out, to be replaced by
sentiment in fiction and in "magazine verse."

It was during this gimcrack era (with its undercur-
rents of violence) of gilt wicker furniture, hand-painted
china, lace curtains, and "sofa cushions" that American
realism, after a long series of false and partial starts,
finally broke through. Three brutal titles announce its
appearance in the novel: *Maggie: A Girl of the Streets*
(1892), *McTeague* (1899), and *Sister Carrie* (1900). And

we must at once add to these fiction titles the title of a book of poems in which the truth concerning American outcasts and misfits—tragic victims of personal and social ignorance and frustration—was told in purely poetic terms: *The Children of the Night,* by E. A. Robinson (1897).

Robinson wrote his early poems in a decaying New England backwater. He was to leave his native scene, in which he had experienced American spiritual forlornness to the full, to become for many years, in New York, a member of one of the "Bohemias" that had begun to form on the shadier fringes of many American cities. These Bohemias, at their beginning, absorbed the defeated and the peculiar, the sensitive and the vicious alike. The reporter and the journalist—"the newspaperman"—were a part of this nexus, along with the socialist, the anarchist, the criminal, the poet, and the painter. Here in the back rooms of saloons, in cheap cafés, in shabby lodgings, a kind of urban hedge-schoolmastering went on: an exchange of ideas, enthusiasms, scattered and fragmentary experience of European arts and ways of life, between old and young. Already, as though in response to a hidden American hunger for information concerning as many European developments as possible, journalists who were themselves amateurs of several arts began to explode into printed enthusiasm for European painting, drama, music, and literature. Huneker was the chief example of this type, and he was to be followed, after 1908, by the young Mencken and Nathan, and Willard Huntington Wright, at first contributors to and later editors of the *Smart Set.*

This pulp magazine, which began by catering to the period's taste for "sordid elegance," soon developed into the principal American purveyor of "modern" ideas and "new writing." Without any pretensions toward either depth of thought or liberality of opinion, with crude and hilarious impudence, its editors attacked American provincialism from the right, as it was already being attacked, by Veblen and others, from the left. They provided, moreover, a constant running picture of contemporary European culture, on all levels, from the *Burgtheaters* of central Europe to Parisian *café-chant-ants*. And along with the unknown and talented writers constantly turning up in its pages, the *Smart Set* provided first-rate factual and fictional reports of untouchable subjects; for a time it specialized in vignettes of American bordellos.

"Truth is so rare, it's delightful to tell it." This Dickinsonian sentence underlies the spirit of the "little American renaissance." Truths long suppressed began to be written and to be published; not only the social truths of the muckraker but the truths of individual lives. Confessions and disguised autobiographies flooded out in prose and in "free verse." And if it is now impossible to read many of these productions without a wry smile, it must be remembered how extreme was the cultural simplicity of the period to which they belong. This simplicity was soon to be altered by young men from the universities who began to apply trained critical analysis to the American scene. A series of rather Jamesian female patronesses also appeared and became active in the company of (in the words of one of them) these young "movers and shakers": Mrs. Jack Gardner in Boston; Mabel Dodge in Florence and New York; Harriet Monroe, along with the somewhat less "genteel" Margaret Anderson and Jane Heap, in Chicago; Gertrude Stein in Paris. And, in the unexpected locus of Philadelphia, about 1907, a school of American painters took hold of realism—"The Eight," John Sloan, Luks, Glackens, and the rest.

Post-Impressionism hit the United States in 1913, with the New York Armory Show; and from this influence American painting never really recovered until the depression of the '30's set in. Both American painting and American music, struck by styles and manners for which they were not totally prepared, became inundated with a wash of eclecticism. American poetry and fiction (more firmly based and more vigorously manned) were able to connect with the Post-Impressionist school directly, without being in any way deflected from their true course. Post-Impressionism in painting is based on an analysis down to basic structure, combined with new and individual (according to each artist) combinations of plastic elements and linear motifs. This anatomization of nature begins with Cézanne; and painting, after him, works toward the discovery, arrangement, or invention of "significant form."

Modern music shows curiosity concerning the hard, inviolable, and unemotional elements of rhythm, tonality, and atonality. Modern poetry, with the Imagists, endeavored to get at the pure definite subject, untarnished by thought, emotion, or moral idea. It was Imagism—invented and directed, throughout its brief life in English, by Americans—which finally turned against the outworn and exhausted forms into which the Georgian poets were able to infuse only a temporary and tepid energy. And it was not the Imagists alone, or chiefly, who developed intense simplicity, both of feeling and of means. Yeats, after 1912, and Pound, working with Yeats and the Fenollosa manuscripts, began to discover a poetic method which combined accuracy with conversational ease and was also capable of applying

form to everyday material. Poetry in English no longer
fled away into medieval settings; it was being made hard
yet flexible, more edged yet more translucent; more
"ordinary" yet more inclusive. It was this modern tone
and these modern means to which Eliot, in *Prufrock*
(about 1916), allied himself, having already discovered
his personal point of departure in Elizabethan drama
and the irony of Jules Laforgue. Yeats and Pound
achieved modernity; Eliot was modern from the start.

In the face of post-1918 confusions, as well as in the
confrontation of adverse "conservative" criticism, it is
important to realize and to state that the large and true
poetic talents, in Europe, England, and America, since
before 1914, have either worked in form or toward the
discovery of form. Moreover, since these poets rein-
forced their findings with methods passed over or dis-
carded by nineteenth-century taste, they engaged in a
task of restoration as well as of originality. The line of
modern poetry is a persistent—though sometimes devious and diverted—line toward new structure, new largeness, and new power; directed by an undeviating search,
not for an absolute and all-embracing aesthetic "machine," but for a commodious and flexible carrier of
complicated thought and sensibility. And at the same
time that it searches for form, it has an added implicit
task: to heal the split between thought and feeling inherited from a century of "progress." "It is on the tragic
side of the nineteenth century that thinking and feeling
go separate ways, or, as T. S. Eliot expresses it, 'the substantial unity of the soul is destroyed.' " *

In these later and central years of the twentieth century, it is becoming evident that the experimental side

* Sigfried Giedion, *Mechanization Takes Command* (Cambridge: Harvard University Press, 1948) , p. 328.

of literature must adjust itself to "reality" and to the changes in the human situation. Without abolishing a continued "openness" toward experiment, writers must not insist upon a stubborn *avant-gardism* when no real need for a further restless forward movement any longer exists. To move forward is not always a crucial need. The moment comes for a consolidation of resources and for a canvassing of the ground already gained; for a recognition of the point reached. In addition, since one of the less authentic features of modern art has been the *rational* exploitation of the irrational (as in the case of Surrealism), a constant need for the examination of all experiment on the grounds of its authenticity exists. The fact that charlatans, power-lovers, and *blageurs* function within the experimental side of the contemporary arts does not, however, invalidate these arts' tremendous accomplishment of clarification, discovery, and restitution. "O the inexhaustibility of the *motifs!*" writes the aged Cézanne in a letter. Modern art and literature, without any help from a constricting environment, have proved that the *motifs,* of both inner and outer nature, are indeed inexhaustible.

Interpretation, rather than exploration, is the task of the moment and of any imaginable future. Interpreters early in the field have been struck by the fact that man has surrounded himself with objects which are to him emotionally opaque: which he cannot love.* Natural "things" are penetrable by the imagination, and certain modern poets have spent lifetimes in rendering the essence not only of "the fruits of the earth" but of those human artifacts into which some spiritual life has been poured by means of the sensitive touch of the human hand. Is it possible to treat, if not with considerate af-

---

* Sigfried Giedion, in *Space, Time and Architecture* (Cambridge: Harvard University Press, 1941), explores this dilemma at length.

fection (as distinguished from "Futurist" idolatry), at least with intelligent placement, these machines that are products of machines, these tools that are the product of tools? Surely our fear of the destructive machine is linked with our emotional blankness toward non-destructive ones. It is significant that the modern poet to whom the French, since 1945, have given almost complete enthusiasm is Guillaume Apollinaire. Apollinaire, in his mature years, expressed a true joy in (if not a perfect acceptance of) the details of his environment, both mechanical and non-mechanical. "Zone" bathes airplanes, advertisements, the Paris street, and its traffic in a light which had not been seen formerly and has not been seen since.

The novel was the last literary form to be struck by Impressionism; and once penetrated by this force, it ballooned out into incredible proportions, becoming, as some observers have noted, a kind of Luciferian universe in the hands of Joyce. The novel remains "the most plastic of *genres*—the most *mobile,* industrious and inventive." * Its future possibilities are obvious, and enormous. Poetry, on the other hand, has come to the end, and perhaps exceeded, its explorative and experimental side. Eliot has recently remarked that although he values "the exploration of certain poetic possibilities for its own sake . . . for the future it is a tenable hypothesis that this advance of self-consciousness—the extreme awareness of and concern for language which we find in Valéry—is something which must ultimately break down owing to an increasing strain against which the human mind and nerves will rebel." †

All objects await human sympathy. It is only the hu-

---

* Thibaudet, *op. cit.,* p. 534.

† T. S. Eliot, *From Poe to Valéry* (Washington: Library of Congress, 1949), p. 16.

man that can humanize. It is now equally as difficult to flood outer reality with emotion as it once was to discover the inner springs of feeling and conduct. The world, already imaginatively dissolved, anatomized, and reconstituted, must now be *felt* through experience, and experienced through feeling. *Four Quartets,* the *Duino Elegies,* and Apollinaire's songs and contemplations have already opened the way.

1 9 5 0

§ *Edith Sitwell*

1 LAUGHTER IN A SWITCHBACK WORLD

Miss Sitwell has for a long time rendered her vision of the world through the baroque tradition, that stiffens the cloud into plaster and sunlight into metal rays. It is a vision, one would suppose, rigidly encased from reality's accidents and consequences. The eye that has seen too much has built up a panorama wherein the sea and clouds move, but as by a set of levers, and soft living things become wood, gold, and lacquer—a switchback world, peopled by personages called up from a mechanical *Commedia dell' arte,* devoid of mewing human sounds, with three gestures for love, and a raucous cry to signify despair. As though something in her heart or mind coveted the unreality of a child's fantasy, it is a fairy tale she tells and retells, however full of hard surfaces and sophisticated implications. Her technique is beaten out in nursery rhythms, and the meaning swings brazenly upon the rhyme. As in children's jingles, the rhymes clap to, like hands beating, and up springs the image, like a bird.

Bucolic Comedies, although sprinkled through and prefaced by paragraphs from Miss Sitwell's essays perfectly black with disillusion, sustained unbroken these myths and distortions of childhood. In *The Sleeping Beauty* the despairing voice sprang at last openly out of her song, and in *Troy Park* the same voice, unmistakably Miss Sitwell's own, speaks again. She at once stands within the clever clockwork kingdom she has made, and contemplates her own dead childhood.

Laforgue's shadow rests lightly upon Miss Sitwell. She sees men and women as the "terrible approximations" outlined by a caricaturist. The apish creatures scuttling upon adult business jig to a harried ragtime: the country gentleman skillfully shoots birds, the Countess airs her curled dogs, the red-faced man stumbles through a wet kitchen garden. Behind them rise lodging houses, "tall and lean," hotels, the *Metropole* and *Grand*—all the clutter of grownup existence. From these the hidden and resentful child grown old escapes into long poems mixed as dreams, full of lime-blossoms, honeycomb, amber, cherries, nutmegs, and waterfalls.

The child went through this cold bucolic world;
The mirage dew upon the ragged flowers
And ass-voice, pig-voice, hen-voice without end
Took on the tones she trusted. Oh, false friend
And our own false heart, falsely crying . . .

Miss Sitwell's epithets, at times deft inventions forced into life by the exigencies of her technique, have often a fortuitous brilliance of their own which justifies them. Again she can look at leaves and shadow with the profundity of true emotional vision. It is only occasionally that her sincerity is to be doubted, and then, perhaps, it is a note of that sharp laughter which she turns upon herself and upon her crowded images, that sounds. We may laugh completely, as children do, at the nonsense of:

. . . the navy-blue ghost of Mr. Belaker
The allegro negro cocktail shaker,

and, in "Country Cousin," at the free variation on a phrase of Gertrude Stein's:

My coral neck
And my little song
Are very extra
And very Susie . . .

but she has other and sadder laughter. Words can be heard with the long accent of memory upon them:

Alas my lovely one, in a remote
And still land of the spirit was my home
And this has faded like a song, and only
On the clear brink of sleep or in the heart
Of music can I find it and return
Through the long lands and be a child again.

With such simplicity Miss Sitwell has brought reality into her scene, before so carefully unreal. The carrousel world has cracked because a human voice has cried within it out of mature horror and despair. It must enclose, hereafter—along with the Margravine, Queen Claud, and the Noctambulo—the "mad Cassandra tongues of birds" that shout "Troy is burning," and some echoing "cold laughter of the water."

1 9 2 5

2 SATIRIST TO SYBIL

We look back on the Russian Ballet, which burst upon
English eyes and ears just before the war of 1914, and
see that much of its color and design has become dowdy
and frumpish. This aging process does not apply, however, to one of the literary phenomena of the period to
which the Russian Ballet contributed—the early poetry
of Edith Sitwell. For Miss Sitwell, a true modern, was
not taken in by the even then slightly obsolete luxury of
something like Rimski-Korsakov's *Scheherazade;* she
went straight to the puppet booth of Stravinsky's *Pe-
trouchka,* and took over the role of the master pup-
peteer. How crisp, how inventive, and how tireless she
was, rigging up her backgrounds and clothing her
wooden dolls, and how many bizarre and satirical charades she devised for them! She had imitators (they
crowded into *Wheels,* which she edited from 1916 to
1921), but she alone had the key to her artificial little
universe. She alone could present the opposition between the puppet booth and the Fair outside. She had
something to satirize—the padded upper-class Victorian
and Edwardian scene, through which she had evidently
been dragged as an unwilling child at the end of a governess' arm. And she had a dramatic instinct concerning
the difference between reality and artifice, so she could
intensify this difference by bringing her reader, from
time to time, up against the question: Are these indeed
puppets, or is there human pathos and laughter in these
wooden breasts?

Human pathos, as time went on, became more and

more a part of Miss Sitwell's imaginary world. Emotion, of a backward-looking kind but nevertheless full-bodied and poignant, exists in *The Sleeping Beauty* and in the more satiric *Bucolic Comedies,* both published in the early twenties. Her fairy-tale invention never flagged, but her figures were now dimly illuminated, more by the shadow of memory than by the glaring limelight of her times. The scene had shifted to lost childhood, the tone had become nostalgic, and there was a premonition of the moment when the Fair, with its shocking sights and sounds, would break through the walls of her tiny stage, when all the half-human dolls would die, insofar as they were human, or be put out of commission, insofar as they were dolls. This moment came, and the carnage and wreckage are perceivable and understandable in *Gold Coast Customs* (1929) and such shorter ensuing poems as "The Hambone and the Heart."

"One cannot think of her in any other age or country," Yeats said of Miss Sitwell, but he goes on to trace her later nightmare visions to Webster and to Swift. *Gold Coast Customs* is Swiftian in its absolute rejection of humankind. Her first full glance at the real world is distorted and warped by horror, and the symbols she improvised to express her anguish are materialist ones, at the very boundary of sanity—symbols of money and blood, gold and cannibalism. It is not only the Fair but the jungle that finally engulfs the puppet booth, and for the next ten years Miss Sitwell is almost wholly silent.

The latest poems, written during and since this last war, are, in the opinion of many critics, Miss Sitwell's finest. She has adopted an entirely new set of metaphors —metaphors that, as Yeats remarked, she raises to myth-making proportions by carrying them over from poem to poem. Her symbols are now large and rather Biblical, and her tone is prophetic. She expresses her faith in a revelation that mankind can help to bring about and share, and she speaks with a new largeness of rhythm. But she has lost, in her progress toward the sibylline, all her whipping satire and all her sense of humor. She is no longer receptive to those short but intense moments of vision usual in her early works. She is more of a Romantic; she is more ordinary in general, and she is far less painstaking in technique, for a sibyl does not need the help of formal poetic devices; the cryptic utterance is effective enough in itself. Her newest book, *A Song of the Cold,* exhibits the prophetess in full panoply, but since she is only sixty-one, she may develop, as time goes on, a less monumental attitude. She has cast a good deal of her poetic bread upon the waters, and it is possible that she will be rewarded for her courage and intransigence by its multiplied return.

1 9 4 8

3 COLD PRINT

Women poets, when they assume the role of sibyl, draw to themselves certain undeniable advantages. They immediately take on ancient authority; they are able to indulge at length in rather loosely written verbal incantation and they are not required to make much sense. It is interesting to note how the popularity of Edith Sitwell increases the more she goes in for an incantatory tone and gnomic meaning. Her new volume of fifteen poems, *Gardeners and Astronomers,* will surely continue to delight her admirers. Charmingly designed and illustrated with line drawings of fish, constellations, leaves, thorns, flowers, butterflies, and an armillary sphere, the book has a seventeenth-century flavor, magic and science operating side by side. This, certainly, is a learned sibyl, who can call upon philosophers, emperors, kings, and queens as well as upon the astronomers Hipparchus and Kepler. (Her gardeners seem to be anonymous.) Anyone who has heard Miss Sitwell read knows how effective her poems are delivered aloud. In cold print, however, they often sound as though they had been composed aloud; they remind one of improvised arias for a baroque opera. The trouble with the sibylline is that it has no staying qualities. We are left with the memory of this poet's predominant theme—her love of the sun and of proud, warm-blooded creatures, including Man, and her hatred of cold, darkness, cruelty, and the reptilian in general. Miss Sitwell is so skillful and so dazzling that she almost persuades us that spiritual intensity follows upon verbal intensity, which may or may not be true.

1 9 5 4

§ *Colette*

Chéri and *Mitsou* are the first of Colette's novels to be published in translations in America. From the long list of her books, written in the thirty years since 1900, one could choose other titles of perhaps equal brilliance. Her first literary period began in 1900, with the publication of the Claudine series; her mature literary career started with the appearance of *La Vagabonde* and *La Retraite Sentimentale,* some ten years later. For twenty years Colette has been the most widely read and most sincerely respected woman writer in France. *Chéri* was published originally in 1920; *Mitsou,* published in 1917, was her first really objective novel. *Chéri* and its sequel, *Le Fin de Chéri,* have already become contemporary classics. *Mitsou,* whose last pages drew tears from the eyes of Marcel Proust, is hardly more than a sketch for a novel of character, yet it stands unmatched in subtlety in the literature of our time.

Colette's excellence, long recognized by a European public that includes her fellow artists, is not easy to

define by English-speaking standards. That she is a born
writer and an exceptionally sensitive woman is evident.
Her full-bodied gusto, her fresh senses and compassion
unspoiled as a child's, are immediately clear to the running eye. She is not erudite. Her pages are singularly
free from allusion and echoes of literature. She can be
compared to little but herself because she has written
her discoveries down just as she herself made them. She
has lived her life—as a provincial girl, the wife of a
Parisian man-about-town, a dancer in music hall, a
woman of letters—and written of it concurrently. She
has not checked the development of her talents by re-
grets for the past or yearnings into the future. The steps
of her life, the ripening of her perceptions, appear as
clearly in her novels as in the facts and dates of her
biography.

The novelist, and particularly the novelist writing in
English, works in a dangerously malleable form. His narrative, roughly, must adjust itself to a rising action, a
knot, and a resolution; through this diagram, and because of it, characters must appear and change. In this
loose texture, under these few demands it is difficult to
detect maneuvers and sharp practices. Animus, stupidity, inaccuracy, and condescension, if disguised by a neat
and fashionable manner and a long wind, can easily pass
unnoticed. The good novelist is distinguished from the
bad one chiefly by a gift of choice. Choice, itself a talent,
as taste is a talent, is not however, enough. Only extreme
sanity and balance of selection can give to prose fiction
the dignity and excitement inherent in more rigid forms
of writing: drama, poetry, and the exposition of ideas.

Colette makes perfect choices. She writes with the
naive freedom of the amateur who has only himself for
audience, and with the artist's unwavering adherence to

form. Her simplicity of manner seems odd to the English reader, accustomed to the extremes of romantic rhetoric and to banal situations put down by writers hardened to their medium and not open to their material. The dated touch of nineteenth-century attitudes of mind still lies heavy upon modern fiction. In spite of loud assurances to the contrary, novels infected by their audience, warped by their authors' biases, bleached by literary form and custom, are the novels that, with few exceptions, come from the presses. Colette, backed by a tradition that includes *La Vie de Henri Brulard,* puts down what she knows—what her sharp senses and hearty nature have told her as the truth. This, we can conclude, is her only secret.

The stories of Katherine Mansfield, so obviously influenced by Colette, illustrate the Frenchwoman's method of attack without giving a hint of her quality. For Katherine Mansfield's talent leaves off where Colette's begins. The Englishwoman's sensibilities could touch nostalgia, pity, and regret. They could not seek out the difficult human relationship, grasp it in essentials, reduce it to form. Where Colette struggles with the problem on its own terms, Katherine Mansfield shied away.

In *Chéri,* Colette chooses for her subject one of the most difficult situations in the rather limited gamut of relationships possible between men and women: the love of an aging woman for a young man; the dependence of a young man upon the passion and tenderness of an older woman. She makes her problem perfectly clear and does not slight its implications. Chéri is not a casual boy picked up by Léa late in her career. She has known him from childhood. She is the friend, contemporary, and confidante of his mother. Like his mother, she is a successful courtesan; unlike her, she is healthy, intelligent, and gay. Léa does not make the first move; it is the boy who chooses her. From the beginning, the psychological set is probable. And from the first kiss of these lovers, so ill assorted according to conventional standards, throughout the course of their love affair, Chéri's marriage, Léa's flight from unexpected sorrow, to Chéri's final rejection of her love and power, the mother-son basis of the bond between them is not for a moment forgotten. The last scene between Léa and Chéri is so complex and so moving that it stands beyond casual appraisal. These two, characters in a novel easily classed as scabrous, take on a tragic nobility. *"Léa,"* says a contemporary critic, *"se dompte comme une heroine cornélienne."* This seems improbable, but is nevertheless true.

Mitsou is so lightly blocked in, so delicately developed, that it barely merits the heavy title of novel. Mitsou, the little singer in a music hall, is the only character that has a name; the others are known by titles, like the people in an allegory or a harlequinade. Brief stage directions report the action for the most part; the scenes are perhaps five in number. Mitsou before the mirror of her dressing-room, dressing, under the eyes of the young officers, "with a cheerless ease and an absentminded immodesty which banished all coquetry"; Mitsou in the apartment furnished according to her own taste, and paid for by the Man of Means, an apartment "extraordinary, in spite of her good intentions"; Mitsou at her desk, writing serious little letters, full of grammatical errors and the newly awakened gentleness of first love—that is all we have, with the exception of Mitsou and her Lieutenant, in a strangers' embrace, seen against the ornate jumble of ornaments in her bedroom. What more could one do for this sober, well meaning child, who does not miss her performance even though her lover goes away tomorrow? Colette does not attempt to do more. She defines her lightly, wakens her briefly, and lets her go.

Turning the light formality of French fiction to her own uses, Colette has colored French prose, for a long time rather grayed by reflections from Parisian streets, with the varied green of provincial gardens. Honest, sensuous, and witty, she has produced a solid body of work that owes little to masculine attitudes. Other translations of her books as excellent as these two should not be long deferred.

1 9 3 0

§ *Flowering Judas*

Katherine Anne Porter's stories, here collected for the first time, have appeared over a period of years in *Transition, The American Caravan,* and in commercial magazines appreciative of distinguished writing. In each of the five stories in the present book, Miss Porter works with that dangerous stuff, unusual material. Two stories have a Mexican locale. Two contain passages which describe lapses into the subconscious and the dream. "Magic" briefly explores the survival of frayed but savage superstition. "Rope" follows the rise and fall of an hysterical mood, and "He" sets against simple human devotion an idiot's non-human power and suffering.

It is to Miss Porter's high credit that, having fixed upon the exceptional background and event, she has not yielded, in her treatment of them, to queerness and forced originality of form. With the exception of "Magic" (which I should prefer to think of as an experiment, since its effect is false, for reasons only too easily defined—the use of the fustian maid-to-mistress mono-

logue, for one), the stories do not lean upon the doubtful prop of manner for its own sake. Miss Porter has a
range of effects, but each comes through in its place, and
only at the demand of her material. She rejects the ex-
clamatory tricks that wind up style to a spurious intensity, and trusts, for the most part, to straightforward
writing, to patience in detail, and to a thorough imaginative grasp on cause and character. She has "knowledge
about reality," and has chosen the most exacting means
to carry her knowledge into form.

The fact, and the intuition or logic about the fact, are
severe coordinates in fiction. In the short story they
must cross with hair-line precision. However far the
story may range, the fact and its essence must direct its
course and stand as proof to the whole. The truth alone
secures form and tone; other means distort the story to
no good end and leave within the reader's mind an impression far worse than that produced by mere banality.
Joyce's "Ivy Day in the Committee Room" depends
wholly upon the truth of the fact; Chekhov's greatest
stories, say "The Duel" and "Lights," have command of
reasons in the first place, of emotion, taste, and style sec-
ondarily. The firm and delicate writing in Miss Porter's
"Flowering Judas," a story startling in its complexity,
were it not based on recognizable fact, would be to no
purpose. As it is, its excellence rises directly from the
probity of the conception. It is as impossible to question the characters of the fanatical girl and the self-
loving man—the "good revolutionist," who, softened to
a state beyond principle, is fit only for a career—as it is
to find a flaw or lapse in the style that runs clear and
subtle, from the story's casual beginning to the specter
of life and death at the end. "Rope," after "Flowering
Judas," is perhaps the most remarkable story in the

book. It makes no claim; its integration becomes apparent only when the reader tries to recount it to himself in any other form than its own. The mood is put together so accurately that its elements cannot be recombined.

"Maria Concepcion" does not entirely come up to Miss Porter's standard. A slight flavor of details brought in for their own sake mars its intensity, and one does not entirely trust Maria's simplicity of motive. For the most part, however, the stories in *Flowering Judas* can claim kinship with the order of writing wherein nothing is fortuitous, where all details grow from the matter in hand simply and in order. Miss Porter should demand much work of her talent. There is nothing quite like it, and very little that approaches its strength in contemporary writing.

1 9 3 0

§ *The Ladies and Gentlemen*

Virginia Woolf's aims, in *Three Guineas,* are incontesta-
bly noble ones. But her style is so elegant, so circuitous,
and so soothing that the reader is halfway through the
book before he realizes what is going on. So that it is just
as well if the critic state at the outset that one should substitute "upper-class Englishwoman," or even "lady," for
Mrs. Woolf's term "educated man's daughter."

Ten years ago Mrs. Woolf, in *A Room of One's Own,*
turned the English patriarchal system inside out. In the
present book the exposé of upper-class Englishman's
tyranny over upper-class Englishwoman is continued.
These women were considered, by their brothers, fathers, and husbands, about on a par with these gentlemen's dogs or horses, which must be well taken care of,
make a fine display, and, if sold, fetch a good price. One
sex, the masculine, had all the material power, all of
the "higher education," and most of the expensive fun.
Fathers prevented their daughters from earning a living,
and husbands kept their wives from nearly everything
except child-bearing.

The First World War broke up the hard grip of such feudal holdovers. Women, in the national emergency, went into hospitals and munitions factories—the ladies, as Mrs. Woolf points out, sometimes still attended by their maids. After the war women won the right to vote and admission into many of the professions. Time passed, and a new war became probable. But now conditions had changed so that it was possible for an "educated man" to write to an "educated man's daughter," asking her advice on how war could be avoided.

Three Guineas is Mrs. Woolf's answer to such a request. The question of male privilege, it is clear, has never ceased to agitate her. She brings up a whole new set of horrid facts proving the continued strength of male domination. From history, biography, and the newspaper, she wheels up evidence that woman's battle, in the upper income brackets, is not yet fully won. Women in the professions are still mistrusted, badly paid, and kept under. And what are these professions? How good are the assumptions on which they are based?

We, the daughters of professional men, are between the devil and the deep sea. Behind us lies the patriarchal system, with its nullity, its immorality, its hyprocisy, and its servility. Before us lies the public world, the professional system, with its possessiveness, its jealousy, its pugnacity, its greed. It is a choice of evils. Each is bad.

Are women of Mrs. Woolf's class, then, to walk into man-made and time-hardened employments, without lifting a finger to change them? At this point Mrs. Woolf exposes her scheme for depositing some female goodness and sensitiveness in the social set-up. Let "educated men's daughters," she says, exercise disinterestedness to the point of fanaticism. Let them "cultivate the

virtues which have taught the daughters of educated
men before this—Florence Nightingale, Emily Brontë,
Christina Rossetti—i.e., poverty, chastity, and freedom
from unreal loyalties." Let them refuse to sell their
brains for money; hold that obscurity and censure are
preferable to fame and praise; fling back badges, orders,
and degrees in the giver's face; rid themselves of the
pride of nationality, religious pride, school pride, college pride, family pride, and sex pride. Cleave to the
example of Antigone, says Mrs. Woolf. Remember Antigone's profound statement concerning the duties of
the individual to society: "It is not my nature to join in
hating, but in loving."

This Outsider's Society, then, would consist of educated men's daughters "working in their own class—how
indeed could they work in any other?" A long, tart note
is here inserted which states that, since the middle class
is much in need of improvement, and since the lower
class probably resent upper-class interference with their
problems, the line had better be drawn definitely and
finally. Upper-middle-class Englishwomen, thus fenced
off, are to erect, upon the class-consciousness and class
education dinned into them from the first moment they
were dandled before the nursery fire, a moral pattern so
severe that it has never been adhered to by anyone who
was not by nature an artist or a saint. That this Outsider's Society will ever materialize, under these conditions, is unlikely.

So that, while *Three Guineas* can be read for its
flashes of that psychological insight and witty realism
for which women are so famed, one must check Mrs.
Woolf continually in her conclusions. Her style itself is
a danger. At its worst, it curves into the suavity of well-
managed rhetoric under which all kinds of beating

about the bush may go on unnoticed. With it she can deflect points on which she has no opinion or merely a class opinion. What about these male regalias, for example? Are they, as she says, the paraphernalia of a sex, or the awesome decorations of a class?

Mrs. Woolf has looked at women of the lower classes. She has even written and published an introduction to a collection of their life stories (*Life As We Have Known It,* 1931). She looked at them, she admits, "with bewilderment and curiosity." She found them "magnificent." But she decided, upon thinking the matter over, that "it is better to be a lady," since ladies "desire ends, not means." In *Three Guineas* Mrs. Woolf has had to venture a little outside of a lady's prerogatives. Perhaps because she is not used to considering means, she has not considered them very thoroughly. Forgetting that she is "an educated man's daughter," Mrs. Woolf should go on being an artist. Patently, being a lady is difficult, but artists have managed to make something of even worse situations and inheritances.

1 9 3 8

§ *Hart Crane*

Hart Crane, whose *Collected Poems,* edited with an introduction by Waldo Frank, was published this spring, was born in Garrettsville, Ohio, in 1899. He committed suicide by leaping from a boat bound north from Mexico on April 27, 1932. He began to write poetry at the age of fifteen; at the time of his death he was revered by many of his contemporaries as the greatest American poet since Whitman. The violence of his life had become a legend and the merits of his work a center of controversy. His poetry, incoherent, of emotional extremes compact, was seized upon as a symbol of the cultural chaos in which it was produced.

Mr. Frank's introduction is long, and, to anyone uninitiated into the metaphysical mysteries, rather puzzling. In it he exhibits one modern critical tendency: the desire to lift the poet out of his true place and ascribe to him the function of the seer; to accredit to a work of literature some mystic revelation. Thus, Crane was a seer, according to Mr. Frank, in spite of the fact that he possessed no "inner nucleus." Moreover, he was a product of "the great tradition," although "because of the time that fleshed him . . . he could not employ traditional concretions." And in Crane's long poem *The Bridge,* according to Mr. Frank, in his guise of St. John, the symbol of American life finally appears. *The Bridge* offers us, as it were, the Word made Steel, for our spirit's consolation.

If we may be permitted to examine Crane's poems a trifle more realistically, we see at once that the poet's quarrel with himself—that quarrel which Yeats names the first cause in the poetic process—was far more grievous than his quarrel with his world. This inner feud was so intense that suicide was his only solution. And in the matter of "traditional concretions," although Crane's work undeniably bore the impress of the three great and inexplicable American romantics, Poe, Melville, and Whitman, it took its immediate color from modern French writing: Surrealism-out-of-Rimbaud-out-of-Victor Hugo. One certain proof of Crane's genius was his ability to build remarkable poetry from the materials offered by a literary movement crammed with blighting and senseless *blague.* He took over much of its form and many of its attitudes, but impregnated it with the intensity of his own powers. All questions of "the greatest since . . . ," of seerhood, of the voice out of chaos, the cave, or the cloud, put to one side, Crane was a poet of genius whose untimely death was a certain loss to American literature.

1 9 3 3

§ *The Letters of Gerard Manley Hopkins*

1

Gerard Manley Hopkins is without doubt the chief Providential Influence (in the sense of where would they be without him?) now acting upon the youngest generation of those who speak in English numbers. The combined authority of Eliot, Pound, and Yeats, supreme for so long, has begun to fade; the echo of their measures is now the exception and not the rule. The young have turned to a contemporary of their great-grandfathers for prosodic guidance.

The main facts of Hopkins' career—his lifelong friendship with Robert Bridges, which began at Oxford in the sixties, his early conversion to Catholicism, and his subsequent induction into the Jesuit order—are now generally known. His poems at the time of his death, in 1889, remained in manuscript; the first edition of his work, collected by Bridges, appeared in 1918. His revolutionary prosodic theories and his extraordinary poetry impressed, but somewhat unnerved, the friends to whom his work was entrusted. All this comes out, along with the quality of Hopkins' critical temper, in *The Letters of Gerard Manley Hopkins to Robert Bridges* and *Correspondence of Gerard Manley Hopkins and Richard Watson Dixon,* published this winter in two volumes under the editorship of C. C. Abbott. These letters are the most important recent addition to the annals of English poetry. They are the record of an intellect at once passionate, cool, sincere, and undeviating, and of a spirit fiery beyond description. Totally unknown to the great figures of nineteenth-century literature, Hopkins scrutinized their work with an intensity which allowed no stupidity or inexactitude of expression to escape unscathed. His remarks on the Brownings, for example, are brilliant. And the letters record, by implication, the progress of Hopkins' long poetic martyrdom: the conflict between his great gifts and his perfect and unquestioning obedience to the rules of his order. The two volumes are edited with a care which resembles reverence, and are illustrated with holographs and portraits.

1 9 3 5

2

"It has always seemed to me that poetry is unprofessional," Hopkins wrote when he was twenty. Because he held, throughout his life, to the practice of his belief, his prose works come to the modern reader singularly pure: in the form of letters to intimate friends and notebooks. The present collection,* under the same reverent

* *Further Letters of Gerard Manley Hopkins, Including His Correspondence with Coventry Patmore.* Edited with Notes and an Introduction by Claude Colleer Abbott.

editorship of Professor Abbott, contains "all further letters which have come to light" since 1935, when Hopkins' letters to Bridges and the Hopkins-Dixon correspondence appeared. *The Notebooks,* edited by Humphrey House, were published in 1937. The letters in this volume are divided into three sections: miscellaneous letters to family and friends; a long continued (1863-1888) series of letters to A. W. M. Baillie; and, at last, the Hopkins-Patmore correspondence in full.

Casual letters are at once a touchstone and a giveaway. They are certain to show all the cheapness and attitudinizing of a writer; rant, seedy thinking, sentiment, and obstinate prejudices come to the surface in such documents to be seen with great clearness. In the case of Hopkins, his letters prove, as his editor says, that the man was all of a piece; the letters "bear the imprint of the same rare mind and spirit, they have the same disciplined honesty and intensity of conviction" as the poems. So there is now disclosed to us for the first time the hidden stream of scholarly discussion which ran steadily beneath the public literary scene of the '70's and '80's. And here are the simply-expressed but profound and hard-bitten conclusions reached by a man who had shut himself away from life—a man who feared his own nature, and, admitting his fear, took every precaution that that nature should not function freely.

Hopkins' remarkable scholastic record has not been fully emphasized. He was a brilliant student of Jowett's at Balliol, a fact which his superiors in the Jesuit order took into account when they appointed him Lecturer and Examiner in Greek to the University College in Dublin. His interest in Greek metrics never flagged, and his technical theories, as well as his technical practice, have opened, and will continue to open, new doors into poetic richness and freedom. Even more impressive, in these letters, than his scholarship are his unfailing curiosity and poetic insight. He was a man "for whom the visible world triumphantly existed." His eye microscopically took in every detail of the objects upon which he fixed his attention. His love for appearance was so great that the worst penance he could impose upon himself was to turn his eyes away from nature. His ear, sharp and interested, picked up turns of speech peculiar to a countryside. He was excited by ecclesiastical architecture no more than by the architecture of swallows.

In the field of the arts his musical interest ranged from Purcell to Wagner (about whose works, since he had no opportunity to hear them, he desired detailed accounts). His remarks on paintings are often profound. ("I have invented a Canaletto with genius: his name is Guardi.") And his critical insight into literature flashes out in a comparison, anticipating many like comparisons made in recent years, between what Keats might have lived to be, with what Shakespeare was. And again, his ideas about the "overthought and underthought" in Greek tragic poets ("underthought conveyed by choice of metaphors, etc., and only half-realized by the poet himself") foreshadow recent ideas of scholars concerning the underlying symbolism in Shakespeare's plays.

Baillie was not a poet, but his learning and sensitiveness and his interest in what Hopkins had to say often brought, from Hopkins, a full rush of explanation and exposition. Hopkins' theories concerning the kinds of poetry—an account which proves him to have been, at twenty, a critic of the first order—were sent to Baillie.

The Patmore correspondence, which occurred during the last six years of Hopkins' life, when he was thirty-nine and Patmore sixty, has been published in part elsewhere—in Basil Champneys' *Life of Patmore* and by Father Lahey in his *Life of Hopkins*. Champneys hesitated to publish the letters in full, on the ground that they were too technical for the general reader. Patmore during this time was preparing the revised (third collected) edition of his *Poetical Works* (1887). Patmore's reputation had gone into eclipse. *The Angel in the House*, a generation earlier, had been second only to Tennyson's poems in popularity. Since Hopkins had expressed his admiration for the later "Odes"—attracted by their free form and intense emotion—Patmore asked his advice on revisions. The younger man's comments, in every case, go straight to the heart of Patmore's basic faults of style and tone. Hopkins' respect for Patmore (who, like himself, was "curious and learned in prosody") kept him from delivering a criticism in the bald manner of Tennyson, who once said that some of Patmore's lines seemed to be hammered up out of old nails. Hopkins not only points out Patmore's ambiguities, incomplete sense, and bad phrasing, but attacks his lack of true ear, frequent lack of taste, his affectation, insincerity, and Tory tub-thumping. Patmore took all this, it must be said, in good part. He saw, as might be expected, nothing but "strangeness" in Hopkins' poems. However, he wrote to Bridges, after the death of Hopkins:

. . . there was something in all his words and manners that was at once a rebuke and attraction to all who could only aspire to be like him . . .

and added that Hopkins' genius was unmistakable.

These letters bring out, finally, the tormented plans —almost amounting to manias—of Hopkins' later years. His discussion, with Baillie, of the probable derivation of Greek words from Egyptian (which led nowhere)

and his determination to write music show the beating
about of a rich nature against the rigidity of the rule it
worked under. Much sympathy has been poured out concerning the conflict between Hopkins' character and
the severity of the Jesuit life. But where could this fiery
spirit, these delicate sensibilities, have fitted in the Victorian world, big as it was with ideas of optimism and
progress, and punctuated as it was by the suicides of
sensitive young men? "Great from the hard forming
hand" Hopkins had chosen in youth "he triumphs, ut-
terly defeated." Seen from our time, the design, the
"instress," of Hopkins' life is so clear that it seems not
only that life's best, but indeed its only possible, pattern.

1 9 3 8

§ *Feats on the Fjord*

Those people who wish young poets to be deadly serious and all of a piece will be annoyed and baffled by Auden's travel book, *Letters from Iceland,* written with Louis MacNeice, a new collaborator. These letters, rhymed and unrhymed, are consistently amusing and frequently brilliant, but they do not repeat the tone of books written by emotional travelers, philosophical travelers, trippers, or escapists. Both Auden and MacNeice are on to the kinds of attitude which can be struck by the English, whether poets or not, in strange landscapes. They have chosen to stick to an amateur and detached standing; as travelers they have kept outside the ranks of explorers, old Etonians of the Peter Fleming tradition, and Wordsworthian nature lovers. When, in the northern wilds, they came upon a real professional English traveler, "handsome, sunburnt, reserved, speaking fluent Icelandic," they were more amused than abashed. Auden, having contracted to do a travel book on Iceland (he was drawn to that country because of his Icelandic name and a childhood interest in the sagas), spent the summer of 1936 on the island, at first alone and later in the company of MacNeice and other friends. Rejecting from the first the idea of the necessity to brood and moon over *ultima Thule,* or to indulge in romantic *poèsie des départs,* he was rather at a loss how to begin. Iceland had been visited by other men of letters and had produced some great native prose. It offered to the view glaciers, waterfalls, geysers, a volcano, and many rocks coated with sphagnum moss. One traveled through it by bus (in which conveyance Icelanders are always sick, Englishmen never) or on horseback. Auden learned to ride, stayed at inns and farmhouses, and struggled to be off-hand about the scenery. ("One waterfall is very much like another.") He soon succumbed to a certain "effect of travel, which is to make one reflect on one's past and one's culture from the outside." He had brought along a volume of Byron, and he began to cast into a variation of the *Don Juan* stanza, with light-verse freedom, the thoughts and part of the life-history of an English poet of twenty-nine, then isolated at the top of Europe, where modern roars and squawks penetrated but faintly. The "Letter to Lord Byron," which makes up five chapters of the book, is always a remarkable technical *tour de force,* and in spite of its tendency to slip into rather self-preening triviality, has its moments of insight. Through this disused Byronic stanza form, Auden once more helps to break up the limiting measures which have hardened around modern poetic expression, and which force poets into stock attitudes, usually of pomposity or gloom. This stanza can accommodate the casual mention of everyday experience, as an example written after Auden's return to England shows:

Autumn is here. The beech leaves strew the lawn:
  The power stations take up heavier loads;
The massive lorries shake from dusk till dawn
  The houses on the residential roads;
  The shops are full of coming winter modes.
Dances have started at the Baths next door
Stray scraps of MS strew my bedroom floor.

Louis MacNeice, a poet of Auden's time at Oxford, who has brought a special kind of North-of-Ireland talent into the younger English group, joined the amateur expedition. Things went on much the same. The friends played rummy in the evening and traveled through the severe and ungrateful countryside by day. MacNeice's serious contributions to the book—three poems—do not suffer by comparison with Auden's fine introductory poem, "Journey to Iceland." His lighter contributions are extravagantly funny. The two noticed different things. The spectacle of a whale being torn to pieces by winches gave Auden "an extraordinary vision of the cold controlled ferocity of the human species." MacNeice was impressed by children singing "The Music Goes Round and Round" in their native tongue.

The authors have not shirked the factual side of their job. The book has maps, charts, and guidebook information on food, transportation, money, etc., as well as quoted accounts of historic events, a bibliography of books on Iceland, and a set of Icelandic proverbs. Nor have Icelandic arts and letters, or the character and habits of modern Icelanders, been neglected. The photographic illustrations are excellent.

A good many readers must still exist who hope that bleak landscapes have an elevating influence on the human spirit, who believe that the uplift element in gla-

ciers must be considerable. To them this book will be a
disappointment. It will also disappoint those who, in
their secret heart of hearts, expect portentous statements from serious and gifted young poets. Auden and
MacNeice often sound, it is true, a tiresome schoolboy
note. Their continual determination not to be taken in
by cant makes them sheer away from emotion. The
"Last Will and Testament" at the end of the book, for
example, spirals up through sheer brilliance into a region where only *Coterie-sprache* can breathe. On the
other hand, it is a sign of health that both young men
are capable not only of humor but of hilarity. And they
never project individual fear and frustration out into
current blanket hatreds. Their will and testament ends:

We leave our age the quite considerable spark
Of private love and goodness which never leaves
An age, however awful, in the utter dark . . .
And to the good who know how wide the gulf, how deep
Between Ideal and Real, who being good have felt
The final temptation to withdraw, sit down and weep,
We pray the power to take upon themselves the guilt
Of human action, though still as ready to confess
The imperfection of what can and must be built,
The wish and power to act, forgive and bless.

                                        1 9 3 7

§ *The Oxford Book of Modern Verse*

It is no small task to gather into one anthology, and to reconcile critically, the schools of English poetry which have flourished since the death of Tennyson. William Butler Yeats, the editor of *The Oxford Book of Modern Verse* (1892-1935), has attempted it. The book opens with Pater's lines on the "Mona Lisa," printed as *vers libre,* because Pater, according to Yeats, was the one writer who had the entire uncritical admiration of the post-Victorian generation. It proceeds through Victorian holdovers (Bridges, Blunt), through the smoky lyrical flames at the end of the nineteenth century (Wilde, Dowson), into the comparatively airy and open years at the beginning of the twentieth. The Georgians take up the tune on their oaten pipes; the Imperialists, the seafarers, the Imagists arrive along with a few Hindus and Irish; Pound brings in echoes from Provence, Alexandria, and China; Eliot (the other American included) changes and distills. Sitwellian fireworks begin to fizz and whir, and war breaks up the game. Twenty years after the war a new school appears; young men who were children in 1914 begin to write at white heat, disabused with a wrecked and disordered world.

Yeats, who all his life has suspected politics, will not admit that it is political passion alone which now moves the young. "Suffering has compelled them to seek beyond the flux. . . . Here stands not this or that man but man's naked mind." His preface closes on a note of belief in the sincerity and intellectual passion of these young men. He does not assign the influence of his own sincerity and intellectual passion to them, although there is more Yeats in all of them than many of them would care to admit.

Yeats' preface is simple in tone, catholic in appreciation, profound in judgment. Hurrahs for his side and contempt for the side of others do not occur in it. Some poetry, because he cannot read it without pain, he omits. (Wilfred Owen's work, which Yeats rejects because "passive suffering is not a theme for poetry," is the one real omission from the book.) Some poetry (Hopkins') he reads with great difficulty, but includes at length. He has several rather peculiar enthusiasms (for W. J. Turner, Herbert Read, Dorothy Wellesley, and C. Day Lewis). On the other hand, he singles out poets whose gifts have been somewhat overlooked: Sturge Moore and Oliver Gogarty. He includes one discovery, Margot Ruddock, whose poems remind him of Emily Brontë's. And he appreciates Tagore along with Auden and MacNeice, Edith Sitwell at her emotional best, Pound at the high point of his style, D. H. Lawrence at the most intense of his sensibilities. He neither overemphasizes nor underestimates the stream of Irish song let into the stream of English by Synge and by the later translations of Lady Gregory and Frank O'Connor. His selection from his own work is superb.

"I think England had more good poets from 1900 to the present day than during any period of the same length since the early seventeenth century," Yeats says, in closing his argument and findings. A clear, heartening statement to hear after the many hollow groans often emitted concerning our time. On the evidence here presented, the reader is inclined to agree with one of the good poets of all time.

1 9 3 6

§ *The Progress of T. S. Eliot*

1 FROM DESPAIR TO FAITH

The later poems of T. S. Eliot, for years fugitive and hard to come by, are at last joined to his early work in the recently published *Collected Poems*. So the record, up to now, of the poet who has changed the accent of poetry written in our period is at last completely available to us. We can trace Eliot's "horror of a life without faith" from its first complete statement in "Gerontion," through its elaboration in "The Waste Land," to its logical conclusion in "Sweeney Agonistes." "Sweeney Agonistes," still a fragment and likely to remain one, twitching to music-hall rhythms, reduced men and women to gargoyles who gibbered in a world where even the comparative nobility of despair was not possible. Faith began to stammer in "The Hollow Men," and from that point on, Eliot's belief mounts beyond his irony and pessimism, not in an unbroken line, but in a line renewed when broken. It is now possible to read the beautiful poems of the transition period ("Journey of the Magi" through "Difficulties of a Statesman") in their proper order, as well as the latest brief lyrics, the nonsense rhymes, and the fine "Choruses from 'The Rock.'" The last poem in the collection, "Burnt Norton," rather long and, compared to the crisp early poems, rather vaporous, brings the later phase to a conclusion that resolves on a note of balanced calm and even a mild sort of joy.

Of the quality of the poetry there is little need to speak. Eliot, the self-styled "minor poet," brought back into English poetry the salt and the range of which it had long been deprived. From Dante through the Symbolists, he took what he needed from the varied stream of poetic resources; he swung the balance over from whimpering Georgian bucolics to forms wherein contemporary complexity could find expression. The *Collected Poems* are more than a work of poetic creation; they are a work of poetic regeneration.

1 9 3 6

2 THE RELIGIOUS ENCOUNTER

Eliot's plays and poems, subsequent to his espousal of the Anglican faith, have not been entirely joyful. They have been well streaked, in fact, with his early defeatism and despairs, and the social-satirical note has seemed to be vanishing from them by degrees. *The Family Reunion,* a verse play with a contemporary setting, will appear to the reader waiting for pure spiritual joy to sound, after the fanfares attendant upon conversion, almost too good to be true. The new play presents an integrated Eliot, completely in control of himself and so filled with insight that the old Eliot comes in for some pretty close dissection, if not caricature. It is no small feat to bring off a Christian (a Jungian, a Sophoclean) theme of reconciliation with the conscience (the unconscious sense of guilt, the Eumenides) and at the same time to expose, down to the last set phrase, the hollow conventions of an upper (in this case, English) class. It is no small feat to surround and examine an early phase of the self by means of a later one.

The play is divided into two parts of three scenes each. In the first scene of Part I, it is the social irony which first attracts the attention. The two non-ironic characters—Harry, the eldest son, who returns to his mother's house ridden by real or imagined guilt—and his aunt, Agatha, who is addicted to clipped sibylline speech and an occasional piece of late-Eliot incantation—sound definitely suspect. There has been just about enough sensitive foreboding in Eliot. Cellars and attics, "the noxious smell untraceable in the drains," "the attraction of the dark passage, the paw under the door" sound so like parody that one is put on guard. A new element, however, soon appears to exorcise the old horror. Downing, Harry's "man," who has "looked after his Lordship for over ten years," is sheer practical common sense, and this Figaro-like conception is reassuring. Eliot, one feels, cannot be planning to recede once more into neurotic terrors while Downing, offstage, cleans up the car. And a complete recession does not, in fact, occur. We are drawn, it is true, with the struggling Harry, right down to childhood and back, straight through the necessary confrontation of the Eumenides. Eliot probes from the outside into the neurotic's tendencies toward cruelty and suffering in a manner one would not have thought possible. Harry, able at last to face his pursuers and accept them, liberates himself. He is then free to escape the deathly house, his mother's relentless will, and the stupidity of his relatives. His sibylline aunt bids him Godspeed. Downing goes with him, and the spectacle of master and man riding off to spiritual liberty in a well-kept car is the play's one faintly ridiculous effect.

Eliot of late years has talked at great length about the value of religious experience. *The Family Reunion* is the first incontrovertible evidence that he has thoroughly experienced the phenomenon. It is interesting to note that other than traditional Church of England symbols have contributed to this play.

Any person who has ever experienced the smallest success in the struggle for spiritual reconciliation will recognize that Eliot here demonstrates in detail the uncheatable nature of the combat. And James never flayed the upper-class English with more delicate skill.

1 9 3 9

3 FROM FORM TO CONTENT

Four Quartets is the first T. S. Eliot volume of serious poetry to appear in America since his *Collected Poems,* published in 1936. The first three poems included have been in print for some time, however. "Burnt Norton," with which the book opens, is familiar as the final piece in *Collected Poems,* and "East Coker" and "The Dry Salvages" were published in the *Partisan Review* in 1940 and 1941 respectively. Taken together, the four rather long works—"Little Gidding" is the other one—show Eliot experimenting in his tireless way. They also show a crucial turn in his thinking, and in his general approach toward the Anglican religion, which he embraced, along with British citizenship, in 1927.

The four poems are linked together by two devices. First, the basic construction of "Burnt Norton" sets the form of the others. Each has five sections. Each has a lyric in its second section, followed without pause by a meditation—development of theme, as it were. A second lyric stands alone in each fourth section as a detached melody. These lyrics and reflections, falling in their allotted places, are supposed, no doubt, to have the effect of the changes in the sonata form. This intended effect comes through, although not, of course, as definitely as in music. The second device is the use of place names as titles to all the poems. Eliot being the subtle inheritor of the Symbolist tradition, these specific localities afford him points from which to range or on which to brood. Burnt Norton is an English country house with a rose garden. East Coker is the town in Somersetshire from which Eliot's forebears emigrated to America in the seventeenth century. The Dry Salvages, according to the author's note, are "a small group of rocks, with a beacon, off the N.E. coast of Cape Ann, Massachusetts." And Little Gidding is the site in Huntingdonshire where, in 1625 or so, Nicholas Ferrar set up an Anglican religious community, which flourished in a quiet way until its destruction by the Puritans about twenty years later. Eliot, therefore, weaves back and forth between his native America and his adopted Britain. He has touched his own presumably Puritan sources and also celebrated, as a convert to the Anglican communion, a shrine belonging to what has been called the golden age of the Church of England.

The form and background once straight in our minds —Eliot gives no explanation of either beyond the note

quoted above—we can read the poems for mere enjoyment, for they are certainly as beautiful as anything he
ever wrote. The lyrics, especially the second in "East
Coker" and the two in "Little Gidding," show what the
poet can do in the province of pure emotion when all
irony has been eliminated.

It has been said that some of Eliot's utterances about
religion have been suspiciously melodramatic. Eliot, in
making religious tradition a frame for his art, chose—
the artist's inevitable choice—cohesion and integrity.
But a choice of form was evidently not enough. It is
interesting to trace Eliot's shift from formal interest in
his religion (its history, rituals, and so on) toward a far
from formal interest in his own post-conversion spiritual
development. The four poems in this book, together
with his play, *The Family Reunion* (1939), are records
of that development, wrung out of him despite all obstacles of reserve. Eliot's conversion was accompanied
by a certain amount of pride and arrogance. In "Burnt
Norton," however, the classic procedure of spiritual
death and rebirth begins and "the dark night of the
soul" is heralded. The poem bears all the marks of deep
depression. It is faint and minor in tone, circular and
repetitive in thought. A flight back to childhood is considered, and the way out, through darkness and mental
suffering, is recognized to be necessary only in an academic way. Here, human sympathy is also academic, if
not actually lacking. This is the middle Eliot manner
fading out and running down.

But in "East Coker" the suffering has been faced,
lived through, understood, and the poet is back on his
feet. The old lamenting and beseeching have completely disappeared. This is a terribly bitter poem, but the
bitterness has some of the early Eliot edge, and it is di-

rected outward, toward reality. The passage on renunciation at the end of section three; the "wounded surgeon" lyric, in a wonderfully effective stanza form; the surprising and unexpected direct personal comment on self and career with which the poem ends—all these are new and fine. The key becomes major, the effects broader. The broadening persists throughout "The Dry Salvages," and in "Little Gidding" many of Eliot's themes— one could almost say fetishes—are brought together in a real feat of reconciliation.

Eliot here stands at a distant remove from the "aged eagle" role in which he presented himself, with considerable affectation, in *Ash Wednesday* thirteen years ago. He has learned lessons in patience and sympathy, a firm basis for renewed poetic strength.

1 9 4 3

§ *Euripides in Modern Dress*

The "classics," as the whirligig of taste turns, generation after generation, come in for some rather odd
transformations. Homer's Homer becomes Pope's Homer; Ezra Pound rewrites Callimachus; and the *Ion* of
Euripides, in the eighteenth century, becomes *Creusa,
Queen of Athens,* with all "the supernatural element"
left out. Gilbert Murray, in his translations, did his best
to completely muffle the original Greek with bad Tennyson and worse Swinburne. Modern poets are now endeavoring to disinter Greek drama from nineteenth-
century gilt and ruffles. H. D., in her current translation
of the *Ion,* makes Euripides into an Imagist, and that is
a queer effect, too.   She admits what she is doing. She
is out after "the core of Greek beauty," so she shears,
compresses, and prunes the varied and sinuous texture
of the Greek into brief cries and bright, detached images. She is out for pure symbols of the Greek intellect,
so everything is made static, reduced to marmoreal
form. She concedes the fact that "so-called rationalists"

have found in Euripides "irony lurking at every corner." But she prefers to think, and write, in terms of
"miracle." This attitude produces some perfectly beautiful poetry, but reduces the play as a whole, in her version, to nonsense.

For if the *Ion* is not an ironic presentation of a God
wreaking himself villainously on mortals, so that his
blind victims—mother and son—very nearly murder each
other as a result, it is difficult to make out what it is.
Jean Cocteau, in his *La Machine Infernale,* has under-
lined and expanded the fearful irony in Sophocles'
Oedipus Rex. To excise the bitter criticism, which en-
dears him to us as a fighter and a modern, from a play
by Euripides leaves us nothing but the shell of his work.
H. D. has given us a shell, and an exquisite one. But
even pure and burning "miracles" pall, whereas irony
and gumption live forever.

1 9 3 7

§ *The People, Yes and No*

Flaubert kept a notebook record—a *sottisier*—of the stupidities of the French bourgeoisie, whom he despised. Carl Sandburg, over a long period of years, has filled what must have been many notebooks with memoranda of the speech and folklore of the American people, whom he loves. *The People, Yes,* his new book, is the latest collection of such data. His poetry from the beginning has included snatches of speech warm from the tongue of the American crowd. The earlier Sandburg (then, as now, a mystic realist in all the strength of his Scandinavian inheritance) bore marks of prettiness, vagueness, and sentiment—the weaknesses of this type of poetry. With time, a good deal of mist has blown away from Sandburg's thinking and style. *The People, Yes,* sturdily written and closely coordinated for all its seeming lack of form, is an attempt to give back to America its sense of myth and living folklore, without which, it is Sandburg's conviction, vision or no vision, a people dies.

America, Sandburg has found, renovates its folklore from day to day, without the slightest bit of trouble. The wisecrack keeps up the tradition of the saw **and** proverb, and the American people continue to clothe their superstitions, prejudices, fears, hatreds, hysteria, hope, and love with imaginative flights, reduced to a terse sentence, or with dry common sense, wrapped in wild humor. ("The farther up the street you go the tougher they get, and I live in the last house." "A fog so thick we shingled the barn and six feet out onto the fog." "The cauliflower is a cabbage with a college education.") Slogans, slang, popular songs keep coming on, and jokes still lay them in the aisles. Death and destiny, the bad break, disaster in general, can be defied if they can be laughed at. Sandburg, with loving care, has collected the things left out when masses of people have been reduced, by abstract thinkers, to black lines on a graph or white lines on a blueprint. There are few comments he has missed (by the people, for the people) concerning the journey that still begins with birth pangs and ends with the grave.

When Sandburg's mystic political vein begins to flow, the people become "the great pool wherein worn-out breeds and clans drop for restorative silence." They are at once the dupes of "the cockeyed liars and bigots" and the earth around the roots of a true leader—"the strong man, the priceless one, who wants nothing for himself." They give beautiful names to common flowers; are brave, uncomplaining, misled. Concerning them, nobody knows the answer; each man "must work out his guess for himself." Meanwhile, they do their chores, pay the installment on the bungalow, the radio, the car; wander through a frightening world of advertisements; live, die, laugh, and consume. And since generation after generation leaves as a heritage a sediment of superb wisecracks, Sandburg hopes. As long as the people continue to talk and laugh with style and humor, there is no need to despair.

It is pleasant to have Allen Tate's slender volume of fifty-six pages—*The Mediterranean and Other Poems.* For the time may come when the freedom to produce, and enjoy, all kinds of things at once may be taken from us. It is now interesting to note the amount of classic common sense in Sandburg (the Western mystic, the feeler-into, the discarder of form), and the corresponding amount of romantic wishful-thinking and bitterness in Allen Tate (the Southern classicist, of the aristocratic tradition compact). Tate is a pupil of Pound, Eliot, and Valéry, a believer in the classic will, the champion of a special cause. To him the modern world is a damned world, since a set of special values has disappeared from it. For him the voices of Senators Calhoun and Mason still resound, the "irrepressible conflict" between the agrarian and industrial systems still goes on. But all has been translated, in Tate's style and thinking, into something rich and strange. The good old days when Representative Brooks thwacked Sumner on the floor of the Senate, when Mason's home was burned by Sheridan, are not wholly over for Tate, and it is romantic, though disguised, reverberations that Tate hears from that past time. Tate's nonpolitical poems—or, rather, his least political poems—are his best. The title poem of the book is a beautiful lyric, and there is much mature writing in the collection. I make one humble wish: that Villon's line, beginning "En l'an trentiesme de mon age," be overlooked for the next twenty years or so, as a title, a part, or an introduction to English poems. Since Pound embedded it in "Mauberley," it has gone the rounds and is by now, to put it mildly, a modern poetic chestnut.

1 9 3 6

§ *Landscape with Jeffers*

The hero of Robinson Jeffers' latest set-piece of human savagery, *Such Counsels You Gave to Me,* walks off the stage acting in an unusual way for a Jeffers character. He is moved, because of pity, to a moral decision. He chooses to shoulder another's punishment, after considering the advantages of suicide and escape. Previously he has acted in the usual Jeffersian manner: abetted his mother's incestuous passion for himself and stood by at his father's murder. He then turns over in his mind the question of whether anything is anything. Is there any crime, any innocence, any binding "human taboo"? Finally he decides that modern man has certain duties ("life is not rational"), and that retribution is one of them. So he turns away from union with the "clean" California wind and the "sane" California mountains, and chooses to expiate, not his own guilt, but his mother's.

All this is very fine, or would be in a character less queerly constituted than this young man is sure to be. Jeffers decides, at one point in the action, that human taboos can be transcended. God must have gone beyond human taboos. He is rather confused, however, on the stand that both ancient and modern man have taken concerning taboos. And he cannot, try as he will, in this case, force his characters to go beyond them. The mother-son incest theme proves too much for him. Classically and primitively, this breach of taboo brings down automatic punishment on even the unwitting transgressor. The wrath of the gods winds up, as Cocteau has expressed the process, like an infernal machine and fells the culprits. Oedipus actually marries Jocasta, in ignorance. In modern and Romantic tragedy the incest-tainted hero, like Hamlet, is usually stricken with inaction. The hero of Jeffers' poem walks open-eyed into the beginning of an incestuous relationship with his mother. But at the last he sheers off. He talks as though he were capable of anything. In point of fact he is capable of nothing but a great many obscurely expressed wrong reasons for his traditional stirrings of conscience. And he arouses little sympathy in the reader. For he and his mother—who, like most of Jeffers' women, *is* capable of anything—seem not so much puzzled and depraved as simple-minded. And, perhaps unfortunately in the humanity Jeffers professes to despise, the moral struggles of idiots somehow do not count.

The Romantic poet should not continue, over a long period, to excoriate the humanity of which he is a member. The satirist can manage analysis and defamation of the human race. He stands outside. The Romantic is involved in the action. The more he strives to identify himself with clean and mindless nature, the more he must degrade his characters and increase the enormity of their crimes. Meanwhile, his own importance increases by leaps and bounds. He is soon no longer con-

tent to be chorus, commentator, or prophet. He tends
toward the state of God himself. Jeffers says:

I the last living man
That sees real earth and skies
Actual life and real death.
The others are all prophets and believers
Delirious with the fevers of faith.

And again:

To be truth-bound, the neutral
Detested by all dreaming factions, is my errand here.

Notions of this inflated kind now frequently appear
everywhere in Jeffers. His lyrics, the forms he has many
times successfully filled with the intense emotion and
remarkable descriptions of natural beauty, are now viti-
ated by pronouncements. It is a pity that his mixed,
parochial, and rather Presbyterian disgusts must thus
gain headway. A man who has, from the beginning,
turned away from the arts, "sports and gallantries, the
stage, the antics of dancers," as childish nonsense, must
at length grow peevish even surrounded by noble landscapes. "Bitter earnestness," for the dramatic poet, can
be a faculty which cuts both ways.

"In very truth, the man who can see all creatures in
himself, himself in all creatures, knows no sorrow."
Such a man is also protected against ultimate confusion
and obsession. Jeffers' great talents, allowed some humble relation to the race, which, whatever its faults, can
at least laugh and change, might have escaped the limits
that now increasingly distort them.

1 9 3 7

§ *Rilke in His Age*

1

Rainer Maria Rilke, the Austrian poet who died in Switzerland in 1926 at the age of fifty-one, is a rare modern example of the poet who, "having learned to give himself to what he trusted," finally "learned to give himself to what he feared"; an artist who neither became stunted through, nor desired to escape from, the demands of his nature and his art; a poet whose work grew with him. In a period when the facing of inner truth is in no way a popular occupation—since too many flights away from the task, from war to suicide, are not only accessible but even morally respectable—a dedicated career like Rilke's becomes an heroic career. His talent for detachment, his distrust of the state of being loved (*"être aimé, c'est vivre mal et en péril"*), have laid him open to the charge of neurotic irresponsibility. We have only his work to assure us of the ultimate hollowness of this charge, and that work is strongly reassuring. Rilke was often exhausted, often afraid, often in flight, but he was capable of growth and solitude, a process and a state denied to the coward's or the delinquent's existence. And he stands as an example of integrity held through and beyond change—one of the few examples of such integrity that our times have produced.

The steady growth of interest in Rilke has brought on several attempts to make him available to English-speaking readers. Four of his prose works have appeared in English translation: *The Journal of My Other Self* (originally *Die Aufzeichnungen des Malte Laurids Brigge*), *The Life and Death of Cornet Christopher Rilke, Stories of God,* and *Letters to a Young Poet.* His last and greatest group of poems, the *Duineser Elegien,* have been translated by E. and V. Sackville-West in a finely printed and limited edition published by the Hogarth Press in 1931. As early as 1918 Miss Jessie Lemont translated some of the earlier poems with more awe than skill, and Ludwig Lewisohn and Jethro Bithell have done other renderings. Lately Stephen Spender has tried his hand at the difficult task.

It is always a question what use translation of any poetry serves. And the greater the poetry, the more closely it is limited to existence behind the barrier of the language in which it was originally written. When the work is subtle in meaning, intensely accurate in perception, profound in feeling, and the product as well of great technical virtuosity, the translator may well hesitate before attempting his task. Rilke may be classed with Baudelaire and Valéry as a poet complete appreciation of whom demands some knowledge in the reader of German and French.

J. B. Leishman, whose devotion to Rilke's work is undeniably deep and sincere, began to produce, in 1931, his series of translations with a volume of selections from all periods of Rilke's career, entitled *Poems.* Whatever his native qualifications for the task (and to lift Rilke into English requires extraordinary qualifications), and whatever his failure and successes, there is no doubt that the earlier book, together with the two volumes now under discussion, with their meticulous notes and long biographical and critical prefaces, give for the first time to the English reader a comprehensive notion of the quality, the range, and the power in one of the great poets of our time.

Requiem and Other Poems (1935) contains, among other things, versions of seventeen poems from the two volumes of *Neue Gedichte* first published in 1907 and 1908—the books wherein the great and mature Rilke for the first time came into view. The period which produced this poetry began after Rilke's meeting with Rodin. Rilke's early work had been filled with the mysticism, the sentimentality, and with that "unwillingness to renounce the attractions of the obscurer depths of the soul," which are peculiarly German. As he later expressed it, until he met Rodin nature had remained for him "a general occasion." His religious feeling, his seeking for God, had been at its worst a kind of adolescent *Schwärmerei* which his visits to Russia had fostered. The poems written immediately before his first visit to Paris (in spite of their great sincerity of tone and their growing mastery over effects) contain poems dangerously near religiosity of feeling.

He was born in Prague in 1875. His father's family was of German peasant stock which claimed some distant aristocratic admixture. From a rather pampered and enervating childhood he passed, at the age of eleven, to the hard life of a military school, which he endured for five years, an experience he never fully recovered from, and to which his distrust of close human relationships may perhaps be traced. He began to write—and publish—very young, and in 1899 and 1900, after an abortive attempt at training in the law and an unfortunate and silly early love affair, he made two visits to Russia. There he met Tolstoy and felt some vague sympathy with the tenets of Tolstoyism. In 1901 he married Clara Westhoff, a young sculptress, and through her became interested in Rodin. He first went to Paris in 1902, and on his second visit lived with Rodin as secretary for a year (1905 to 1906).

Malte Laurids Brigge (1910) and the *Neue Gedichte* (1907) are the direct products of the influence upon Rilke of Paris and of Rodin. Rodin taught him that the moment of inspiration must not be waited for but must be summoned and seized; and in Paris he learned to live "that simple life of a love that has endured, that without ever praising itself on that account, advances to everything, unaccompanied, inconspicuous, worthless. Proper work, abundance of tasks, all begin for the first time beyond this endurance."

Malte Laurids Brigge takes up, with extraordinary courage, the spiritual dissection of a modern city where it had been dropped by Baudelaire. (It was by reading Baudelaire that Rilke comforted himself during his first terrible Paris days.) In the Paris streets Rilke laid himself open to the strongest impacts of fear, horror, and loneliness. The cripples, the beggars, the madmen, the paupers, the terrible sick in those streets, became for him the doorways to meaning, to the secret which must, he believed, be hidden from mankind. He instinctively used "that mental pathology which seeks to understand human personality by studying it in its rare or morbid states, states in formation or deliquescence." And he not only looked upon suffering people in search of the secret. He went to "things"—sculpture, flowers, cathedrals, paintings, an open square, or a countryside. He detached himself from a subjective approach; for the first time he became objective. "His former tone . . . had been that of prayer, of the examination of conscience, of the act of faith. It had been an interior monologue which looked for God." He now looked upon "the thing" with the intensity which had earlier produced that profound and moving poem "Der Schauende" (Mr. Leishman's translation of which, in the *Poems* of 1931, is, up to now, his most inspired version of anything in Rilke). He was granted access to that "inscape" which Hopkins and the great mystics have felt to be present in all objects in nature.

The *Neue Gedichte* (1907)—short, closely written, compressed into most exigent form, using the most subtle possible powers of language, rhythm, rhyme, and assonance—are of course ultimately untranslatable. The grace in them, the light which seems to fall from the depth and height of the universe upon them, their tenderness and precision, can exist only in the original German. Mr. Leishman's methods of approximation have their moments of success and failure. His extreme respect for Rilke's work has led him to use the simplest and most direct English, singularly free from rhetorical padding. But his keeping to the side of simplicity often makes the language too light and too ordinary: he is hardly ever successful in rendering Rilke's extraordinary nouns and verbs, the structure of the refracting crystal of his style. The poems are always given, however, in their original scheme of rhyme and rhythm, and the complications of the German (that language *"si malleable, si capable d'abstraire et de personnifer à la fois"*) are handled with a good deal of authority. One poem, "Lied vom Meer," whose subtlety should warn off any translator from an attempt upon it—a poem which rises and subsides like a wordless cry—Mr. Leishman has attempted with unfortunate results. And in the translations of the two tender and profound poems that make up *Requiem* he again fails, because the looseness of the form demands a language more weighted, more resonant, than the English without effects into which it has been turned.

Die Sonette an Orpheus (eighteen of which in Mr. Leishman's earlier versions are included in the *Requiem* volume, and all of which, with the original German printed opposite the English versions, are included in the *Sonnets to Orpheus*) are part of the last work which Rilke accomplished. These poems, written in 1922 after ten years' silence, were "given" to Rilke when he was at last able to take up the task of completing his *Duineser Elegien,* begun in 1912 and interrupted by the First World War. "After months of solitary contemplation, utterance and release came to him in February, 1922, when, in a tempest of creative activity with which there is no parallel, except perhaps in the lives of some of the great musicians, the remaining eight elegies, the fifty-five *Sonnets to Orpheus,* and a number of poems he classified as *Fragmentarisches,* were written within three weeks."

These sonnets have been called, and are without doubt, among the profoundest poems of our time. In them Rilke expressed more deeply and, in spite of their difficult and compressed form, more fully and clearly than in any other work, his hard-won knowledge concerning love, existence, and death. Orpheus is taken as the symbol of the Mediator: the god with the lyre to whom both worlds are open, who not only knows the secret but works and expresses the secret in his song. Here Rilke made, instinctively and in his own medium, discoveries concerning the nature and workings of the unconscious, startling in their accuracy. For in his later maturity he was able to bring over into the modern world—when the "great traditional therapies" had broken down as guides to man's thoughts or answers to his suffering—the love which we can only call Christian, because of its profound pity and humility. Like Yeats, Rilke had spent his life creating a religion for himself. But beyond Yeats, who came to believe in man's pride and intellect as guides and symbols, Rilke, stubbornly confronting the real world with his sensibilities, continually testing one by the other, came at last to explain the one by the other, and made a connection between them. Unlike many converts to Roman or Anglo-Catholicism in our day, he did not walk into a ready-made spiritual system and close its door behind him. In the self-imposed isolation of his later years he rediscovered the worth of traditional and mythical residues, and drew from them insights of clinical worth and exactness. He belongs to the company of those who, in our day, have uncovered forgotten truths concerning the human psyche and its relation to its world. His poetry is great because of its spiritual validity, as well as for the validity of its complicated and subtle art.

His belief that "one must praise, in spite of all"; that one must renounce, let go, die and be reborn, endure; "that egoism and childish revolt must be silenced"; that the things which rouse the most terrible grief in us (such as the death of the young) must hold for us the deepest meaning; that it is our force which must use the mechanisms of a changing world for its own ends, not the mechanisms which must weaken our force; that we exist (as the rose, "that inexhaustible thing," exists), the fruit of powers beyond us, within us, which we must in some manner trust: such belief, such openness, such adulthood give back to us the healing of which cynicism, hatred, and an insistence on the complete sufficiency of material systems deprive us.

Sei—und wisse zugleich des Nicht—Seins Bedingung,
den unendlichen Grund deiner innigen Schwingung,
dass du sie völlig vollziehst dieses einzige Mal.

Zu dem gebrauchten sowohl, wie zum dumpfen und stum-
men
Vorrat der vollen Natur, den unsaglichen Summen,
zahle dich jubelnd hinzu und vernichte die Zahl.

Although a cult of Rilke would be unfortunate (as modernly all cults tend to become), it is important that his work be made more accessible to students of modern poetry and modern thought. For his work is one of the strongest antidotes to the powers of darkness—hatred, split allegiance, guilt, and regression—that our time has produced. And although the daring, yet accurate imagery, the compressed thought, and the compressed texture of this difficult poetry must come to us in a muffled and watered form, whatever hand attempts its Englishing, we must be grateful for some means of approach to its music and its meaning. With this Mr. Leishman's translations have provided us. Rilke himself believed that translations were of some value; he translated certain works of Gide, Valéry, Mallarmé, Baudelaire, Louise Labbé, and Michael Angelo.

Valéry wrote after Rilke's death:

To have lost him means to have lost one who combined in himself not only the comprehension of all the beauty

Europe has produced and a deepened recognition of the riches which spring from our complexity, but one who possessed an immediate and creative sensibility—the spirit of a coming age.

1 9 3 7

2

Rainer Maria Rilke finished the *Duino Elegies,* now translated into English by J. B. Leishman and Stephen Spender, in 1922. Together with the fifty-five *Sonnets to Orpheus,* written in the same burst of creative energy, they mark the summit of his career.

The *Elegies* are extremely difficult in the original German for stylistic reasons alone. They are an amalgam of two tendencies: the German, wherein, with dangerous ease, abstractions can be personified and the concrete abstracted; and the Symbolist, which tends to throw up plastic and bizarre images in order to express subtle states and intuitions. Rilke's power over language was immense, and he could work in the most exigent forms. The *Elegies,* however, are written in what seems to be a relatively untrammeled manner. Actually, their style, based for the most part on the hexameter, is laborious and condensed. The language everywhere is welded and weighted, and nowhere blurred or diffuse. Rilke, in his struggle to indicate the mystery of man's destiny, to "open up a universe without barriers," pushed language to extraordinary limits, suiting the range of his insight. The translator's task is therefore one of almost insuperable difficulty. One badly chosen word will throw a whole passage out of tone, and one expanded phrase almost obliterate the meaning.

J. B. Leishman has spent years translating Rilke into English and in writing long, painstaking glosses on the meaning of his poetry. Because of his sincerity, patience, and love for Rilke's work, he has had some remarkable moments of success in his task. Stephen Spender, who is his collaborator here, has translated Rilke before this. He has, however, always brought Rilke over into Spender rather than the opposite. His choice as collaborator was not entirely wise, for whatever Spender's gifts may be, they are not exceptionally disciplined or austere; they often suffer from vagueness and a delight in throwing language around. His taste, moreover, is not sure. The one earlier translation of the *Elegies* into English, by E. and V. Sackville-West, erred by making the tone too literary in a traditional English way. The present translation often fails by coalescing with the German, by sliding over punctuation (and italics), by frequent awkward and even ridiculous use of words. It is true that efforts have been made to duplicate the interior assonances and the neologisms, and to indicate the fundamentally ungrandiose tone by means of elisions and ordinary speech. What has not been carried over in any way is the underlying emotional pulse of the poetry, so moving in the original.

Leishman has contributed an illuminating preface and many notes. The reader who wishes to pursue further studies will find an enormous amount of reference material here. It would be valuable, too, if Leishman's earlier translations were published in America.

Rilke, during the last ten years, has been treated to exegesis in four languages. His integrity will bother the new utilitarian school of criticism, certainly. He is a perfect target for its simplifications. He will be outlawed as a "dilettante," because he lived in castles (Duino was one) and actually, for a time, in a tower (Muzot). He dedicated the *Elegies* to a princess. He spent his life looking and feeling and contemplating; he loved solitude; he drew nourishment from works of art. In the *Elegies,* however, the ills of our time are traced back to their source, to the spiritual infection of a world without values. The cheapness of this world is delineated in the "Tenth Elegy" with tragic insight. And Rilke's suggested cure is of a clinical exactness.

1 9 3 9

§ *Asian Exoticism*

American readers may now examine T. S. Eliot's translation of St.-J. Perse's *Anabase,* the poem which, both
before and since its first appearance in England in 1930
has influenced many poets, including Eliot himself. The
present edition, like the earlier, presents the French
text opposite Eliot's version and is introduced by the
original preface, wherein Eliot makes some attempt to
clear up the poem's impenetrability. Because poetry,
since 1930, has tended to become more impenetrable
rather than less, and because we are now familiar with
several watered versions, by American and British imitators, of this particular poem, we are more free than
Mr. Eliot once supposed we could be, to appreciate the
power of the original work and to enter into enthusiasm
about it.

Anabasis, as it is called in this translation, deals with
the beauty and terror of the earth, and with the beauty
and brutality of the civilizations man imposes upon it.
It deals as well with what lies beneath and extends beyond man's ingenious arts and plans: his spiritual journey, begun and continuing in isolation, and at last faced
with that symbol of further mystery, the sea. Perse's
poem is filled with that special Asian exoticism of which

our time approves. The sentiment projected onto the East by the nineteenth century (which populated the desert with Byronic heroes and multiplied, in copper-plate vignettes, gazelle-eyed maidens diaphanously swathed, under palms) has now been supplanted by something quite different. It is Eastern harshness, barrenness, Eastern cruelty and strength that appeal to heightened and disabused modern taste. *Anabasis* encloses these qualities, as *Seven Pillars of Wisdom* enclosed them. Effects of violence, severe and barbaric splendor, and terrible solitude are here compacted into sentences which seem dislocated by the intensity of the material they are made to bear. St.-J. Perse is the pseudonym of M. Alexis Saint-Leger, an ambassador of France, who as a diplomat spent many years at the French Embassy in Peking and as an explorer has made journeys into the Gobi Desert. It is the work of a many-sided personality. The spiritual and the actual, bathed in hard, open light of arid lands, are combined to produce the poem's special atmosphere.

The original French often rises into sonority and ecstasy (never purely rhetorical) that are sometimes flattened and deadened by Eliot. For example, "To the scale of our hearts was such vacancy completed!" certainly does not adequately render the feeling of *"A la mesure de nos cœurs fut tant d'absence consommée!"* But an occasional stiffness of phrase is better than the complete softening the poem has been subjected to in the hands of other manipulators. *Anabasis* is difficult, like all excellent things. But it repays, to put it materialistically, careful examination. For it is easy to forget, at present, things undertaken in "the darkness of the spirit," in a world "given over to explanations."

1 9 3 8

§ *The Decoration of Novels*

Edith Wharton has told how she was haunted, before the books in which they ultimately appeared were written, by her characters, or, even, by their disembodied names. In her autobiography, *A Backward Glance,* she mentioned a name then in her mind: Laura Testvalley. *The Buccaneers,* Mrs. Wharton's last and unfinished novel, gives Laura Testvalley her scene and character. She is a governess, granddaughter of a hero of the Risorgimento (Gennaro Testvaglia), cousin to Dante Gabriel Rossetti, once employed by a duchess, and later governess in an "old" New York family. She goes on to the higher wages offered by a "new" family (whose money is based on "deals" and financial manipulation); takes the fortunes of the younger daughter in hand and pilots her, over the heads of the disapproving Newport and New York sets, to London, and into a titled marriage. The manuscript breaks off before the novel's dénouement: Laura's sacrifice of personal happiness in order that her former pupil, now the ranking duchess of England, may escape from her dull duties and her dull duke into "deep and abiding love" with a lover. The outline left by Mrs. Wharton describes the entire plot very clearly.

It is interesting to see how Henry James' insistence on "form" in the novel was simplified by his friend and follower, Mrs. Wharton, into mere adherence to plot. The plot must proceed, through all its ramifications, even though characters be wrenched out of shape to serve it. Minor figures, put in purely to prop up the plan, soon are shuffled away, and are featureless from the beginning. The long arm of coincidence snaps up the roving actors and places them down neatly in surroundings cleverly arranged to suit their situation. The background is filled in with great color and accuracy; there is continual movement; the details of life in drawing room, ducal seat, and dower-house, on Saratoga verandas, in a ruined Cornish castle, on American railway platforms, all suitably lighted by the atmosphere of the '70's, are written down by a mistress of genre. But *The Buccaneers,* for all Mrs. Wharton's cleverness and skill, is dead at the heart. The book brings out, however, the way in which Mrs. Wharton's work formed a bridge from the nineteenth-century novel to the magazine fiction of the present where, in a superficially arranged scene, manners, clothes, food, and interior decorations are described carefully and at length; how she contained in herself, as it were, the whole transitional period of American fiction, beginning in the bibelot and imported-European-culture era of the late nineties, and ending in the woman's-magazine dream of suburban smartness.

The essential numbness in her novels—with the exception of *Ethan Frome,* where her talent for local color and her insight into the simpler ingredients of human character succeeded, because she did not attempt too much—goes back to the fact that she based her values not upon a free and rich feeling for life but on a feeling for decorum and pre-Wall Street merchant respectability. James praised early in her career "her diabolical little cleverness, the quality of intention and intelligence in her style, and her sharp eye for an interesting kind of subject." Added to these gifts was a highly trained taste, a thorough acquaintance with the "great world" of her time, and a passion for artistic people, provided, of course, that their background and manners conformed to the rather stuffy standards of the late nineteenth-century upper bourgeoisie. She admired, it should be remembered, not only Henry James but also Paul Bourget. An example of her fundamental bias against the disordered life of the artist is her astonishment when she discovered that George Sand's home, Nohant, showed no sign of the wild life which had streamed through it; it did not look *déclassée,* but on the contrary traditional and respectable. (The sympathetic attitude expressed in James' two essays on Sand is in strong contrast to Mrs. Wharton's surprise.) And Mrs. Wharton's mildly ironic description of life in great English houses should be put against the true dissection apparent in James' approach to the same subject. For the difference between a subject treated with ingenuity and one treated with imagination, Nan St. George, the "new rich" girl in *The Buccaneers,* and her family can be set beside Daisy Miller and hers. We love the living people and merely watch the puppets.

1 9 3 8

§ *William Butler Yeats*

William Butler Yeats, at the age of seventy-three, stands well within the company of the great poets. He is still writing, and the poems which now appear, usually embedded in short plays or set into the commentary and prefaces which have been another preoccupation of his later years, are, in many instances, as vigorous and subtle as the poems written by him during the years ordinarily considered to be the period of a poet's maturity. Yeats has advanced into age with his art strengthened by a long battle which had as its object a literature written by Irishmen fit to take its place among the noble literatures of the world. The spectacle of a poet's work invigorated by his lifelong struggle against the artistic inertia of his nation is one that would shed strong light into any era.

The phenomenon of a poet who enjoys continued development into the beginning of old age is in itself rare. Goethe, Sophocles, and, in a lesser degree, Milton come to mind as men whose last works burned with the gathered fuel of their lives. More often development, in a poet, comes to a full stop; and it is frequently a negation of the ideals of his youth, as well as a declination of his powers, that throws a shadow across his final pages.

Yeats in his middle years began to concern himself with the problem of the poet in age. He wrote in 1917, when he was fifty-two:

A poet when he is growing old, will ask himself if he cannot keep his mask and his vision, without new bitterness, new disappointment. . . . Could he if he would, copy Landor who lived loving and hating, ridiculous and un-conquered, into extreme old age, all lost but the favor of his muses. . . . Surely, he may think, now that I have found vision and mask I need not suffer any longer. Then he will remember Wordsworth, withering into eighty years, hon-oured and empty-witted, and climb to some waste room, and find, forgotten there by youth, some bitter crust.

We can trace, in Yeats, the continually enriched and undeviating course of an inspired man, from earliest youth to age. We can trace the rectitude of the spiritual line in his prose and poetry alike. And there is not a great deal of difference between the "lank, long-coated figure . . . who came and went as he pleased," drama-tizing himself and his dreams in the streets of Dublin (the youth who had known William Morris and was to know Dowson and Wilde), and the man who, full of honors in our day, impresses us with his detachment and subtle modernity. Yeats, the fiery young Nationalist, rolling up with his own hands the red carpet spread on a Dublin sidewalk "by some elderly Nationalist sof-tened or weakened by time, to welcome Viceroyalty," is recognizable in the poet of advanced years who does not hesitate to satirize certain leaders of the new Ireland.

Yeats' faith in the development of his own powers

never failed. He wrote, in 1923, after receiving from the
King of Sweden the medal symbolizing the Nobel Prize:

It shows a young man listening to a Muse, who stands
young and beautiful with a great lyre in her hand, and I
think as I examine it, "I was good-looking once like that
young man, but my unpractised verse was full of infirmity,
my Muse old as it were, and now I am old and rheumatic
and nothing to look at, but my Muse is young." I am even
persuaded that she is like those Angels in Swedenborg's
vision, and moves perpetually "towards the dayspring of
her youth."

1

The Irish literary and dramatic movement, in general
belief, rose, late in the nineteenth century, in some
vague manner from the temperament of the Irish people. As a matter of fact, Ireland in Yeats' young manhood was as ungrateful a soil for art as any that could
be found, in a particularly materialistic time. The native Celtic genius that Arnold had felt to be so open to
the influence of a "natural magic" had been, for over a
century, drawn off into politics. The Anglo-Irish tradition, having produced in the eighteenth century Swift,
Congreve, Edgeworth, Goldsmith, Berkeley, and Burke,
flowered no longer.

The Land Agitation (the struggle of the peasantry
against their landlords) and the Young Ireland and
Fenian Movements (the struggle of the Irish people
against English rule) from the '40's on had absorbed the
energies and the eloquence of talented young Irishmen.
Irish writers, as Stephen Gwynn has said, having been

taught by Swift that written English could be used as a weapon against their oppressors, never forgot their lesson. The Catholic Emancipation Bill, by the efforts of Daniel O'Connell, was passed in 1829. In 1842 the Young Ireland Movement was given a newspaper by Thomas Davis: the *Nation,* whose motto was "to create and foster public opinion in Ireland and make it racy of the soil." The *Nation* also fostered a school of Irish poets. Their audience was eager for stirring and heartening words; the verse which spoke to it most clearly was the rhetorical and sentimental ballad, celebrating the Irish race and inciting it to action and solidarity. This verse, when it was not written in the sentimental and insipid vein made famous by Tom Moore, was filled, as has been pointed out, with the hortatory gusto of Lord Macaulay. Versifiers used its forms with skill, and one or two—Clarence Mangan and Sir Samuel Ferguson—touched them with real color and depth of feeling. But there is no doubt that Irish literature, in the years between 1848 and 1891, had fallen upon barren times.

The year 1891 brought Parnell's death. The tragic end of a leader intensely hated and loved, and the loss of much political hope thereby, threw the national consciousness violently back on itself. Yeats has described the situation (he was twenty-six at the time). "Nationalist Ireland was torn with every kind of passion and prejudice, wanting, so far as it wanted any literature at all, Nationalist propaganda disguised as literature. All the past had been turned into a melodrama with Ireland the blameless hero, and poet, novelist, and historian had but one object, to hiss the villain, and only the minority doubted the greater the talent the greater the hiss. It was all the harder to substitute for that melodrama a nobler form of art, because there had been, however different in their form, villain and victim."

At the breakup of the Catholic State in the wars of the seventeenth century, "Irish laws and customs, the whole framework of the Gaelic civilization, had been annihilated." Music, literature, and classical learning, loved by even the poorest of the Irish, had been driven into hiding, with only "hedge-schoolmasters" and wandering bards to keep them from oblivion. During the years when the *Nation* was coming to be the literary force behind Irish Nationalism, traditional Gaelic survived in the minds of Gaelic-speaking peasants. Elsewhere it had disappeared, and from these minds and memories it was rapidly fading. After generations of poverty and oppression, the orally transmitted songs and histories had become fragmentary. Few educated Irishmen knew them, since no educated Irishman knew Gaelic. The Irish language was forbidden in the national schools, and the sons of Anglo-Irish landlords and rectors who passed through Trinity College in Dublin learned English culture and English literature. Standish James O'Grady had published his *Bardic History* in 1880, but, since O'Grady was a champion of the aristocracy, the book made little impression on the partisan-minded country as a whole. When, in 1894, an Irish landlord with some literary ambitions, Edward Martyn, said to another of the same class, George Moore, "I wish I knew enough Irish to write my plays in Irish," Moore replied, "I thought nobody did anything in Irish but bring turf from the bog and say prayers." And Yeats has testified in an essay on the Irish Dramatic Movement: "When we began our work we tried to get a play in Gaelic. We could not even get a condensed version of the dialogue of Oisin and St. Patrick."

2

Where so much of the spirit of art had to be revivified, so many of its forms repaired, and so tight a mold of fanaticism broken, a man was needed who had in himself some of the qualities of the fanatic—a man who was, above all else, an artist, capable of making an occasional compromise with a human being, but incapable of making one with the informing essence of his art. New light and air had to be let into the closed minds and imaginations of a people made suspicious and hysterically provincial through persecution and disaster. It was impossible to weld the opinions of factions, but all could be drawn into "one net of feeling." A man of sensibility, however, was not enough. Not only insight and imagination, but ruthlessness, fervor, disinterestedness, and a capacity for decision and action, were required.

William Butler Yeats first appears, in the memories of his contemporaries, as a rarefied human being: a tall, dark-visaged young man who walked the streets of Dublin and London in a poetic hat, cloak, and flowing tie, intoning verses. The young man's more solid qualities were not then apparent to the casual observer. But it was during these early years that Yeats was building himself, step by step, into a person who could not only cope with reality but bend it to his will. He tells, in one of his autobiographies, of his determination to overcome his young diffidence. Realizing that he was "only self-possessed with people he knew intimately," he would go to a strange house "for a wretched hour for schooling's sake." And because he wished "to be able to play with hostile minds" he trained out of himself, in the midst of harsh discussion, the sensitive tendency "to become silent at rudeness."

The result of this training began to be apparent before Yeats was thirty. George Moore has recorded how, on meeting him in London (having been badly impressed by his "excessive" getup at a casual meeting some years before), he thought to worst Yeats easily in argument. The real mettle of his opponent soon came into view. "Yeats parried a blow on which I had counted, and he did this so quickly and with so much ease that he threw me on the defensive in a moment. 'A dialectician,' I muttered, 'of the very first order'; one of a different kind from any I had met before."

This intellectual energy, this "whirling" yet deeply intuitive and ordered mind, with its balancing streak of common sense, had come to Yeats through a mixed inheritance. The Yeats blood, perhaps Norman, had been Anglo-Irish for centuries, and it is notorious that English families transplanted to Ireland often become more Irish than the native stock. Yeats' paternal grandfather and great-grandfather had been Protestant rectors, in County Down and County Sligo respectively, and there had been eighteenth-century soldiers and government officials on this side of the family. Yeats' mother was a Pollexfen; her stock was Cornish—that is to say, English-Celtic. Her father, William Pollexfen, a lonely strong man whom Yeats as a child loved and feared ("I wonder if the delight in passionate men in my plays and poetry is more than his memory"), had settled in Sligo as a shipowner, after a career as master of ships. Yeats spent several of his childhood years and many of his adolescent summers near the town of Sligo, and from that Western countryside, so full of the beauties of lake, mountain, and sea, and from its people, who still had Gaelic in their speech and legends in their memory, he drew the material of his early poetry.

Yeats has told of the deep emotional reserves in his Sligo-born mother, "whose actions were unreasoning and habitual like the seasons." From his father, John Butler Yeats, a man of original mind who had been trained in the law but turned to painting and to the pre-Raphaelite enthusiasms current in the '70's and '80's, Yeats early heard that "intensity was important above all things." The father's passion for Blake, Morris, and Rossetti soon was shared by the son. Yeats had some English schooling; he later was an art student in Dublin. During this period he became a Nationalist. The elder Yeats had friends among Unionists and Nationalists alike, and, well acquainted with the liberal English thought of his time, enthusiastically espoused the cause of Home Rule. His son's Nationalism was both intellectual and emotional. He became the friend of John O'Leary, an old Fenian who had returned to Dublin after imprisonment and exile for youthful conspiracies; and Maude Gonne, a great beauty and successful agitator, was also an influence helping to channel his youthful ardor toward the more heroic and mystic side of the Nationalist movement. In both of these people Yeats felt imaginative and courageous character which transcended political bigotry and dogma. At no time, from the beginning of his career onward, did he for a moment yield to the hard letter of Irish politics. It was the spirit in those politics he wished to strengthen and make serviceable. His ends, and the means to bring about his ends, were always clear in his mind. "We cannot move the peasants and the educated classes in Ireland by writing about politics or about Gaelic, but we may move them by becoming men of letters and expressing primary truths in ways appropriate to this country."

His art was poetry, and, almost from the first, he used that art as a tool, his avowed purpose being to rid the literature of his country from the insincere, provincial, and hampering forms of "the election rhyme and the pamphlet."

3

The music of Yeats' early poetic efforts was in part derived from Morris and Shelley. The earliest poems, published in the *Dublin University Review* in 1886, paid youth's tribute to romantic subjects and foreign landscape: Spain, India, Arcadia. The poems in *The Wanderings of Oisin,* published in 1889, celebrated Irish landscape as well. Actual Sligo place names appeared in them, and, along with imaginary words put into mouths of legendary Irish figures, Yeats had built poems on the single line of a song, or around a few words heard from peasants. Sligo continued to be the home of his imagination during the next ten years, when he was much away from Ireland, working as a journalist in London. His best-known early poem, "The Lake Isle of Innisfree," came to his mind in a London street, and expressed his homesick memory of an islet in Lough Gill, a lake near the town of Sligo.

In England he not only was drawn into the end-of-the-century literary movement, but played an active part in shaping it. With Ernest Rhys he founded, in London, the Rhymers Club, to which Lionel Johnson, Ernest Dowson, and Arthur Symons belonged. He knew

Wilde and was published by W. E. Henley in the *National Observer*. Yeats went to Paris in 1894, at a time when Villiers de l'Isle-Adam's *Axël* was exerting its power over the young for the first time. This poem, "the swan song of romanticism," a mixture of Gothic gloom, Rosicrucian occultism, and Symbolist poetry, was to influence more than one generation of young writers. "*Axël* or its theme," Yeats wrote thirty years later, "filled the minds of my Paris friends. I was in the midst of one of those artistic movements that have the intensity of religious revivals in Wales and are such a temptation to the artist in his solitude. I have in front of me an article which I wrote at that time, and I find sentence after sentence of revivalist thoughts that leave me a little ashamed." Contact with such enthusiasm, however, did much to confirm Yeats' own belief in the importance of standing out for *l'art pour l'art*. He had been exposed, at exactly the proper moment in his young career, to literary excitement heightened into a kind of religious fervor. He brought back seeds of this stimulation to Ireland: to a soil which had lain fallow for a long time.

Meanwhile, in Ireland, an interest in Gaelic was growing. Douglas Hyde, a brilliant student at Trinity in Dublin, had learned Gaelic and had begun to translate Gaelic songs and legendary material into the beautiful Tudor English still spoken in the West. Gaelic idiom had been brought over into this speech, and Yeats immediately recognized the language, English yet un-English, in which he wished to write. His poetry soon took to itself not only Gaelic effects of alliteration and assonance, but Gaelic effects of rhythm: that "gapped music" so delicate that it seems to come from the rise and fall of intonation in the Irish voice.

Many Irish people, particularly the young (as Joyce has testified), were haunted by the harplike fluidity of these songs, and imaginatively stirred by the traditional symbols, the heroic Druid figures Yeats revived. But political societies and the press turned against his aesthetic purposes. The poems in *The Wind Among the Reeds* (1899) were termed "affected," "un-Irish," "esoteric," "pagan," and "heretical." Yeats in later years was to admit a "facile charm, a too soft simplicity," in his early work. He soon began to clear his style of its symbolic trappings, to make it austere, flexible, resonant—an instrument of great lyric and dramatic range. Had he clung to the early style, with its long swing, almost like incantation, its heavy imagery, he would have limited himself unduly. Coming when they did, however, these evocations of Celtic beauty, heroism, and strangeness wakened, as more severe music could not then waken, Ireland's ears to the sound of its own voice speaking its own music.

4

Yeats had the good fortune to form, in the late '90's, one of the most important friendships of his life. He met Lady Gregory when his need for a staying influence was crucial. He had not entirely escaped the results of the romantic violence let loose (more into their personal lives than into their poetry) by the poets of the decade, in their revolt against respectable bourgeois strictures. He has indicated the nature of his own crisis in *Dramatis Personae*. "When I went to Coole [Lady Gregory's estate in Galway] the curtain had fallen upon the first act of my drama. . . . I must have spent the summer of 1897 at Coole. I was involved in a miserable love-affair. . . . Romantic doctrine had reached its extreme development. . . . My nerves had been wrecked."

Lady Gregory, whom Yeats met through Arthur Symons and Edward Martyn (Martyn's demesne, Tillyra, adjoined Coole), was a woman of much cultivation and generosity of spirit. Yeats had lost the power to impose upon himself regular habits of work. Lady Gregory, who was later to write out the Irish legends in the simple speech of the peasants of her countryside, took him from cottage to cottage collecting folklore. Coole and its environs were to give the mature Yeats a background for his later work, as Sligo had given him a scene for his earlier. With his technical apprenticeship and his most excessive enthusiasms behind him, Yeats turned away from the middle-class culture of Dublin to the people of Galway farms and villages. "Folk is our refuge from vulgarity." Once he had regained "a tolerable industry," his grasp on reality was further strengthened by the struggle to found what was to become the Abbey Theatre. To this task he and Lady Gregory, with the help of Edward Martyn and George Moore, now applied themselves.

Yeats knew that nothing was read in Ireland but "prayer books, newspapers, and popular novels." He also knew that the Irish had been trained, by politics and the Church, to listen. They were a potential audience, in the primary sense of that word. He had already formed in Dublin the National Literary Society, with the intention of giving "opportunity to a new generation of critics and writers to denounce the propagandist verse and prose that had gone by the name of Irish literature." He now wanted a literary theatre. He had written plays, but had no stage, unless it were the stage of small halls, where they could be presented.

Against him were ranged the entrenched powers of the commercial theatre, the Church, and the press, the last two informed with the special Irish fear of "humiliation" and misinterpretation, bred from Ireland's peculiar political situation. "But fight that rancor I must." He fought it for more than ten years, not only for the sake of his own plays, but for the plays of other Irish dramatists, particularly Synge. His own plays caused mild trouble. Synge's *Playboy*, presented in 1904, brought on a week of riots and emptied the Abbey Theatre for months. But Yeats held out, against an enraged Dublin and an intimidated company. By 1912 the public had learned how to listen to imaginative drama with appreciation, to satiric plays without resentment. The Irish Dramatic Movement had come through, at the cost of great energy and courage expended by its founders. Yeats then turned away from the "popular" theatre, and began to write plays which could be presented in a room by a few amateurs and musicians, plays which could carry his special music and dramatic formality with the least theatrical machinery.

5

"We should write out our thoughts," Yeats has said, "in as nearly as possible the language we thought them in, as though in a letter to an intimate friend." And again: "If I can be sincere and make my language natural, and without becoming discursive, like a novelist, and so indiscreet and prosaic, I shall, if good or bad luck make my life interesting, be a great poet; for it will no longer be a question of literature at all."

If we grant naturalness, sincerity, and vigor to Yeats' late style, we still have not approached its secret. Technical simplicity may produce, instead of effects of tension and power, effects of bleakness and poorness. What impresses us most strongly in Yeats' late work is that here a whole personality is involved. A complex temperament (capable of anger and harshness, as well as of tenderness), and a powerful intellect, come through; and every part of the nature is released, developed, and rounded in the later books. The early Yeats was, in many ways, a youth of his time: a romantic exile seeking, away from reality, the landscape of his dreams. By degrees—for the development took place over a long period of years—this partial personality was absorbed into a man whose power to act in the real world and endure the results of action (responsibility the romantic hesitates to assume) was immense. Yeats advanced into the world he once shunned, but in dealing with it he did not yield to its standards. That difficult balance, almost impossible to strike, between the artist's austerity and "the reveries of the common heart"—between the proud passions, the proud intellect, and consuming action— Yeats finally attained and held to. It is this balance which gives the poems written from (roughly) 1914 on (from *Responsibilities,* published in that year, to poems published at present) their noble resonance. "I have had to learn how hard is that purification from insincerity, vanity, malignance, arrogance, which is the discovery of style."

Technically, the later style is almost lacking in adverbs—built on the noun, verb, and adjective. Its structure is kept clear and level, so that emotionally weighted

words, when they appear, stand out with poignant emphasis. "The Wild Swans at Coole" (1919) opens:

The trees are in their autumn beauty,
The woodland paths are dry,
Under the October twilight the water
Mirrors a still sky;
Upon the brimming water among the stones
Are nine and fifty swans.

Equipped with this instrument, Yeats could put down,
with full scorn, his irritation with the middle-class ideals
he had hated from youth:

What need you, being come to sense,
But fumble in a greasy till
And add the halfpence to the pence
And prayer to shivering prayer, until
You have dried the marrow from the bone;
For men were born to pray and save:
Romantic Ireland's dead and gone,
It's with O'Leary in the grave.

.   .   .   .

Was it for this the wild geese spread
The grey wing upon every tide;
For this that all that blood was shed,
For this that Edward Fitzgerald died
And Robert Emmet and Wolfe Tone,
All that delirium of the brave?
Romantic Ireland's dead and gone,
It's with O'Leary in the grave.

On the other hand he could celebrate Irish *salus, virtus,*
as in the poem "An Irish Airman Foresees His Death,"
and in the fine elegies on the leaders of the 1916 Easter
Rebellion.

And Yeats came to be expert at the dramatic presentation of thoughts concerning love, death, the transience and hidden meaning of all things, not only in the form of a philosopher's speculation, a mystic's speech, or a scholar's lonely brooding, but also (and this has come to be a major Yeatsian effect) in the cracked and rowdy measures of a fool's, an old man's, an old woman's song. *The Tower* (1928) and *The Winding Stair* (1929) contain long meditations—some "in time of civil war"—upon his life, his times, his ancestors, his descendants; upon the friends and enemies of his youth.

The short plays, composed on the pattern of the Japanese Noh drama, which Ezra Pound had brought to Yeats' attention—*Four Plays for Dancers* (1921), *Wheels and Butterflies* (1934), *The King of the Great Clock Tower* (1935)—Yeats made the vehicle for the loveliest of his later songs, for all his later development of pure music:

Come to me, human faces,
Familiar memories;
I have found hateful eyes
Among the desolate places,
Unfaltering, unmoistened eyes.

Folly alone I cherish
I choose it for my share,
Being but a mouthful of air
I am content to perish.
I am but a mouthful of sweet air.

The opening song in the play *The Only Jealousy of Emer* illustrates the variety of stress, the subtlety of meaning, of which Yeats became a master:

A woman's beauty is like a white
Frail bird, like a sea-bird alone

At day-break after a stormy night
Between two furrows of the ploughed land;
A sudden storm and it was thrown
Between dark furrows of the ploughed land.
How many centuries spent
The sedentary soul
In toil of measurement
Beyond eagle and mole,
Beyond hearing or seeing,
Or Archimedes' guess,
To raise into being
That loveliness?

A strange unserviceable thing,
A fragile, exquisite pale shell,
That the vast troubled waters bring
To the loud sands before day has broken.
The storm arose and suddenly fell
Amid the dark before day has broken.
What death? what discipline?
What bonds no man could unbind,
Being imagined within
The labyrinth of the mind,
What pursuing or fleeing
What wounds, what bloody press
Dragged into being
This loveliness?

6

From youth on, Yeats has thought to build a religion
for himself. Early "bored with an Irish Protestant point
of view that suggested, by its blank abstraction, chlorate
of lime," he eagerly welcomed any teaching which at-
tested supersensual experience, or gave him a back-

ground for those thoughts which came to him "from beyond the mind." "Yeats likes parlor magic," George Moore maliciously remarked, in the '90's. At that time, when religious belief and man's awe before natural mysteries were rapidly breaking up, the wreckage of the supernatural had been swept into mediums' shabby parlors and into the hands of quacks of all kinds. Many men of Yeats' generation took refuge in the Catholic Church. But Yeats kept to his own researches. He had experimented, when an adolescent, with telepathy and clairvoyance, in the company of his uncle, George Pollexfen, a student of the occult. He later studied the Christian Cabala and gradually built up, from his own findings and from the works of Blake, Swedenborg, and Boehme, his theories of visionary and spiritual truth. But he was never, as Edmund Wilson has pointed out, a gullible pupil. He invariably tried to verify phenomena. And today, when we know more than we once knew concerning the meaning of man-made symbols, the needs of the psyche, and the workings of the subconscious, Yeats' theories sound remarkably instructed and modernly relevant. His *Anima Mundi* closely resembles Jung's universal or racial unconscious, and even his conceptions of Image and Anti-Image, the Mask and its opposite, are closely related to psychological truth.

Of late years, after a lifetime spent in efforts to break up the deadening surface of middle-class complacency, Yeats has drawn nourishment from the thought of the relation of eighteenth-century Anglo-Irish writers to their society. These men—Swift, Berkeley, Grattan— had behind them, he believes, a social structure capable of being an aid to works of imagination and intellect. The ideal of the artist built into his background, sustaining it and sustained by it, Yeats has termed "Unity of Being." He has striven all his life to give Ireland a sense of what such a society can be, and to make himself an artist worthy of the energy which built "the beautiful humane cities."

In age, he shows no impoverishment of spirit or weakening of intention. He answers current dogmatists with words edged with the same contempt for "the rigid world" of materialism that he used in youth. He is now content to throw out suggestions that are not, perhaps, for our age to complete, as it is not for our age fully to appreciate a man who reiterates: "If we have not the desire of artistic perfection for an art, the deluge of incoherence, vulgarity, and triviality will pass over our heads." But adherence to that creed, and that creed alone, has given us the greatest poet writing in English today, and Ireland the greatest it has ever known.

Move upon Newton's town,
The town of Hobbes and of Locke,
Pine, spruce, come down
Cliff, ravine, rock:
What can disturb the corn?
What makes it shudder and bend?
The rose brings her thorn,
The Absolute walks behind.

1 9 3 8

§ *Light and Adult*

Some years ago, W. H. Auden, with a collaborator, produced an anthology designed to lure English schoolboys toward the forbidding subject of "poetry." Now, in the preface to *The Oxford Book of Light Verse,* which he has edited, he has set himself the task of proving why poetry has lost, in great measure, its power to express ordinary life and delight the general ear. The fault, he says, lies with the results of the Industrial Revolution, which broke up an agricultural society, moved people from their bases, made the division between classes sharper, and drove the poet into gloomy romanticism and into specialized groups of his own kind: "introspective, obscure, and highbrow." A good society, Auden concludes, is the only society which can survive, and a poet in such a society will be able to "write poetry which is simple, clear and gay; light and adult."

Long ago, from an entirely different point of view—that of the "pure artist"—Yeats gave much the same reasons for poetry's muddle and decline. Poetry, he said, flourished in "the hut and the castle." It is the middle classes, bred in strength by the Industrial Revolution, that have no appreciation of poetry's impact. From simple working people come folk songs, gay snatches of all sorts, chanteys, proverbs, and nursery rhymes. From levels of society where leisure allows a cultivated taste to flourish comes verse written with high skill: epigrams and various forms of verbal play. The middle classes, with skimpy standards and frightened, insecure taste, produce nothing but a great dislike for "vulgarity" and a passion for verse reeking of sentiment or sounding, in some vague way, uplifting and "noble."

Auden takes light verse to include verse "which is neither emotional nor obscure, but . . . casual in content, popular and unpretentious in form, and easily understood." Light verse, he adds, can be serious. (Eliot proves this with his early *Poems,* although Auden does not mention the fact.) But light verse, primarily, is to be enjoyed. To quote Yeats again: "Only that which does not teach, does not cry out, does not persuade, does not condescend, does not explain, is irresistible."

There is no doubt whatever that the poems in Auden's collections are irresistible. From Chaucer through Skelton and the anonymous writers of lovely little carols, ballads, and rhymes (how nice to see "Hey, diddle, diddle" appreciated!) from Shakespeare's and Ben Jonson's songs to Herrick and "Hudibras"; from Marvell to Dryden ("London Bridge" comes in around here); from Swift's verses on his death, that masterful combination of cultivated form and ordinary speech, to Gay, Pope, Burns, and Blake; from a fine collection of rough Irish ballads on to Lamb, Landor, Tom Moore, Byron, Barham, Hood, and Praed (who is said to have influenced Pushkin), the lightness, the fancy, and the realism flow. Then, after an anonymous alphabetical song on the Corn Laws, we are treated to the full nonsensical talents of Lear, Carroll, and W. S. Gilbert. Auden has long been enthusiastic about American folk songs; he includes un-hackneyed Negro spirituals along with "Casey Jones," "The Man on the Flying Trapeze," and "Frankie and Johnny" ("orally collected"). We get light verse from unexpected people: Hardy, Lawrence, Housman, V. Lindsay are printed near Yeats. The more professional modern writers of gay rhyme have been omitted. The whole anthology is so completely clear of the musty, the pompous, the would-be, and the hateful sides of mankind that it makes confidence in the human breed mount. It would be fine to have a New Society to match it.

1 9 3 8

§ *Stephen Spender*

1 HEADS WILL ROLL

Stephen Spender's *Trial of a Judge* is described as a tragedy in five acts. Its action is, briefly, as follows: A liberal judge with ideas of abstract and absolute justice condemns a group of Fascists for the brutal murder of Petra, a half-Jewish intellectual. Soon after this he is faced with the problem of how to treat some Communists who have been unlawfully carrying revolvers and who have inadvertently shot a policeman in the arm. He condemns the Communists, too. His wife, who is a reactionary, and his friend, who is a member of the government, bring pressure to bear upon him. He reprieves the Fascists. He then listens to the Communists, sees a Communist killed, retracts the reprieve, and grants the Communists a new trial. The Fascists, now in power, arrest the judge and bring *him* to trial. He clings to the idea of humane values, and Petra's fiancée says a few words about the necessity of love, but this show of antique European idealism does not save him from a prison cell and death at the hands of a Fascist firing squad. A chorus of Red prisoners, in the last act, chants a hymn of hope for future freedom and peace. They sort of forgive the judge, too, for his liberalism, which made him see with a "hypocrite mind."

Mr. Spender makes no mystery of his Communist sympathies, so perhaps it is not too Red-baiting to say at once that *Trial of a Judge* is straight post 1935-Party-line liberal-scaring. (The Red faction in the play is so up-to-date that it calls upon the laws of democracy and the police, at one point, to protect it.) Going one step further into hypocritical-liberal dissection, and considering the play as a piece of writing, the critic must say that it marks a new low in Mr. Spender's career, is frightful poetry, and, academically speaking, no tragedy at all.

For tragedy must have some root in human motives. The human motives in the first act of *Trial of a Judge* go completely off the rails. The mother of the murdered man, for example, appears, and in our old-fashioned way we feel sympathy for her bereavement. This is the wrong reaction, we soon perceive. She is really a maundering old fool and, it later turns out, a symbol for Established Religion. The fiancée pregnant with the murdered man's child again touches our hearts, but once more our sympathy is misplaced. She takes up at once with the brother of her lover, and we feel foolish and confused, although we realize that her action must Mean Something. Mr. Spender, with loud cries of "Death!" from Communists and Fascists, and of "Heads will roll!" from the Fascists, endeavors to waken us to the fact that our gentle reactions put us right before the Fascist firing squad with the judge. But by the time the last act came on, with its final volley, this reader, for one, no longer cared. If peace and freedom are to be ushered in with such a farrago of mixed metaphors, dictated thinking, Eliotonian tigers (there are three of these), and Salvation Army choruses, perhaps it is better for anyone who admires good writing and insists upon keeping intact a sense of humor to seek out a grave and curl up in it. Without giving a series of silly speeches first.

There is a beautiful image of an airman looking down on a town on page 56.

1 9 3 8

2 RUINS AND VISIONS

Stephen Spender's new book, *Ruins and Visions,* is his first collection of shorter poems to be published in America since 1934. Spender's work has been preferred by some to the more astringent writing of Auden, and for a discernible reason. At bottom, Spender is not really "modern" at all; he writes in a style clogged with rhetoric and adolescent emotion and has a strong strain of nineteenth-century hope and hero worship, but his gift is undeniably real, and that he is a perfectly sincere and touchingly idealistic character is apparent. His gentleness and idealism show up even in the most obvious of his propaganda verse.

Ruins and Visions cannot be said to show a startling degree of integration. Reality, however, has moved in on the poet and he is now less sure of the efficacy of the abstract will. "I have deliberately," he says in the preface, "turned back to a kind of writing which is more personal, and have included within my subjects weakness, fantasy, and illusion." As a matter of fact, the later poems are far less illusory and fantastic than many of his earlier ones. He has left behind those long, sagging colloquies with himself, so characteristic of the delayed adolescent; he no longer wants to be somewhere where he isn't or return to somewhere where he once was. He is less sentimental about the perfect quality of love presumably to be found in the proletarian inhabitants of a house "at the edge of the railway lines." Perhaps, these later poems say, courage and patience in bearing an actual situation are as worthy as the determined effort to keep outside "the grownup world of cheating compromises." The reader should watch for the real majesty and sensitiveness of phrase, which become more conscious and controlled as the book goes on, and not be too easily tripped up by the sentences which mean nothing and are put in here and there like gargoyles.

1 9 4 2

§ *James on a Revolutionary Theme*

For all the varied critical attention given, in the last twenty years, to the novels of Henry James, those of his middle period are seldom read. When they are read, their real intention is often missed or is interpreted in some peculiar, special way. F. R. Leavis has recently pointed out several flagrant misinterpretations of James (including the classic mistake made by the critic who thought Isabel Archer divorced her husband and married an American businessman at the end of *The Portrait of a Lady*) and has explained the neglect of the early and middle James by the fact that readers, steered toward the works of the late, "difficult" period, and baffled by these, make no further investigation. The three books which, appearing in the center of James's career, fully exemplify the virtues of his early manner—*The Bostonians, The Princess Casamassima,* and *The Tragic Muse*—are those most completely ignored.

The Princess Casamassima, it is true, has recently come in for some attention, since critics interested in

novels concerned with revolutionary activities have discovered that in this book James deals with revolutionaries in the financially depressed London of the '80's.
Although I cannot claim to have unearthed every scrap
of material written about this book, I have read a fair
amount and can say that not one commentator has
shown signs of understanding the design James has so
clearly presented in it. Usually *The Princess* has been
put down as a melodramatic and rather fumbling attempt at a novel dealing with a revolutionary theme.

Several good reasons exist for these critical miscon-
ceptions, but before we deal with them, it would be well
to get clear in our minds, since one of the charges against
the book is that its material has not been thoroughly
grasped, exactly what degree of mastery over his material, of insight into his characters, James had reached
when he wrote it. *The Princess* was probably written
concurrently with *The Bostonians*. Both novels were
complete failures when they appeared (in 1886). James
believed in both books, although for reasons that remain
obscure he did not include *The Bostonians* in the definitive New York Edition. But *The Princess* was included,
with a preface which delicately but firmly pointed up
the book's intention.

During the '70's James had produced no completely
successful long work. And certainly *Watch and Ward*
(1878) and *Confidence* (1880) are not only the most
clumsy novels ever signed by James but the most clumsy
pieces of fiction ever signed by a man of genius. They
display the unsure approach of the writer who is doing
it all from the outside—from the notebook, the stiff plan,
the bad guess. Through some spurt of development
James, in 1881, wrote the finely balanced, deeply observed *Washington Square* and *Portrait of a Lady*. He

was now able to base his books upon his characters, as
opposed to supporting the action with some artificial
diagram of conduct. Each character now casts light and
shadow and is in turn accented or illuminated by the
darkness or brilliance of the others. James had not finished profiting from Balzac, but he was now Turgenev's
intelligent pupil as well. The realistic method was becoming more effortless at the same time that the technique of suggestion took in more territory with greater
ease. So that the chance of James' fumbling, at this
period, any problem he put his hand to is small.

The Princess Casamassima, it is true, opens with a
block of Balzacian realism mixed with Dickensian melodrama that is extremely hard for modern readers to
accept. In the later chapters of the book detail and suspense are to be brought in with sureness and ease; every
part of the situation is to be elucidated by that sure technical skill so characteristic of the pre-theater James. The
first three chapters, however, are thick with underlining
and filled with a kind of cardboard darkness. The characters are so overloaded with reasons that they closely
approach the line dividing drama from burlesque. The
delicate little boy called Hyacinth, the son of a French
working girl who is also a murderess, and an earl, her
victim; Miss Pynsent, the tender old maid who has
raised the child; Mr. Vetch, the battered fiddler with
leanings toward anarchism—at first glance these appear
cut out of whole cloth. And in spite of a few flashes of
insight, the scene in which Hyacinth witnesses his mother's death in prison is dated and overcharged. Thus
balked at the outset, it is little wonder that the reader
expects to find a measure of falseness everywhere in the
story.

Given the remarkable figure of Hyacinth and the remarkable fact of his sharply divided inheritance, what use does James make of them? It may be best to give the story in bare outline. Hyacinth, grown to young manhood, is apprenticed to M. Poupin, an exiled veteran both of '48 and the Commune. (Hyacinth's own maternal grandfather, James tells us at an early point, died on the Paris barricades.) Poupin teaches him revolutionary principles along with the trade (James considers it a minor art) of bookbinding. The youth then meets the two people who are to bring about the crisis in his life. The Princess Casamassima, separated from her husband and foot-loose in London on her husband's money, first dazzles Hyacinth with her interest in revolutionary plots and then with her interest in himself. And Paul Muniment, son of a north-country miner, an active, realistic, and inscrutable worker deep in revolutionary activities, attracts the ardent boy. Hyacinth actually gives over his life to Muniment, promising in a moment of enthusiasm that he will be the instrument for an act of violence whenever the need arises. Muniment accepts his pledge and binds Hyacinth fully, by a vow taken before witnesses. Hyacinth tells the Princess, after she has given him some minor glimpses of the great world, of his origin and dedication. Miss Pynsent dies; her small legacy enables Hyacinth to go to the Continent. He comes back changed. What he has seen has convinced him that certain objects, of which he had no former notion, should be preserved, not destroyed. The Princess has meanwhile met Muniment. She brings her charm to bear on him, with the secondary purpose of extricating Hyacinth from his vow; but primarily to get herself deeper into true conspiratorial circles. Hyacinth, whose determination to do what he can to further the cause of the people remains unchanged in spite of his secret change of heart, thinks that the pair have cast him off. Then the call comes: a duke is to be assassinated and Hyacinth is picked by the mysterious instigator of these affairs to be the assassin. The revolutionary group, at this news, splits into two factions: those who wish to save Hyacinth and those who are willing to let matters take their course. Muniment, although he professes sympathy for Hyacinth and says that he is free to choose, does nothing. The Princess rushes to save the boy and to offer herself in his stead. She and a kind, methodical German conspirator meet at Hyacinth's lodgings. But the boy has already shot himself, with the revolver meant for the assassination.

Critics have construed this story according to the set of their own convictions. Van Wyck Brooks, for example, although appreciative of James's success with Poupin, Vetch, Miss Pynsent, and others, considers Hyacinth an insufferable little snob. And Hyacinth is, according to Brooks, an embodiment of James's own yearning after the glories of the British upper classes.

This unfortunate but remarkably organized youth . . . is conscious of nothing but the paradise of which he has been dispossessed. . . . In real life the last thing that would have occurred to a young man of Hyacinth's position would have been to "roam and wander and yearn" about the gates of that lost paradise: he would have gone to Australia, or vanished into the slums, or continued *with the utmost indifference* at his *trade* of binding books. But this attitude represents the feeling of Hyacinth's creator. [Italics mine.]

C. Hartley Grattan believes that Hyacinth's "sense of deprivation" vitiates the worth of his radical impulses:

The conviction that it is senseless to do anything, no matter how small the act, to destroy the upper classes leads to the climax of the novel in Hyacinth's suicide.

But Grattan admits James' insight into his material.

When the social-minded young English disinterred the book some years ago because of its theme, Stephen Spender wrote in *The Destructive Element:*

The observation of political types in this book is really remarkable and curiously undated . . . Paul Muniment . . . is a true revolutionary type. He has the egoism, the sense of self-preservation, the cynicism of a person who identifies himself so completely with a cause that he goes through life objectively guarding himself from all approach, as one might preserve for the supreme eventuality a very intricate and valuable torpedo.

Spender's evaluation of Hyacinth is this:

Hyacinth, with his strong leaning toward the upper classes and yet feeling that he is somehow committed to the cause of the workers, might today have become a Social-ist Prime Minister: a Ramsay MacDonald who . . . would dismay his followers by going over to the other side and be-coming the most frequent visitor at large country houses and of dinners at Buckingham Palace.

Now Hyacinth, in the very essence of his character as James with great care and at considerable length pre-sents it, could never become what Spender thinks he could become, any more than what Brooks thinks James should have made him become. Before turning to Hya-cinth, let us examine the character of the Princess. Who is she? What is she? What has she been, and what is she likely to be? The development of her character must have meant a good deal to James since she is the only figure he ever "revived" and carried from one book to another.

She was Christina Light in *Roderick Hudson,* the character in that early work who evokes the mixed feelings of admiration and exasperation that James was later to call up through many of his women. She is the daughter of an Anglo-American shrew and adventuress who forces her, by a threat of scandal, into a marriage with the highest bidder. James managed to bring out, even at a time when his art was still imperfect, Christina's marred idealism and ignorant pride, so that they freshen every page on which she appears. The coarser and weaker people, in contrast with her straightforwardness, show up in a sorry way. Roderick Hudson, with whom she falls in love and whom she tries to galvanize into some kind of manhood, crumbles, after losing her, in much the same way, James makes us feel, as he would have crumbled had he won her. Brought up to deadening shifts, she has one flaw. She is not truly courageous. She marries the prince at once after receiving the shock of her mother's revelations.

In the later book she is the single person who is continuously presented from the outside. James never "goes behind" her. We are never told what she thinks or how she feels; we merely see her act. James clearly presupposes a knowledge in the reader of her early tragedy. To watch her casting her charm and enthusiasm about; to see her reacting more and more violently against her money and position; to see her—after Muniment has told her that it is her money alone which interests his circle, and has prophesied her certain return to her husband now that the Prince has stopped the flow of that money—rushing in desperation to offer herself as a substitute in the affair of the duke's assassination—all this can puzzle us if we know nothing of the beautiful girl who moved through the scenes of *Roderick Hudson*.

Now "the cleverest woman in Europe," she bears a grudge against society strong enough to force her into repudiation of everything her trained taste fully values. When Hyacinth bares his own tragedy to her, the relation of the two is lifted out of a stupid contrast between a revolutionary-minded woman of the world and a talented pauper. For what the Princess knows, as she listens to him, and what the reader should also know, is that she is herself illegitimate. James, far from being taken in by it, deeply realizes that the life she represents is as undermined by the results of cruelty and passion, for all its beautiful veneer, as Hyacinth's own. Having failed in her youth to face a crisis and see it through, she knows in her heart that when she thinks of herself as "one of the numerous class who could be put on a tolerable footing only by a revolution," she is thinking dishonestly. It is her despair and her defects which push her toward extreme revolutionary enthusiasm, as much as her generosity of spirit. But in Hyacinth she recognizes—after she has emerged from her first sentimental ideas concerning him—complete devotion, consistency, and fineness. This boy "never makes mistakes," and is incapable of going back on a given promise. She shows him specimens of English county families, toward whom her own reaction is: "You know, people oughtn't to be both corrupt and dreary." But what Hyacinth tenders them, as he tenders her, beneath his devotion, is a kind of gentle pity.

For this son of a criminal and an aristocrat is not, as he has been made out to be, a little snob, an affected artisan with a divided nature and ambitions beyond his station. James with every subtle device of his mature art, from the first sentence describing him to the last, shows the boy as an artist, a clear, sensitive intelligence, filled with the imagination "which will always give him the clue about everything." James has endowed him, indeed, with the finest qualities of his own talent; and this is what is meant when James says that Hyacinth had watched London "very much as I had watched it." Hyacinth is, like James, "a person on whom nothing is lost." If the character has a fault, it is that James has distilled too purely into his creature the sharp insight, the capacity for selfless devotion, the sense of proportion, the talent for self-mockery and gentle irony which seldom exist in genius without an admixture of cruder ingredients. But James wanted a cool and undistorting mirror to shine between the dark and violent world of the disinherited on the one hand and the preposterous world of privilege on the other. Such a clear lens (Maisie, Nanda) James was later to place in the center of psychological situations. He was never again to place it, and with the final polish of genius added, between social classes. For that matter it has never been placed there, up to the present, by anyone else, although Conrad, in *Under Western Eyes*, a book almost certainly modeled on *The Princess*, examined the revolutionary side of the picture through the clear spirit of Razumov. We are used, in fiction dealing with social problems, to the spectacle of the artist absorbed or deflected into one class or another. James kept Hyacinth detached to the end. And though the solution for the artist, in the insoluble situation James has constructed, is death, as the symbols of the two extremes he has instinctively rejected (after he knows that his own life must exist independently, apart from either) stand by his deathbed, we feel that what they both have been left to is not exactly life.

The book is full of wonderful moments. Short mention should be made of the ultimate opacity and brutality of Muniment, as he is shown in contrast not only to Hyacinth but to the more humane members of the revolutionary circle; of James' masterly analysis of Hyacinth's spiritual coming of age, resulting, on his return from abroad, in increased self-sufficiency and a more complete grasp of his work; of the complex rendering of Hyacinth's rejection of the thought of violence when his mother's murderous hands come before him; of the superb portraits of the solidly disillusioned Madame Grandoni, the morbidly jealous Prince, and those true fools and snobs—Captain Sholto and Muniment's horrible invalid sister. The scenes of submerged London have been praised. What is even more astonishing than these is James's knowledge of the relentless mechanisms of poverty—poverty's *minutiae*.

It is interesting to trace down the source of James's understanding of Muniment. We remember that the elder James was surrounded by socialists of the Fourier school, and that he "agreed with Fourier that vice and crime were the consequences of our present social order, and would not survive them." The younger James had, no doubt, seen Muniment's counterpart multiplied about him, in Fourier's more fanatical followers, in his childhood.

"Very likely . . . all my buried prose will kick off its tombstones at once," James wrote to Howells in 1888. After, it would seem, Stendhal's hundred years.

1 9 3 6

§ Country Things

Robert Frost's *Collected Poems: 1939* brings together
six books, beginning with *A Boy's Will,* first published
in England in 1913, and ending with *A Further Range*
(1936). A preface called "The Figure a Poem Makes"
describes Frost's experience with a poem's beginning
and development ("There is a glad recognition of the
long lost and the rest follows"). *A Boy's Will* should
bring back to some readers the freshness its delayed
American appearance let into literary parlors: a fragrance wholesome as the smell of new hay, which, more
than twenty years ago, showed up the sad, unaired condition of American poetry. The lambrequins and anti-
macassars then disturbed have been put aside and all
sorts of new and foreign breezes have since flowed in
and out. Frost's first book was close to English prewar
Georgian verse (also bucolic), but was saved from that
school's sentimentality by the sensitive accuracy (akin to
Thoreau's) applied to the long-neglected New England
landscape.

North of Boston, which also had to be imported, as it were, from England, did something more: it put New England speech into literature. Reading these poems again one is struck by their solidity in comparison to even the best of a thousand poetic narratives derived from them. Frost never stretched his narratives to any great length. His good sense has kept him from running any of his tendencies into the ground. That same good sense, on the other hand, has kept him from developing, in any broad way, beyond his first work.

Frost has for a long time been one of the most popular poets of our day. Some of this popularity can be put down to the fact that he has always expressed, with imaginative sincerity, American nostalgia for a lately abandoned rural background. His love for the soil, his intimate knowledge of "country things," and his rejection of an industrial civilization's special values appeal strongly to readers who have been compelled to accept these values. If Frost had allowed his philosophy to remain completely implicit in his poetry, he would have escaped the occasional querulous tone apparent in his later books. It is not the province of the pastoral poet directly to preach. If one has chosen nature and eschewed cities, the choice must be absolute and unrationalized. If the pastoral poet sees fit to defend his chosen mode of life, he immediately lays it open to criticism in turn—is it not a backward and recessive development of the civilization he has thought to escape? Frost has broken out every so often in diatribe against the city and its machines, although, since his recognition by the public—late enough, one admits—the results of his successful dealings with that machine, the printing press, have enabled him to live as he pleases.

The best of Frost's lyrics are immune to criticism.

They appear in his latest book as surely as in his first. But one reads *Collected Poems: 1939* waiting for a crack of upheaval, with some roughness of unforeseen growth thereafter. The tone is curiously static throughout. The emotion in the best lyrics, and particularly in Frost's greatest lyric, "To Earthward," does not "broaden down" from youth to maturity; it sounds intermittently. And the reader who holds these lyrics in deep respect somewhat feels that Frost's later carping and conservatism should never have appeared in his work at all.

"More than once I should have lost my soul to radicalism if it had been the originality it was mistaken for by its young converts," Frost says in his introduction. For the poet, the point is to lose his soul to whatever wisdom or folly, and then to regain it. "The best way out," he once said, "is always through." The ordinary man may be able to conceal his evasions; in the poet, the evasion shows. In the later Frost, the mold, unbroken, has stiffened a little.

1 9 3 9

§ *The Pure in Heart*

Modern fiction of the subtler kind when written by women is likely to depict at length the trouble resulting from unsuitable and complicated people falling in love. The stays and obstacles once provided by difference in social position, family feuds, missent letters, and trumped-up misunderstandings have narrowed into drama arising from the fact that the lovers have neuroses that do not match, are in love for the wrong reasons, in love too late or too soon, or are incapable of love at all. Elizabeth Bowen in her previous novels has described such combinations, and Madame Colette has worked with them for years. Miss Bowen has also probed with great thoroughness into the reaction of sensitive children, sometimes the offspring of mismatings, thrown into situations of which they hold only one or two clues. *The House in Paris* successfully brought off an atmosphere of emotional tension, resulting when the past, present, and future converged on such a child, who was caught, between journeys, in rooms full of the tragedy to which he owed his being. *The Death of the Heart* turns on a girl of sixteen, the product of a misalliance, who, when introduced into the "edited life" of her half-brother's smart London household, throws upon it the full glare of her innocence, breaks through its surface, and shows the lack of human feeling on which it is based.

Miss Bowen's young Portia Quayne is the daughter of a late second marriage, following an impulsive liaison, between a middle-aged conservative Englishman and a silly but warm-hearted widow. The first Mrs. Quayne with rather mean nobility divorces her husband and casts him off. Mr. Quayne, cut loose from his pleasant country moorings, is forced to live shabbily on the Riviera with his new family. After his death and that of Portia's mother, his son Thomas takes the child into his home, knowing that his father wanted some settled, decorous English experience for her. Portia, still feeling grief for her mother, enters a household built up with great taste and care by Anna, Thomas' wife. Everything in the exquisite house overlooking the park, the aquamarine curtains, the furniture rubbed "so that you can see ten feet into the polish," the ritual of beautiful food, the series of delightful effects—depends upon Anna. Even the family friend—called St. Quentin and a novelist—is choice and seems picked to match the wallpaper. Portia's brother, sunk in the depths of passionate cravings which marriage has not solved, is Anna's. And Eddie, the neurotic, charming young hanger-on, to whom Portia gives the full weight of her innocent affection, is Anna's—not her lover, but her amusement and her foil. It is Anna who at once instinctively ridicules the child, as she ridicules anyone of awkward human worth. Portia, learning of an ultimate betrayal, runs first to Eddie, who of course, although he has worked off some of his warped tenderness on her, rejects her; then

to Major Brutt, another misfit in Anna's *décor*. Major
Brutt telephones the house and tells Thomas that Portia
demands that they come to some decision about her. In
a masterfully-done scene the three disabused adults—
Anna, Thomas, and St. Quentin—thrash the matter out
at the dinner table. ("This evening the pure in heart
have simply got us on toast.") They come to a decision.
They send a servant, Mrs. Matchett, Portia's only confidante in the household, to fetch Portia back in a taxi, as
one would send for a lost parcel.

Miss Bowen has elsewhere spoken of "the limitations
of English narrative prose, with its *longueurs* and conventions dangerous to truth." In her novels she has
taken every precaution to reduce these conventions to a
minimum. The strokes come close, and every stroke
tells. Miss Bowen is particularly good at reflecting one
character in another, always making it clear that some
people see things partially while others take in every detail. Matchett, the self-contained upper servant, with
her toughened sympathy and snobbery and her pride of
the good artisan, sees everything. Eddie sees everything
—in his way—and himself, "at once coy and insolent,"
only too well. Matchett can sum people up. Of the "sac-
rificing" first Mrs. Quayne she says: "I couldn't care for
her; she had no nature"; of Anna: "Oh, she has her taste
and dearly loves to use it. Past that she'll never go."
Eddie says of Anna: "She loves to make a tart out of another person. She'd never dare to be a proper tart herself." Thomas has an occasional moment of insight into
the society about him; "self-interest, given a pretty
gloss." But Portia, not yet absorbed into "the guilty
plausibility of the world," sees more than everything.
She detects the impossibility of a natural human relationship between these people who write letters, go to
dinner parties, talk at tea—always "stalking each other."

She watches "thoroughly"; she tries to shake some human response out of Eddie; she importunes; she nags with the implacable fury of first love. At the end she gives the show away to simple, kind Major Brutt. "Anna's always laughing at you. She says you are quite pathetic. . . . And Thomas thinks you must be after something. They groan at each other when you have gone away. You and I are the same."

Miss Bowen's talent is so rich and so searching, and this novel stands so far outside the class of novels which resemble packaged goods put up for the trade, that one is tempted to give her nothing but praise. She sees deeply, but not widely enough. Corruption has not lately entered the class of which she writes; the heart is not dying in these people; it never lived in them. And her tone, too keyed up, never lets down for a moment; the *longueurs* are deleted to such an extent that they are missed. Beautifully-done descriptions of times of day and the weather edge the action—to a tiresome degree. The backgrounds for emotions are chosen with care; one, an empty seaside boarding-house on a Sunday morning, is almost unbearably appropriate. Miss Bowen can cook the vulgar English to the same crispness to which she treats their betters. But *The Death of the Heart* is too packed, too brilliant, for its own good. What Miss Bowen lacks is a kind of humility. She has forgotten more than many novelists ever knew, but what Turgenev, for example, knew, and was chary of expressing, she cannot quite deal with. Once in a while the reader hears the accent of self-satisfaction, if not display, in the novelist. But for all that, *The Death of the Heart* deepens our view of the horrors experienced by open innocence up against a closed world.

1 9 3 9

§ *Poet in Spite of Himself*

American readers eager for acquaintance with Valéry's work have been meagerly served. Just after Valéry's reception into the French Academy in 1927, Malcolm Cowley translated *Variété I,* the collection of essays by which Valéry tried—not entirely successfully—to explain the researches into pure thought and "pure poetry" that had occupied him during twenty years of silence. Now, after a long lapse of time, and after Valéry has published many volumes in France, a new translation of miscellaneous essays appears, made up of pieces chosen from three books, *Variété II* (1930), *Pièces sur l'art* (1934), and *Variété III* (1936), together with an essay on Villon and Verlaine, published in France as a finely produced separate volume in 1937.

Faced with the last-named essay, the reader familiar only with the first, ten-years-old translation, may well be puzzled about Valéry's development. For the essay on Villon and Verlaine is, obviously, a well-made piece of hack writing. It is not profound or even subtle; it might have been turned out by a journalist in the ordinary run of his work. Where are the evidences of labor and strain which Valéry once insisted must go into the act of writing? Where are the results of his belief in literature's difficult function? This essay, taken by itself, is proof of the change which has come over the man who once disdained to utter any thoughts at all; who admired, in literature, not so much works themselves as the "genesis" of works, and the spiritual elements which, in fusion, bring about the initial impetus in the artistic process. We see here a result of the circumstances which have transformed Valéry from a poet and thinker who, as he has said of Poe, "tried to unite a sort of mathematics with a sort of mysticism" into Valéry the academician, expected to have ideas on all sorts of artistic manifestations, have them often, and have them publicly.

Valéry's general ideas were never particularly varied, and they tended, as he has lately himself admitted, to harden into *idées fixes*. His sensibilities, on the other hand, have always been fine and complex. But he has spent many years in crying down his major gifts. His early strong admiration for Mallarmé, his acquaintance with Mallarmé's arduous poetic practice, and his youth spent in the anti-romantic atmosphere of the Symbolist movement gave him not only a dislike but also a positive feeling of guilt concerning literature sensuously or intuitively expressed. His poetry, he has said, has for him been a set of "exercises." He disparages the element of chance, "inspiration," and insists on the function of the will in art. He has swallowed without a tremor Poe's rationalizations of instinctive creative workings. He has peppered his writings with italics, as though he were constantly bearing down on their essential "thought." Beneath all this underscoring his style flows on fluidly, often with rhetorical magnificence. He is a writer, all his protestations to the contrary, endowed with a natural feeling for sonorous language, operating under the force of a highly refined and subtle intuition. Gifts of this kind cannot be concealed and cannot be forged. The fact that Valéry continually denies them lends to his work as a whole a faint, continual tone of sophistry. We believe in him only partially, and most completely when he has for a moment let down his guard.

One fortunate result of the demands made upon Valéry by his official position is the diminution of his habit of endowing certain artists with his favorite virtues. Although still extolling Protagorean man, "the measure of all things," he can now look more objectively on individual personalities. The essays in the present volume devoted to Stendhal and Baudelaire are truly distinguished pieces of analytical appreciation. The Stendhal essay throws light not only upon Stendhal but upon the complexities of his time. Stendhal, detached and ironic observer of the follies attendant, in the post-Napoleonic era, upon the beginnings of big business, bureaucracy, and middle-class decorum, who insisted upon following his own tastes in art and amusement while his contemporaries "ended by no longer believing in anything but money," Valéry appreciates as an example of free spirit. Again, in the Baudelaire essay, he places the poet in his rightful place as the man who broke through romantic extravagance into modern cleanness of expression and inexorable realism.

In contrast to these solid and illuminating pieces of criticism Valéry's sad views of the breakdown of the human spirit in the modern world—he has been writing and rewriting these views for twenty years—sound feeble and complaining. Defining "the spirit" almost out of existence, he neglects to mention the sources, in ordinary human vitality, from which it continues even now to draw refreshment. How would an illustrious figure from the past view our civilization? he asks. Would not such a one be terrified of it, or disgusted with it? Since no vital response is struck out of himself, Valéry donates to men who might well be delighted with some manifestations of modern vigor his own elegant despair. Valéry is weakest when he allows his sensitiveness, lately absorbed into the chilly conservatism of the public man, to underestimate "the spirit's" essential toughness. Man may bomb himself off the earth, but it is unlikely that human attributes will recede back into the prehuman. And Valéry's illustrious ghost would recognize holdovers from the past in the present: crime, poverty, and riches. The reasons for these hold-overs Valéry never allows himself to go into.

The present translation is uninspired. The translator, William Aspenwall Bradley, has edited the French: the essay "Mediterranean Inspiration," for example, has been cut in half, and the section containing some of Valéry's most fruitful writing, dropped. It would be a good thing if a more representative collection of Valéry's prose were published. His dialogues, considered by some critics to be his most valuable writing, his reminiscences of Mallarmé and Dégas, a selection from his aphorisms and *aperçus*, the essays which establish his connoisseurship in the minor arts, together with many passages which succeed in drawing with great delicacy lines connecting man with the beauty and mystery of nature—such pieces of writing would give readers of translations a better view of the man than has been afforded them up to now. Such a book would be an antidote to the unhealthy tendency toward formula rather than feeling, in literature at large and in Valéry himself. It would present Valéry the poet *malgré lui*—his most valuable role. True poets are rare. There are always plenty of real and disguised academicians.

1 9 3 9

§ *On the Death of William Butler Yeats*

I have been busy with a single art, that of . . . a small unpopular theater; and this art may well seem to practical men, busy with some program of industrial or political regeneration, of no more account than the shaping of an agate; and yet in the shaping of an agate, whether in the cutting or the making of the design, one discovers, if one have a speculative mind, thoughts that seem important and principles that may be applied to life itself, and certainly if one does not believe so, one is but a poor cutter of so hard a stone.

August, 1912

Yeats' break with his early style and subject matter—though the break never was, and never needed to be, complete—dates from 1909 or a year or two earlier. It has been said that this break was the result of his entrance into practical affairs. This statement is only partially true. Yeats' youthful ambition was to be a man of action, and he was more active in organization—in the Nationalist movement and literary societies—in his twenties than at any later time. It was only when he broke with the popular theater, which had interested him for ten years, and refused to make any further attempt to satisfy middle-class ideals of art that the resonant tone characteristic of the later poems sounded for the first time.

Synge died in 1909. Two years earlier the "Playboy" riots had occurred. And it was in this same period that Yeats witnessed the scandal raised by popular opinion and the Irish newspapers over the question of whether the city of Dublin should build a gallery to house Sir Hugh Lane's gift of Impressionist paintings. He witnessed, that is, in an acute form, the hostility of the middle class toward disinterested artistic expression, as it had been witnessed a generation earlier in France. The bourgeois mind demanded that art be moral or useful, and not only discredited the artist's function but outlawed the artist. Flaubert and Baudelaire were summoned before courts of law, and in Ireland the citizens of Dublin attacked Synge with outright violence.

Ireland, because of its ambiguous political status, threw up bourgeois culture late. And it was there produced in such a clear form that the transformation of the countryman's economy into that of the town dweller is an easily visible process. Yeats wished to give his country not only a sense of its former greatness but also a feeling for the nobility of the arts in general. After the bigotry aroused by *The Playboy*, he began to see that his ideal was antipathetic to his audience.

I believed . . . that a new intellectual life would begin, like that of young Ireland, but more profound and personal . . . I could not foresee that a new class . . . would change the nature of the Irish movement . . . Power passed to small shopkeepers, to men who had risen above the traditions of the countryman without learning those of cultivated life . . . and who, because of their poverty, ignorance, and superstitious piety, are much subject to all kinds of fear. Immediate victory, immediate utility, became everything, and we artists, who are servants not of any cause but of mere naked life . . . became as elsewhere in Europe protesting individual voices.

This was written in 1907. In 1909 Yeats begins to speak of "the mask," and to write those direct poems filled with scorn for "Paudeen" and Paudeen's wealthy "betters." *Responsibilities* (1914) developed this phase fully. The role of action was finally refused, and the artist's role finally accepted.

The common admonition administered to a writer when he refuses to express the opinions and ideals current in his lifetime, choosing instead his own subjects and symbols, is that he thus risks preciosity and final sterility. Yeats, in refusing to cater to the middle, had two fields open to him—"aristocratic" and "vulgar" expression. These ends of the scale are equally rejected by the bourgeoisie: subtlety puzzles and coarseness shocks them. Yeats wrote his new plays in a form derived from the aristocratic Noh drama of Japan. He interested himself in the most "unserviceable" subjects—the Cabala, spiritualism, Hindu philosophy, Byzantine civilization. In *A Vision* he built up a whole mystical system and applied it to historic facts. The later plays are so wrapped in symbol that they approach sheer incantation, and Yeats steadily refused to make their intention clear. He said to a musician who was to write music for these plays: "Lose my words in patterns of sound as the name of God is lost in Arabian arabesques. They are a secret between the singers, myself, and yourself."

The revolt against the idea of art's usefulness could hardly be pushed farther than Yeats in this manner ex-

tended it. Did the poems, then, written in this vein, in
the last thirty years of his life, from the age of forty-four
to the time of his death at nearly seventy-three, suffer?

On the contrary, they went on to ever greater degrees
of power and suggestiveness; they touched the borders
where poetry becomes ultimate evocation, and the regions where religion rises from universal mystery.

These lovers, purified by tragedy,
Hurry into each other's arms; those eyes
By water, herb, and solitary prayer
Made aquiline, are open to that light.
Though somewhat broken by the leaves, that light
Lies in a circle on the grass; therein
I turn the pages of my holy book.

For two years, between the ages of sixty-seven and
sixty-nine, Yeats wrote no poetry. "I had never been so
long barren." Then began a new period of creation, to
which we owe the great poems which have been appearing in English and American magazines during the last
few years. In these poems "aristocratic" and "vulgar"
forms unite. The songs and meditations are often
"coarse" and written in as simple a form as street ballads or broadsheets. Yeats never abandoned the ballad
forms first learned from Sligo peasants in his childhood:
one or two appear in every volume, and the "Crazy
Jane" songs in *The Winding Stair* (1933) are late and
intense examples of the type. The last ballads go beyond
even these; there is nothing quite like them in literature. The last lyrics of Goethe, written in age, seem literary in comparison. These poems are unstained by any
breath of false resignation or "ennobling" feeling. They
express the sane bawdiness of healthy old age, in phrases
written, nonetheless, with every distinction, every

knowledge of effect, every delicate sympathy native to a sensitive nature. Meditation and speculation are there, but behind them, to the last, still exist "naked life" and the vivid sensual world.

Any artist old or young can take courage from these poems. And he can discover in Yeats' prose writing— which developed, like the poetry, from elaboration into simplicity, and documents fully the struggle of a long life—old evils again to be combatted, however new and disguised their modern forms. A battle has been fought against them up to the very last days of a man recently dead, who emerged the victor.

1 9 3 9

§ *Make It New*

.

The English edition of this volume is called *Guide to Kulchur*. Because this title so perfectly sets the tone of the book, it is odd that the American edition is called merely *Culture*. Certainly Pound is the last person to wish a cold, unironic title set at the head of his irreverent remarks. The extreme oddness of these essays, to the reader inexperienced in Pound, may automatically invalidate many of his conclusions, some of which are valuable. It would be a good thing, therefore, if the new title at the outset were canceled and the old title written in.

Pound's ideal reader is a person who has experienced real discomfort on being shut up, in a railway train, lecture hall, or concert room, with well-modulated voices expressing careful, well-bred opinions on the subject of the arts. Such a reader will remember his own impulse to break into argot and obscenity. This is exactly what Pound has done here, for 349 pages. He has published in the last ten years a number of diatribes against the

canned reverence accorded literature. He now goes for
reverences pertaining to the whole field of culture, including mathematics, philosophy, painting, and music.
He is against the pious respect which "stiffens around
mankind's achievements in all fields—the religion of
culture well adapted to the emotional needs of polite
societies." He is all for breaking up, throwing out, bit-
ing the thumb at, pulling the beards of, disinterring,
freshening, "making new." He refuses to attack moldy
but sacred academic rigmaroles from a distance. A critic
like Roger Fry, from whom Pound has learned much, is
content to pin down the pretensions of philistines, culture addicts, and *avant-garde* snobs with well-bred wit.
Pound walks into the field armed with stink bombs. He
fronts the "specialists," running to seed in their limited
circles, with his own eclecticism, which makes free of
many. He is at times shallow, misinformed, inaccurate,
but he smashes his way through the fences and pulls
down the walls between archives.

Pound is a provincial American who, after receiving
degrees from two provincial American universities, went
to Europe and never came back. He combines in himself at present two strongly marked and—one would suppose—completely irreconcilable types: the brilliant
American village atheist, and the European dilettante
to whom "novelty is a positive virtue." At the beginning
of his career, sick to death of the hangovers from the
English nineteenth-century critical and artistic values
then infecting American poetry, he determined to ex-
hume poetry in general from the grave into which scholars and moralists had lowered it. He was after poetry in
all languages, poetry of all ages. The preface to *The
Spirit of Romance* (1910), "a book which never had a
public," announced this ambition. Recently he has

added a passionate belief in the theories of Major Douglas to his belief in pure poetic values. He is now a soldier of an Economic Faith Militant, as well as a fighting
aesthete. His unexpected jumps between these poles of
enthusiasm, his uncontrolled and frequently hysterical
attempts to link the two passions together, his tub-
thumping for Mussolini's planned economy make it a
simple task to cull ridiculous and half-baked statements
from his text. Certainly Pound has few disciples at present, and every critical observer has had a period of dis-
liking his methods. The only way to be fair to a man
who, in spite of all his faults, has spent his life cutting
away dead wood in the sacred grove is to read *Guide to
Kulchur* with an eye alert for its virtues rather than its
defects.

"Great literature," Pound has said, "is simply language charged with meaning to the utmost possible degree." One of the sternest of Pound's English critics has
admitted this statement to be "a very good corrective to
the academic and general habit of discussing literature
in terms of Hamlet's and Lamb's personalities, Milton's
universe, Johnson's conversation . . . and Othello's or
Shelley's private life." In contrast to academic failure to
see, or acknowledge, the human vigor at the center of
human art and thought, here are some sentences from
Pound:

In my student days no senior had the faintest inkling of
Dante's interest, Shakespeare's interest in living . . . The
history of culture is the history of ideas going into action.
. . . You can write history by tracing ideas, exposing the
growth of a concept. You can also isolate the quality or
direction of a given time's sensibility. That means the history of an art . . . Properly, we shd. read for power. Man
reading shd. be man intensely alive. The book shd. be a

ball of light in one's hand . . . I suspect that the error in educational systems has been the cutting off of learning from appetite . . . How to see works of art? Think what the creator must have known and felt before he got around to creating them . . .

Snap judgments, wrong insistence, and, although this is rare, lack of ordinary common sense lie scattered about on these pages. On the other hand, the book is almost completely free from *idées reçues*—except, of course, economic ones. What is lacking is the increasing mellowness and the real, as opposed to hysterical, breaking through into new thought one expects, not entirely sentimentally, from a seasoned artist of fifty. Pound's original substance has not been tough enough to go forward, in spite of and through struggle, into great originality. His taste for the obscure and the esoteric has ultimately weakened his gifts. He likes to fiddle around: to translate Latin translations of Chinese ideograms into English; to put a phrase of Aristotle's, in the original, under a Chinese character. (But it must be remembered that the only interesting and profound discussion of Chinese ideograms in English comes from Fenollosa, through Pound.)

All sorts of memories of Pound's real service in clearing up the aesthetic-moral muddles of the last thirty years must be referred to while one reads this book. And two sentences might be added to its title page:

To express anything at all is a crime with the philistine; to express anything vital is a crime with culture.
(Roger Fry)
I am trying to use not an inch rule but a balance.
(Ezra Pound)

1 9 3 9

§ *Finnegans Wake*

1 PROTEUS, OR VICO'S ROAD

Joyce has been writing *Finnegans Wake* for seventeen years. In 1922 *Ulysses* was published in Paris; this book was begun the same year. *Transition* has brought out about half of it, intermittently, under the title "Work in Progress"; and a number of fragments have appeared now and again in pamphlet form. A whole school of imitators has clustered around its linguistic and philosophical example, and its influence has been so strong that critics have been led to write of it in, as it were, its own terms. Something unheard-of and extraordinary was happening to language, history, time, space, and causality in Joyce's new novel, and the jaw-dropping and hat-waving of the front-line appreciators were remarkable in themselves. Because this subjective, or rolling-along-in-great-delight-with-a-great-work-of-art, school of criticism has had its innings with Joyce's books, the plain reviewer might do well to approach the work at first with a certain amount of leaden-footed objectivity, remaining outside the structure and examining it from as many sides as possible.

Joyce himself, as we shall see, has given a good many clues to what the book is about. The first thing that strikes the reader, however, is the further proof of Joyce's miraculous virtuosity with language. *Finnegans Wake* takes up this technical skill as it existed at the end of *Ulysses* and further elaborates it. Then Joyce's mastery of structure and his musician's feeling for form and rhythmic subtlety are here in a more advanced—as well as a more deliquescent—state of development. The chief reason for the book's opacity is the fact that it is written in a special language. But this language is not gibberish—unless it wants to be. It has rules and conventions. Before one starts hating or loving or floating off upon it, the attention might be bent toward discovering what it is, and how it works.

This private tongue is related to what Panurge called the "puzlatory," and it is cousin to the language of E. Lear, L. Carroll, and the writers of nonsense verse in general. It is based on the pun and is defined, by Fowler, as: "Paronomasia (Rhet.) 'word-shunting.' Puns, plays on words, making a jocular or suggestive use of similarity between different words or of a word's different senses." Upon this rhetorical device *Finnegans Wake* is borne, no matter what limits of intelligibility or impenetrability it touches. Two examples may illustrate it:

> For a burning would is come to dance inane.
> Glamours hath moidered's lieb and herefore
> Coldours must leap no more.
> But listen to the mocking birde to micking
> bards making bared!

Now let us examine the texture of the writing. This, as one would expect, is firm. Moving for the most part in a private idiom, Joyce keeps unerringly to style's econ-

omy, precision, and weight. Through a thousand variations, through a confusion of tongues, the fundamental
sinew of the writing persists; the book can be opened
anywhere, and a page read at random, in proof of this.
The remark of Richard Strauss to a young musician
comes to mind: "Why do you write atonally? You have
talent." Joyce is not writing as he is writing to cover up
inexpertness. Prosodically, he is a master, as can readily
be seen if he is compared with his apprentices.

He is a master-musician and a master-parodist. Here,
even more clearly than in *Ulysses,* Joyce brings over into
literature not only music's structural forms—as exemplified by the fugue, the sonata, the theme with variations
—but the harmonic modulations, the suspensions and
solutions, of music: effects in words which parallel a
composer's effects obtained by working with relative or
non-relative keys. Phrases and whole passages are trans-
posed from a given style, mood, tempo, signature into a
more or less contrasting one. Certain proper names—
Finnegan, Earwicker, Anna Livia, Dublin, Phoenix,
Howth, James and John, Lucan and Chapelizod—reap-
pear in truncated, anagrammatically distorted, or port-
manteau forms. The night-river leitmotif reads, at its
most normal: "Beside the rivering waters of, hitherand-
thithering waters of. Night!" Its variants are numerous
and remarkable. Joyce, the parodist, in *Ulysses* always
effectively colored matter with manner. The number of
styles parodied in *Finnegans Wake* is prodigious. But
these present parodies differ somewhat from their predecessors; they are actually more limited. The punning
language in which they are framed gives them all a
mocking or burlesque edge (the prose poems, only, ex-
cepted). This limitation and defeat of purpose—for an
immense book written in two main modes only is sure

to grow monotonous—is the first symptom to strike the reader of the malady, to be later defined, which cripples *Finnegans Wake*.

Thus equipped, then, with his private vernacular, Joyce proceeds to attack what certainly seems to be every written or oral style known to man. A list of these styles would fill pages. The range and variety can only be indicated here. All forms of religious liturgy (Bible, prayer book, sermon, mass, catechism, litany); conversation; letters informal, formal, and illiterate; the fable, the examination paper, the chronicle; fashion notes and soap-box speeches; the hair-splitting argument and the sentimental narrative. And here are dialects and jargons—"every known *patois* of the English language." Slang, journalese, and specialized vocabularies: of heraldry, the race track, the courtroom, the nursery. Also uncounted foreign tongues, from Sanscrit through Anglo-Saxon to modern European, back to pidgin English, baby talk, and the sounds children make before speech. There are also just plain noises, onomatopoetically expressed, from bangs and howls to twitters and whimpers.

The "auditive faculty" of Stephen Dedalus has been expanded so that the functions of the other senses become subsidiary to it. Joyce has put down everything he has heard for the last seventeen years. We now can examine some evidence from Eugene Jolas, the editor of *Transition,* as to Joyce's method of work. Jolas says: "It was necessary [in compiling a complete MS for publication] to go through a number of notebooks, each of which had esoteric symbols indicating the reference to a given character, locality, event, or mood. Then the words accumulated over the years had to be placed in the segment for which they were intended." And what Joyce was up to in general—the underlying theme and philosophical purpose of the book—has been partially elucidated by Joyce to Jolas and others. Jolas says:

We know that Mr. Joyce's ambition has been to write a book dealing with the night-mind of man. . . . We have tried to keep in mind that the dramatic dynamic is based on the Bruno theory of knowledge through opposites, and on the Vico theory of cyclic recurrence. . . . History being, in his earlier words "a nightmare," Mr. Joyce presents his phantasmagoric figures as passing back and forth from a mentality saturated with archetypal memories to a vision of future construction.

Another of Joyce's favorite exegetes sheds a little more light (and it can be definitely stated that light is needed, since the one actual fact which is clear to the reader, without exegesis, is that the action takes place in one night or one aeon of time, and is concerned with a man—a giant, an earth-force—asleep). Stuart Gilbert says:

Joyce's new work is partly based on the historical speculations of Vico. . . . Vico held that there is a recurrent cycle in human "progress," as in the movement of the stars. Societies begin, continue, and have an end, according to universal laws. . . . Every nation passes through three stages, the divine, the heroic, the human. The prelude and aftermath of each cycle is complete disintegration. . . . Vico contemplated the writing of an "ideal and timeless history" in which all the actual histories of all nations should be embodied. . . . "Work in Progress" is, in many aspects, a realization of Vico's project. . . . It is interesting to note that an exceptionally intricate passage in Mr. Joyce's book is, in effect, a fantasia on the quinary scale. . . . Even the difficult passages of the "Anna Livia Plurabelle" fragment become lucid when read aloud in the appropriate rhythm and intonation by the author. In fact, rhythm is one of the clues to the meaning . . . for each of the polymorphous personages of the work has his appropriate rhythm, and many "references" can be located by reference to the rhythm of the prose.

With these few "clues" well in mind, the reader can only open the book, without further explanation, and battle his way into it. Life is too short to read all the glosses which have already multiplied around it and will continue to multiply. Some of its themes are perfectly clear. The pedestrian reviewer can add a few scattered notes, put down during her own two weeks' life with the literary monument.

There is every reason to believe that a *complete explanation* of the whole thing will come, after a longish lapse of time, from Joyce himself. This happened, it will be remembered, in the case of *Ulysses* after about nine years. . . . There is nothing whatever to indicate that Joyce has any real knowledge of the workings of the subconscious, in sleep or otherwise. Carroll has far more intuition than Joyce into the real structure of the dream. There are no sustained passages which give, for example, the feeling of nightmare. The punning style, as a matter of fact, precludes this. It is as though Joyce wished to be superior to the unconscious. . . . At one point he brings in a long apologia for his own method and language. The effect of this interpolation is very queer. . . . Some sections start off with indicated time, but these indications seem to be afterthoughts. . . . The later versions of the fragments already published seem to be changed out of sheer perversity: a clause is omitted leaving nothing but a vestigial preposition; a singular noun is shifted to the plural, and the meaning is thereby successfully clouded. . . . The most frightening thing about the book is the feeling, which steadily grows in the reader, that Joyce himself does not know what he is doing; and how, in spite of all his efforts, he is giving himself away. Full control is being exercised over the minor details and the main structure, but the compulsion toward a private universe is very strong. . . . Joyce's delight in reducing man's learning, passion, and religion to a hash is also disturbing. . . . After the first week what one longs for is the sound of speech, or the sight of a sentence in its natural human context. . . . The book cannot rise into the region of true evocation—the region where Molly Bloom's soliloquy exists immortally—because it has no human base. Emotion is deleted, or burlesqued, throughout. The vicious atmosphere of a closed world, whose creator can manage and distort all that is humanly valuable and profound (cunningly, with God-like slyness) becomes stifling. . . . *Ulysses* was based on a verifiable theme: the search for the father. The theme, or themes, of *Finnegans Wake* are retrogressive, as the language is retrogressive. The style retrogresses back to the conundrum. To read the book over a long period of time gives one the impression of watching intemperance become addiction, become debauch.

The book's great beauties, its wonderful passages of wit, its variety, its marks of genius and immense learning, are undeniable. It has another virtue: in the future "writers will not need to search for a compromise." But whatever it says of man's past, it has nothing to do with man's future, which, we can only hope, will lie in the direction of more humanity rather than less. And there are better gods than Proteus.

1 9 3 9

2 APPROACHING UR

A Skeleton Key to Finnegans Wake, by Joseph Campbell and Henry Morton Robinson, is the first full and painstaking attempt to translate, page by page, the dream-language of Joyce's last work into English. The authors have attempted to trace, furthermore, "in thin lines" the skeletal structure of the enormous and baffling book. They have provided a synopsis of the whole, given indicative names to the four large sections and to the chapters. They have identified and translated many of Joyce's quotations—those in identifiable human tongues. They have tried to keep his alternately looming and dissolving characters straight; listed references and cross-references in footnotes; have labored, that is, to give the reader some intelligible ground to stand on and some recognizable space to move around in. Like archaeologists, whose tasks theirs of necessity so much resemble, they have uncovered one more layer of Joyce's extraordinary verbal buried city. They also supply, in an introduction and conclusion, another fairly impassioned defense of the book as a work of art, and of Joyce as a great conscious artist.

The quality of being *closed* becomes more and more evident as expert attention is directed toward *Finnegans Wake.* The book does not seem, like certain structures of great literature, to be a tower or high place, built on earth and open at the top and on all sides to the Nature about it. Into a limited locale (at its largest, Dublin, on the island of Ireland) are brought all ages of man and some of nature. In one narrow room and one sleeping mind, the developing human faculties, from the brute upward, grow and dissolve and reform. The circle of Vico's history is superimposed upon the circle of Dublin. Macrocosm and microcosm, symbol and reality, inextricably mix.

The present "translation" proceeds page by page; but the translators have of necessity chosen certain passages, and what has seemed to them the core of these passages, for detailed comment. It is interesting to notice what portions of a knotty (or merely repetitive) passage the elucidators have separated out, and what portions— sometimes containing matter which another observer might consider interesting or crucial—they omit. The footnotes, too, while generally filled with the most helpful kind of information, have moments of complete blankness as to what the text seems to present in the most forcible way. The use of this "key" is therefore stimulating to the thoughtful student in more ways than one. It brings up new problems with every step of ground it clears.

Time must pass, and thorough research be made, before certain fundamental questions concerning *Finnegans Wake* can be answered. One question that comes to mind is: are we dealing with a work (always granting that it is a work of incontestable genius) essentially small in inner meaning and even in essential design, a work that has nevertheless exfoliated into a semblance of growth and complexity? Are we dealing, that is, with a work, the product of a man and artist who has never come into maturity? Or are we dealing with an essentially great work, the product of a man and artist who has suffered life and transcended his suffering; who is no longer the victim of his talent, his circumstances, or the tensions within his own character, but has become master of them all? Are we getting from this fantastically distorted and interwoven speech, these amazingly contrapuntalized themes, illumination and truth; or are we being led into the mystery of a childish individual's dreaming game, with the rigmaroles and jokes and tricks of the child (or immature man) presented to us neat?

Joyce's lyric gifts, his full equipment as a trained realist, his ingenuity as a fabulist, his skill as a parodist, his sharp wit and Jesuit-trained learning, his innate musician's ear—these attributes are as clearly evident in *Finnegans Wake* as they are in any piece of writing he ever produced. What difference does it make if we are listening to the operations of sleep; we have heard such operations in great pieces of literature before this. Even if Joyce was a sick man, we are listening to a writer who was in many ways a martyr to his genius and to his age. But we want to penetrate the disguises he has had to throw about himself; or the symptoms he has been forced to assume. We have this desire not out of niggling curiosity, but out of real interest: that we may receive the help and refreshment that any true artist's struggle with his material gives us, particularly when we are caught with him into the same deforming time.

The poet and the "comic fabulist" are equipped with uncommon gifts by which they are able to get around interior "censorship." They have tricks, as it were, to get the information through. They transpose the dangerous and (actually) untellable truths of the subconscious into imaginative terms, not easy to bring, otherwise, into the light of day. What strikes the more detached observer when faced with the extreme opacities of certain portions of *Finnegans Wake* is the certainty that concealed beneath his very eyes is a submerged

fable having to do directly with Joyce, with Joyce's relations to the world, with Joyce's attitude to his time. Is
not the whole book a masked attempt at the fullest
apologia pro vita sua that Joyce has yet given us? And
this last confession and apology certainly must be more
revealing (consciously or unconsciously) than anything
written in his earlier career. Under the ostensible action, under H. C. Earwicker and Anna Livia Plurabelle,
and Shem and Shaun, and the multitude of other clear
or ambiguous figures, from time to time another drama
shows: the drama of Joyce's own life, up to the writing
of the book, and during the writing of the book. It is a
drama terrifically malicious in expression; it flays one
contemporary after another; it brings down all facades
of learning and worship in one mass of mocked-at de-
bris. Joyce is doing more than returning compulsively
to the Dublin from which he is an exile. He is razing
more than Dublin structures with the fires of his love
and hatred.

What exterior situation, then, brought Joyce to the
pass where, to get his secret across, he had to resort to a
kind of desperate cunning? To resort, as well, to the
often monotonous, often trivial, often brutal, ruses of
the accomplished *farceur*? Or to the insistent sobbing
minor lyric passage? (It seems at times that these two
"tones" are the only ones in the book.) Does this work
stand like a terrible half-buried monument, both to the
recent past and the near future: outlining a deforming
epoch when a work of art must become oblique expression—a joking show, a wry song, a cock-eyed cinema-
mythology—in order to exist at all?

"The price of virtuosity is abject slavery to a com-
plaisant tool; that of creative artistry is wilful domi-
nance over a recalcitrant tool." What do we finally see

in Joyce: virtuoso or artist; compulsive neurotic or a writer with himself entirely in hand? This question requires a deeper analysis than has yet been dared by Joyce students and disciples. It is not a skeleton key we need, so much as eyes to see in spiritual (was it?) darkness; and ears with which to separate cunning (are they?) confusions.

1 9 4 4

§ *Unofficial Feminine Laureate*

Edna Millay's new book, *Huntsman, What Quarry?*, is "the first book since the publication of *The Buck in the Snow*," her publishers say, "in which [she] has brought together a new group of her lyrical poems." This statement seems to pass over the appearance, in 1934, of *Wine from These Grapes,* a collection of lyrics and sonnets which showed signs of Miss Millay's successful passage from the emotions and point of view of a rebellious girl to those of a maturely contemplative woman. The present book, although it bears marks of the poet's magnanimity of nature and her basic poetic gifts, is a strange mixture of maturity and unresolved youth. What further complicates its expression is the influence of the hampering and sometimes destructive role of the unofficial feminine laureate which Miss Millay has had to play for so long to her American public.

It is a dangerous lot, that of the charming, romantic public poet, especially if it falls to a woman. The temptation to repeat effects continually reappears; there are "occasional poems," which it seems necessary to write; and it is almost impossible for the poetess, once laurelled, to take off the crown for good or to reject the values and taste of those who tender it. Certainly Miss Millay has never completely granted the demands of groups whose favorite she has remained for so long. But it is difficult to see why she still writes certain kinds of poems. The delightful ballad, peppered with colorful place names; the poems built on picturesque and faintly feudal situations (the hunter and the acorn-gathering girl; the princess and the handsome groom); and the numerous poems which describe pride trampled, though never actually defeated, by an unworthy object of affection—a time and place exist for these, but it is not in the middle of a career. It is difficult to say what a woman poet should concern herself with as she grows older, because woman poets who have produced an impressively bulky body of work are few. But is there any reason to believe that a woman's spiritual fibre is less sturdy than a man's? Is it not possible for a woman to come to terms with herself, if not with the world; to withdraw more and more, as time goes on, her own personality from her productions; to stop childish fears of death and eschew charming rebellions against facts? Certainly some fragments of Sappho are more "mature" than others. And Christina Rossetti, who lived an anonymous life and somewhat resembled, according to the cruel wit of Max Beerbohm, "a pew-opener," explored regions which Miss Millay has not yet entered. And there is the case of Emily Dickinson.

Miss Millay has always fought, and is still fighting, injustice. She is still subject to moods of self-disgust as well as to moods of mutiny against mankind's infringements on its own human decency. Once or twice she contemplates a truce which "slackens the mind's allegiance to despair." And twice—in the poem just quoted and in the recessively titled "The Princess Recalls Her One Adventure"—she writes as beautiful lyrics as she has ever written. But what has happened to the kind of development announced in *Wine from These Grapes,* the most kindly disposed reader cannot say. If Miss Millay should give up for good the idea that "wisdom" and "peace" are stuffy concepts, perhaps that development might be renewed.

1 9 3 9

§ *The Poetry of Paul Eluard*

Paul Eluard, one of the original members of the Dada "school," moved into Surrealism, under the leadership of André Breton, when "the Dada anarchy" was outlawed. He has held closely to the tenets of Surrealism through all their hardening and stiffening, in spite of the fact that his gifts seem perfectly opposed to all that Surrealism once stood for, and all it stands for now. The reasons for his alliance with Dada would be somewhat difficult to determine. It was natural, certainly, that a talent like Eluard's—simple and sensitive, quite unclouded by the fumes of the macabre, and undisturbed by the sardonic horseplay and involved cynicism of his sturdier contemporaries—should be forced, during the twenties, to take on some kind of protective coloring, make some defensive alliance, in order to exist. Such a talent was of the exact kind to move his contemporaries to parody. Eluard's complete complaisance to Surrealist doctrine, before and after Surrealism's alliance with "the revolution," permitted him to go on writing; but his passivity has lapsed, at times, into a kind of masochism, vitiating his work and making his "thinking" ridiculous. He has never rebelled against Breton's manifestoes and excommunications; he is, in fact, the complete complement of Breton, who has been called the Saint-Just of Surrealism. He obediently became a Communist when Surrealism, the party wedded to complete non-utilitarianism and to the exploration of the wayward subconscious, automatism and the dream, developed a dogma equally unyielding, and in many ways paralleling Communist dogma. Eluard has obeyed, it is true, without once changing his fundamental poetic nature. He stands today in the peculiar position of a poet who has remained a depository of one kind of poetic expression (a kind, as we shall see, which is not particularly French), while paying more than lip-service to doctrines in every way inimical to the development of that expression.

Surrealism has received little analytical discussion in English. Because it cast back for exemplars through the 1870 generation in France (Rimbaud and Lautréamont), to Baudelaire, it seemed to gather up Symbolist functions, and, moreover, extend them by adding Freudian theory to the Symbolist base. Actually, this widening and deepening never occurred, and Symbolism was contracted rather than extended, by Surrealism. Since Eluard's poetry is so symptomatic of one result of adherence to Surrealist theory, it is necessary to outline briefly the nature of the Surrealist revolt against Dada, and the uneven history of Symbolism (which did not proceed in an unbroken line, as is generally supposed) after Mallarmé.

In 1898 Mallarmé's chief pupil, Valéry, entered the silence which was to remain unbroken for twenty years.

And although the influence of Rimbaud was not entirely dead, it was subjected to traditional distortions,
chiefly at the hands of Claudel and Rivière, who endeavored to prove Rimbaud a Catholic character and
an embodiment of angelic (though fallen) innocence.
A regression toward convention and traditionalism had
set in. Marcel Raymond describes it in his *De Baudelaire à Surrealisme:*

"Writers seemed prisoners of their culture. Psychological
or physiological drama, recitals of sociologists, physicians
and geographers, poems by archeologists or men of erudition, the literary jests and *divertissements* of mandarins
—all these [pre-1914] works rested on a base of positive
knowledge, considered unshakable and untouchable. Literature was . . . limed in the mass of facts, laws and hypotheses
which the remarkable development of human knowledge
had heaped up . . . during the 19th century. The great
majority of the works of the period proposed to demonstrate
something, whether by describing, analysing, explaining individual or collective phenomena, or by decomposing them
into rational elements. . . . These works were clear and
satisfied the needs of a simple logic. . . . All were determinist or finalist. The creative freedom of the artist could
not function except between walls of truth, utility or good
sense. . . . Poetry, from the early epoch of Parnassianism,
had been towed along behind philosophy and history. Hugo,
Leconte de Lisle, Prudhomme and Herédia had wished to
condense in their verse a world of ideas and facts. It is
true that the Symbolists, coming after the Parnassians, had
. . . opened literary windows and allowed the fog of mystery to come into the study of the man of letters. But, after
1895, the Symbolists were violently attacked: neo-classicists
. . . wrote erudite poetry. . . . All the writers joined in
a common cult of the intelligence: between a poem by
Mme. de Noailles and certain pages of the novels of Régnier,

between the phrases of Anatole France, Maurras, Barrés, and the poems of Moréas, between the tirades of Paul Adam, the invectives of Mirbeau and certain social poems of Verhaeren, the difference was only one of meter and rhyme. . . .

In this situation, it is interesting to remember, it was foreigners like Rilke and Yeats who received refreshment from whatever feeble sparks of Symbolism remained alive. (Villiers de l'Isle-Adam was such a spark for Yeats. Rilke went back to Baudelaire.)

The birth of Dada coincided with the renovation of the "conception" of the universe, and of the spiritual life, by the scientists whose work, conceived and tested before 1914, became generally available thereafter. "Relativist hypotheses made absolute truth recede far beyond the touch of human reason"; the Freudian hypotheses broke down and complicated "the grossly simplified analyses, in the moral field, of the preceding era." Art, always acting as a symptom, and always well before the event (even in its least energetic periods), had already announced the change (Rimbaud, two generations previously). An undercurrent of revolt against officially respectable literature, colored with occultism, interest in the supernatural, the erotic and the sadistic, had begun before the war. Jarry was its chief mystificator. Apollinaire, of Slav and Italian-Swiss blood, born in Rome, brought back into French literature a forgotten interest of the Symbolists: an interest in "popular poetry" —the literature produced by everyday life. Popular songs and the machines and apparatuses then beginning to change the technique of European living appeared in his poetry more often than the esoteric trappings of the macabre. He rarely tried to elevate his tone to match the sublimity acceptable to French writing. He worked best on the level of wit. He was able "to create an atmosphere wherein the banal, the daily, the threadbare theme was transfigured." He was also capable of true pathos, and it was his wit and pathos which were deleted almost entirely from the Surrealist movement whose name derived from one of his invented terms. "It was things themselves [which interested Apollinaire], happenings which ought continually to become 'the marvelous,' if looked at with a certain bias."

Dada, soon dead and denounced by Surrealism, was, in its beginnings, a far more vigorous assault against logic and the weight of bourgeois ideals, than Surrealism, fixed, humorless, and from the beginning out for the dead-end effects of madness and mystification. Symptomatic of post-war derangement, hysteria, and despair, Dada nevertheless contained elements of control over and insight into its aberrations. Its working resembled the forms of hysteria, but it was the hysteria of an intelligent living entity suffering from shock. It never developed the paranoid symptoms of Surrealism. It was able to laugh at its own jokes, be cynical with its own cynicism and cruel to its own sadism, and its dogmatic and persecutory symptoms were mild, if they existed at all. It found room for Max Jacob's *macaroniques* and bold parodies, and for Eluard's pathos. Surrealism, on its first appearance, immediately showed signs of a sobering-up process. It was announced by a call to order, disguised as a manifesto for more freedom. Its championship of automatism, its great show of dives into the depths of the subconscious and flights into the empyrean of *le merveilleux* were accompanied by a reciprocal tendency to law-making, litany-singing, and the issuance of marching orders. Breton's litany on "the marvelous" might be set to four-four time: *"Le merveil-*

*leux est toujours beau, n'importe quel merveilleux est
beau, il n'y a même que le merveilleux qui soit beau."*

It would be simple to produce an analogy between
the functioning of Surrealism and the mechanisms dis-
coverable in a person suffering from a psychosis. The
more the irresponsibility of the "subconscious" is given
rein, the more an increasingly rigid and authoritarian
set of rules is thrown up, which parallel the workings,
in a psychotic individual, of a super-ego, or too harsh
conscience. The "jacobin and jansenist logic" superimposed upon Surrealism allowed it to remain detached
from reality, and worked off the guilt of artists who had
reduced their art to a kind of collection of picture
postcards or a parlor game. Art, under these conditions,
must become more rather than less fixed; its forms become monotonous. The monotony extends to the work
of those "rage types" who take it out in invective (Surrealism is rich in these); it shows itself in the reduction
of form to the bleak list and the tiresome juxtaposition.
Not only is growth impossible, but recession is probable.

Breton and Eluard at one time collaborated in the
writing of a book of poems which imitated the speech
of "victims of mental debility, acute mania, general
paralysis, etc." They "hoped," in their notes to these
productions, "that attempts to simulate the maladies for
which one is usually confined, may one day replace the
ballad, the sonnet, the epic. . . ." Breton wished his
recitals of dreams to be stenographic, and his approach
to "madness, the dream, the absurd, the incoherent, the
hyperbolic and all that opposes the summary appearance
of the real" is one of "precise experiment." The truth
is, that in Surrealism, the dream is treated in the most
primitive way: it is recounted or imitated; Surrealist

poets have gone into the subconscious as one would take a short trip into the country, and have brought back some objects of grisly or erotic-sadistic connotation, or a handful of unrelated images, in order to prove their journey. It has not occurred to them that the journey has been taken many times, that human imagination has, before this, hung a golden bough before the entrance to hell, and has described the profound changes the true journey brings about. It is a journey not to be undertaken lightly, or described without tension of any kind. And the *aller et retour,* if merely approximated, produces approximate expression: the sulphurous, the sadistic, the luxurious macabre, the Grand Guignol; or the childish, fatuous game.

2

"Give the initiative to words," said Mallarmé, and if this command is followed to its logical conclusion, the subject disappears. It is (or has been) a Surrealist pleasure to take the kernel of meaning out of forms into which meaning is most closely compressed. Here are three surrealist proverbs by Eluard and Péret:

Les éléphants sont contagieux.
Les cerises tombent ou les textes manquent.
Les grands oiseaux font les petites persiennes.

Or the definition. Here are two Eluard "définitions":

Un homme vivant monté sur un cheval vivant rencontre une femme vivante tenant en laisse un chien vivant.

Une robe noire ou une robe blanche? Des grands souliers ou des petits?

If the fortuitous brings in (by chance?) a semblance
of wit (as it does, certainly, in the above quotations),
this wit must be countered by the "fortuitous" poem,
dull as a flat joke:

Un grand feu dans la cheminée
Un bon tapis par terre
Quelques chaises autour de la table
Des brosses des charrues des clairons des dentelles

Le tout soigneusement enduit de glu.
                    (*Cours Naturel*, 1938)

It is plain that Eluard is not perfectly freely "giving
the initiative to words"; the element of choice is working, if in a reverse direction. In the two early poems
which follow, Eluard's purity of diction, his taste (comparable in many ways to the taste of the Parnassians),
and his pathos are evident:

LEURS YEUX TOUJOURS PURS
Jours de lenteur, jours de pluie,
Jours de miroirs brisés et d'aiguilles perdues,
Jours de paupières closes à l'horizon des mers,
D'heures toutes semblables, jours de captivité,

Mon esprit qui brillait encore sur les feuilles
Et les fleurs, mon esprit est nu comme l'amour,
L'aurore qu'il oublie lui fait baisser la tête
Et contempler son corps obéissant et vain.

Pourtant, j'ai vu les plus beaux yeux du monde,
Dieux d'argent qui tenaient des saphirs dans leurs mains,
De véritables dieux, des oiseaux dans la terre
Et dans l'eau, je les ai vus.

Leurs ailes sont les miennes, rien n'existe
Que leur vol qui secoue ma misère,
Leur vol d'étoile et de lumière

Leur vol de terre, leur vol de pierre
Sur les flots de leurs ailes,

Ma pensée soutenue par la vie et la mort.
                    (*Capitale de la Douleur,* 1926)

("No play with words," Eluard says. "Everything is comparable to everything, everything finds its echo, its reason, its resemblance, its opposition, its transformation. And this transformation is infinite.")

LA NÉCESSITÉ

Sans grande cérémonie à terre
Près de ceux qui gardent leur équilibre
Sur cette misère de tout repos
Tout près de la bonne voie
Dans la poussière du sérieux
J'établis des rapports entre l'homme et la femme
Entre les fontes du soleil et le sac à bourdons
Entre les grottes enchantées et l'avalanche
Entre les yeux cernés et le rire aux abois
Entre la merlette héraldique et l'étoile de l'ail
Entre le fil à plomb et le bruit du vent
Entre la fontaine aux fourmis et la culture des framboises
Entre le fer à cheval et le bout des doigts
Entre la calcédoine et l'hiver en épingles
Entre l'arbre à prunelles et le mimétisme constaté
Entre la carotide et le spectre du sel
Entre l'araucaria et la tête d'un nain
Entre les rails aux embranchements et la colombe rousse
Entre l'homme et la femme
Entre ma solitude et toi.
                    (*La Vie Immédiate,* 1932)

It is a limitation in Eluard that he is aiming at one kind of poetry and producing another. Loose form and the continually changed image must have beneath them

—or rather, must rise from the very existence of—a ground-swell energy, wildness and ferocity in the poet. When the poetic gift is sensitive, and its projection mild, on the other hand, it is form alone which gives edge to its nuances. Eluard is far closer, as Jean Cassou has pointed out, to the German poet's nostalgia and "suffering" than to the French poet's sublimity and lucidity. And he is certainly more close, in nature, to the Parnassians than to Baudelaire, Rimbaud, or Lautréamont, in all of whom ferocity is present. The French classic line intersected, in Baudelaire, with the macabre and Gothic; classic form was used with passionate feeling and imagination and the results are superb and inimitable poems. Rimbaud and Lautréamont charged language with such force that it broke through form; even Hugo's rhetoric was not adequate for these personalities. Even in Mallarmé the reverberation of emotion sounds through his designs for fans, and his preoccupation with his furniture and lace-curtains; the grandeur of glaciers, thunder, and rubies invades the poetry from which actual "meaning" has been barred. When Rimbaud wished to express pathos, he immediately and instinctively went back to form (in the poems *Bonheur* and *Chanson de la Plus Haute Tour,* for example). The results of imitating a poet, whose form is distorted because it is bearing more condensed meaning and emotion than it can bear, may be observed in the imitators of Hopkins. The tricks are managed, but the true effects not in any way approached.

Emotion, when it rises above pathos, immediately takes on complexity. Eluard, well below the complex level, and attempting to work with the automatic and hallucinatory, at the end is left with his vocabulary (simple, exquisitely chosen), his syntax (also of the simplest), and his one emotional effect: "an amorous and dolorous obsession of an infinitely pathetic character."

Eluard is incapable of the poem of revolt. When he feels that such a poem is required of him, he writes the following undistinguished and adolescent lines:

CRITIQUE DE LA POÉSIE

C'est entendu je hais le règne des bourgeois
Le règne des flics et des prêtres
Mais je hais plus encore l'homme qui ne hait pas
Comme moi
De toutes ses forces

Je crache à la face de l'homme plus petit que nature
Qui à tous mes poèmes ne prefère pas cette CRITIQUE
DE LA POÉSIE
(*La Vie Immédiate,* 1932)

The kindest of Eluard's critics have warned him against the traditional French affectation into which his writing can so easily be led. He shows this tendency in his comparisons, which are likely to compare something of emotional weight to something pretty or abstract, or charmingly strange. Or delicate attributes are given to creatures and objects of a certain natural energy and strength:

Birds perfume the woods
Rocks their great nocturnal lakes

And it is possible, in Eluard, as in any poet, to detect the faked phrase, put in to make things harder, or to render matters, to the casual glance at least, more profound. All the manifestoes in the world cannot infuse import into "agile incest," or "fishes of anguish." This sort of thing, if persisted in, becomes *mignardise et confiserie*.

Eluard's virtues are apparent, and his influence, if not strong, might be importantly pervasive. His basic naturalness, existing uniquely among his contemporaries, preserves in French literature (at a time when such a delicate ingredient might be entirely lost) a *pathétique* equally as valuable as the sublimity, wit, irony, malice, and corrosive rhetorical splendors with which that literature has always been so well supplied. Apollinaire combined this pathos with wit; he has moments which go back to Villon. Pathos alone, or in combination, is contrary to the self-conscious, anti-sentimental, and synthetically tough spirit of the time; but it is a valuable civilized and salutary element, none the less. That Eluard's gifts should have been forced, by the fashion or neurosis of his period, to disguise themselves as "unconscious" (so that their true imaginative flights will not lie open to scorn), and be reduced to the level of a word game, is peculiar enough. That they should have been twisted into the use of propaganda, and made to function under manifestoes, literary and otherwise, will certainly amuse future critics and diagnosticians of his era.

TRANSLATIONS OF POEMS QUOTED IN THE TEXT

A fine fire in the fireplace
A good carpet on the floor
Chairs around the table
Brushes ploughs bugles laces

All smoothly covered with bird-lime

THEIR EYES FOREVER PURE

Slow-passing days, days of rain,
Days of broken mirrors and lost needles,
Days of eyelids closed to the seas' horizon,
Of hours all alike, days of captivity.

My spirit which still glitters on the leaves
And the flowers, my spirit is naked like love,
Its forgotten dawn makes it lower its head
And look upon its obedient and vain body.

Nevertheless, I have seen the most beautiful eyes in the
    world,
Silver gods who hold sapphires in their hands,
Actual gods, birds in the earth
And in the water, I have seen them.

Their wings are mine, nothing exists
But their flight which shakes off my unhappiness,
Their flight of star and light
Their flight of earth, their flight of stone
On the tide of their wings,

My thought sustained by life and death.

NECESSITY

Without great ceremony on earth
Near those who keep their equilibrium
Upon this unhappiness without risk
Very near the good road
In the dust of serious people
I establish relations between man and woman
Between the smeltings of the sun and the bag of drones

Between enchanted grottoes and the avalanche
Between eyes surrounded by dark circles and the laugh of
desperation
Between the heraldic female blackbird and the star of garlic
Between the leaden thread and the noise of the wind
Between the fountain of ants and the cultivation of straw-
berries
Between the horseshoe and the fingertips
Between chalcedony and winter in pins
Between the tree of eyeballs and verified mimicry
Between the carotid artery and the ghost of salt
Between the araucaria and the head of a dwarf
Between rails at a junction and the russet dove
Between man and woman
Between my solitude and thee.

CRITICISM OF POETRY

It is certain that I hate the rule of the bourgeois
The rule of cops and priests
But I hate even more the man who does not hate it
As I do
With all my strength.

I spit in the face of the man smaller than nature
Who does not prefer to all my other poems this CRITI-
CISM OF POETRY.

1939

§ *America Was Promises*

Last year Archibald MacLeish resorted to scaring people, over the radio, with air-raid noises and human
screams in order to waken the population to "Fascist"
dangers. This year he publishes a small book of twenty
pages with a similar end in view. *America Was Promises*
traces, in Mr. MacLeish's languid and faintly eccentric
style, the history of the American people sold out and
misled by "the Aristocracy of politic selfishness." All
hope is not yet lost, however. America is still full of
lovely scenery, exquisite weather, "big fists," and strong
hearts. "America is promises to Us To take them Bru-
tally With love but Take them." And the poem ends
with the plaintive imperative "O believe this!"

This poem is Mr. MacLeish's saddest and most con-
glomerate attempt at "public speech" to date. It opens
with a sort of crepuscular question and goes on through
lines which faintly parody the now public poet's early
"private" writing; there's some *Conquistador* in it, and

even a little *Hamlet*. Mr. MacLeish is evidently aware of the dangers of appealing to the People with a capital "P." He partially skirts that problem by speaking of them at least once in lower case. Yes, Mr. MacLeish has heard of the sentimental come-ons and exhortations of demagogues and evidently does not wish to ally himself with such persons. The difficulty is that he is writing political poetry, even a kind of official poetry, and therefore the strict checks and disciplines of poetry written for itself (as a result of reality making a direct emotional impact upon the unique temperament of a trained and exacting writer) do not hold. If such disciplines were functioning, Mr. MacLeish would certainly have realized, for example, that he was getting off to a bad start with his title. *America Was Promises* is a sentence which even an untrained ear instinctively rejects; it sounds ugly. But it also sounds impressive, and "public speech" is out to impress.

Everything brought up by Mr. MacLeish sounds impressive: the rise and decadence of American fortunes; the dead lying in "Spain Austria Poland China Bohemia"; "the coarse ambitious priest [leading] by the bloody fingers forward." Because of his relaxed form, his righteous anger comes through so feebly, however, that all we are moved to do is sit down and join the author in a good cry. Bury his gifts though he may, Mr. MacLeish is a private, a lyric, poet through and through; it is somewhat of a loss that he did not allow himself to remain one. Evil conditions need a satirist to pin them down and flay them clean. Official poets are seldom satirists. A pity. So we may look forward to many poems from Mr. MacLeish which bear the same relation to the art of poetry that Blashfield murals bear to the art of painting, and we may look forward to a new and better world announced by the rhetorical generalities peculiar to a low level of writing in the old.

Muriel Rukeyser is much younger than Mr. MacLeish; she is twenty-five. Like him, she is interested in the state of society to the almost complete exclusion of any conscious "personal expression." She is highly gifted. She can range freely over the insane manifestations of a world infected with a suicidal death wish; she can fuse the early Auden manner with the brilliant snapshot technique of Surrealism. She is earnest, and she has language. After a single reading of her new book, *A Turning Wind,* one is uncertain what ingredients of life and poetry are lacking. After one has reread it, the suspicion arises that Miss Rukeyser is deficient in a sense of human life. A certain amount of rough joy and silly pleasure, of lying and lust and horseplay, existing in humanity, however ill it may be, is overlooked. Miss Rukeyser has rubbed off the soiled and silly edges which mean nothing, and everything. Her world is at once too nightmare and too noble; it is static and literary. She does not realize that such a world could not last overnight, that the sense of injustice is only relevant when applied to living human beings, and that human beings, although oppressed and cruelly crazy, are also wonderfully funny and healthily vulgar (even to themselves). The day of chaste and noble proletarian myths should be about over. It has been recently proved that there is something hideously oversimplified in crude oppositions and blind idealism. Miss Rukeyser can write with great complexity. She should come into herself completely when she lets down a little, masters a wider range of feeling, and mixes some loud laughs with her high scorn.

The decade which outlawed from poetry personal emotion, individual insight, and straight looks into the flawed human heart now closes. It has been a queer time. And, from all current signs, patriotism and "public speech" have still a long course to run. Art is slow and long, but there's nothing brisker and more vocal than politics.

1 9 3 9

§ *Utilitarianism Disguised*

Max Eastman's *The Enjoyment of Poetry* first appeared in the days when young rebels (in America) had recently dared to cast religion and "morals" aside, shake off science, and step forth as hearty embodiments of "awareness." Mr. Eastman, with the passing of time, has toned down his original picture of the poet as inspired vagabond and of poetry as sheer vitalism. And, although he has built his theories on Marxist science, he has not fallen into the open trap of poetry as propaganda. But he has never gone back on his original belief in the cleavage between science and art, and he will have nothing to do with poetry which is not "general" and not clear. This insistence on clarity certainly seems to be utilitarianism working in a disguised form. And it is an insistence charged with a kind of moral feeling; because modern poets cannot be easily understood, they are to be distrusted.

The poems selected for Mr. Eastman's new *Anthol-*

ogy for the Enjoyment of Poetry are sorted into sections "according as their prevailing values are of sensuous perception, emotion, action or idea" and one "devoted to purely imaginary values." Their division into categories immediately imparts an old-fashioned flavor to the book. We are reminded of a nineteenth-century habit; poems put under the heads of "Life," "Love," "Eternity," etc. And the selections themselves remind us that the romantic-socialist rebellion against the mechanist-economic nineteenth-century world, though it seemed to leave behind "elevating" standards of art, actually dragged them along in its wake. Mr. Eastman is, of course, completely against "taste" as a criterion. "Taste" is a luxury product; it comes out of the drawing room and the "ivory tower" and leads back into these refuges. The poet—and especially the great poet—is out on the open road of life, thrilling to his own heartbeat, to "the vigorous abandon" of his mind: a minstrel. The historic process has shut him off from science and religion, but nothing can stop his search for "intensified experience."

Substituting the word "sensibility" for the outlawed word "taste" and applying this faculty to Mr. Eastman's selections, the reader recognizes good, bad, and indifferent work. At times these poems creak with sentiment, are stiff with rhetoric, or fall flat from their very fullness of "life." Mr. Eastman has not entirely rejected the moderns; here are Hopkins, T. S. Eliot, Yeats, Spender, H. D., Edith Sitwell, and James Joyce (in their clearer moments). But Mr. Eastman tends to reject the truly dramatic poem in favor of the melodramatic, the metaphysical in favor of the "fanciful," the "mystical" in favor of the ghostly, the satirical poem altogether. He chooses descriptive and emotional verse with some authority, since poetry of this kind falls in best with his general theories.

Mr. Eastman's inability to understand what modern poets are up to rises from his insistence that science is still rigid and is becoming more so. The psychological and social sciences, he says, may seem to be less fixed, but this is a delusion. Give them time and they will drive poetry out of the books entirely. He ignores the fact that during the last twenty-five years scientific simplifications have been enlarged. The universe has been extended into pure realms of the imagination, and the subconscious has become a scientifically recognized guide to the world of "practical" affairs. The cog-wheels of the mechanistic universe have stopped turning; science has become humble before the intuitive thinker. All this makes Mr. Eastman rather cross. He seems to want a rigid universe against which the poet may surge and rebel. When poetry expresses complicated emotions, when the poet concerns himself with borderline subliminal states (all of great interest to modern science), Mr. Eastman disapproves. That "unintelligible" poetry can extend consciousness he will not admit. Granted that modern poetry has among its practitioners counterfeit talents, the ability to sense the difference between the real and the imitation requires more sensitive instruments than Mr. Eastman has to hand. Certainly, compared with some of the poems here included, modern poetry has advanced into regions far beyond those in which Mr. Eastman's "life-forcing" values hold.

1 9 3 9

§ *Pound's Later Cantos*

Ten years ago it was the custom for *avant-garde* critics to call those people who were puzzled by Ezra Pound's *Cantos* imbeciles. Such people then were beneath both explanation and contempt. Now it is different. Pound's publishers have gone to the trouble, as they publish his new volume *Cantos LII-LXXL,* to provide a neat little explanatory brochure, which slips into a neat pocket pasted on the inside back cover of the book. This brochure, entitled "Notes on Ezra Pound's Cantos: Structure and Metric," contains two well and clearly written essays, one on Pound's matter and one on his manner. A photograph of Pound, making him look even more scowling than he frequently sounds, embellishes its cover.

Pound's moral ideas are based, we are told, on the discipline of Confucius; his economic ideas, on those of "certain of the Canonist writers on economics," "certain of the economic theories of the corporate state," Major Douglas, and the obscurer economist Silvio Gesell.

Pound believes that everything in the modern mess could be fixed up if "the democracies" would "finance their war and defence with statal economy"—this in spite of the fact that Pound is against war. Pound is no Fascist at heart, we are told, although he likes to live in Italy; and the Chinese have taught him the use of "extreme ellipsis." Also, the *Cantos* actually are not based on the fugue form but may have been strongly influenced by the structure of Dante's "Commedia." Pound has already given us an "Inferno" in the early *Cantos*; in the present "American Colonial and Chinese cantos," we are in the midst of his "Purgatorio." At any moment, as his apologist puts it, Pound may "plunge into the Empyrean." On the metrical side, we are assured, Pound is breaking up the iambic metres, usual and often monotonous in English poetry, with trochees and spondees.

After Pound's long and rather insolent cultivation of opacity and ambiguity, it would be easy to become hilarious at all this blueprinting. And it would be easy to poke fun at Pound himself, since he seems to be almost totally without humor. But one must realize that he is in many ways a great figure. He did an extraordinary job thirty years ago of bringing life to English verse, and his influence has not yet petered out. He has written beautiful poetry. That he now sounds less like a poet than like a case history is tragic rather than comic. Faced with these new *Cantos*, one's warmest charity is certainly called into play. The dullness and brutishness of the Ming and the Manchu rulers, described in the first section, are equalled only by the fustiness and mustiness of John Quincy Adams' notations on life and business conditions with which Pound deals in the second. We are given, in this latter part, not "the idea and ideal of democracy as it was conceived in the mind of one of

the founding fathers," which the publishers rather sentimentally promise us, but the atmosphere of American
Colonial laundry bills and old promissory notes. Pound's
early ability to open up gaps in his narration, through
which we saw tranquil sea- and landscapes and lovely,
cool forms of antique beauty, has totally disappeared.
The only asides are scatological ones, of an extremely
childish and petulant kind, and a few yelps of pure race
hatred. As for the metrics, they often are those of prose
(which is a mixture of iambs, trochees, and spondees).

Perhaps this is Purgatory. If so, we can only hope it is
to be brief. For if Pound plans to make "plunges" into
Paradise, he must be able to put aside his hatred, as
Dante managed to do. If one hates anything too long,
one not only begins to resemble what is hated but one
forgets, one becomes incapable even of imagining any
longer, what it is that one could love. What Pound
would do in a paradise unencumbered by old bills of
lading and growls about usury, it is becoming difficult
to think. Moral indignation is one thing; *l'amor*, which
Dante said moved the sun and other stars, is something
even more difficult.

The ideograms occurring here and there in the text
are certainly beautiful, and it is a great pleasure just to
look at them.

1 9 4 0

2

Official justice has now dealt with Ezra Pound, and this
autumn New Directions has again taken up the task of
publishing his works. Two volumes announce the be-

ginning of this program: *The Pisan Cantos,* twenty
poems written by Pound while he was a prisoner in
the Italian city awaiting trial as a traitor, and *The
Cantos,* which includes not only the Pisan section but
all of his "epic" (in Pound's view, any poem that contains history is an epic) that he has written to date. The
initial sixteen cantos first appeared in book form in
1925, when Pound's reputation was at its height. At the
start, this "epic" exhibited in full the range of Pound's
genius. It is a late work, begun when he was nearly
forty and firmly in command of his difficult style. T. S.
Eliot's *The Waste Land* (1922) dedicated to Pound,
had given the modern world its first major poem in
English. It was time for Pound to commence gathering
together the fruits of his already long career: his scholarship in medieval Romantic literature (chiefly the literature of Provence), and his interest in the culture of
the Italian and French Renaissance, in Greek literature
from Homer to Callimachus, and in Chinese poetry and
ideogram. His episodic and disjunct style suggested
cinema technique, or so critics have decided, for it involved the flashback, breaking up the sequence of time
and of place. Each item made sense but had no apparent connection with any other. And from the first
Pound employed his most obvious trick: the use of
classical tags, often in languages, such as Greek and
Chinese, that need transliteration, or in dead tongues,
such as *langue d'oc.* As we look back with time's perspective, we realize that his various devices, if often used
legitimately, were frequently the result of his mystifying,
or sorcerer, side. The not clearly understood creates
wonderment and awe, but bafflement and irritation as
well. There is something hypnotizing, even for the ini-
tiate, in being confronted with a language one can

barely pronounce, and the uninitiate are likely to be
bowled over by words as simple as "to agathon" when
they come at them in large black Greek capitals. But
it was the Chinese ideogram which really offered Pound
the chance to become a master magician. The ideogram
is lovely beyond belief, yet it thwarts almost any attack
made upon it by non-Chinese reason. There it is; one
is impressed; the spell takes hold, and Pound has the
reader in his mage's power. These Poundian procedures
had their good aspect, however. The poet was breaking
down prejudice against forgotten or neglected cultures.
He was striking across the lines of specialist scholars, so
strict and so snobbish in our day. He was presenting the
past as though it were all simultaneous and were still
going on; he was making the point that in art this syn-
chronization and timelessness actually exist.

Pound's streak of charlatanry, in *The Cantos* as a
whole, was so interwoven with valuable insight that it
was fairly negligible. What became really annoying was
his growing tendency toward obsession. The obsessed
always lack that final ingredient of greatness, humility.
They are also invariably bad-tempered and vituperative.
They hammer and they scold. Finally they stop making
sense, and end up ranting in an exasperated gibberish.
Pound never reached the gibberish stage, but at his
worst he presented a picture of a fanatic who must always be in the right, who cannot turn a hairsbreadth
from the small and concrete toward the large generality,
who bores by quoting from documentation, and who
sets up a pattern that gradually hardens, until we get
nothing but deadly repetition. In the cantos written
just before the war, Pound seemed to have lost his
ability to control his manias, and his increasingly vulgar presentation of them often made him sound less

like a lover of the highest cultures and more like a rude inheritor of none. But he could, at his best, revive, in lines of the most exquisite weight and the purest flow, the classic world, the crystal beginnings of men and gods.

Pound's imprisonment in Pisa seems to have brought him back to art and to life. *The Pisan Cantos* shows a new sense of proportion. He begins to feel pity and gratitude, and he begins to smile wryly, even at himself. I cannot think of any other record by an artist or a man of letters, in or out of prison, so filled with a combination of sharp day-to-day observation, erudition, and humorous insight. The diatribes against usury (Pound's King Charles' head) occur, but they are now a minor theme. The gibes at enemies continue, but they are now mixed with the memories of friends—and what great and brilliant friends! And Pound cannot give enough gratitude to the Negro soldier who secretly made him a desk out of a packing box, to get him "offen th' ground" (he was living in a tent). He speaks with tenderness of a visiting lizard, and he jots down reminiscences of his art and life, beginning with the moment when, as a young poet, he thought of dumping the entire edition of his first book into a Venetian canal. All this may help us to understand the stresses that beset this American poet, whose art time will in the end surely honor, and without whose influence and energy we should not have modern poetry in English as we know it today.

1 9 4 8

§ *The Poet in New York and Elsewhere*

Federico Garcia Lorca, Spain's greatest modern poet, who was shot at the age of thirty-seven in Granada in the early weeks of the Spanish war, was, like Yeats, fortunate in having direct access to a living folk tradition. Again like Yeats, Lorca was open to the *avant-garde* movements of his time. Yeats came under the influence of French Symbolism; Lorca had his Surrealist period. The poems in the first section of his *The Poet in New York* (well translated by Rolfe Humphries from the poet's perhaps incomplete typescript) are thoroughly Surrealist. They were written in 1929 and 1930, when Lorca, already famous in Spain for his songs and ballads, lived in New York as a student at Columbia and travelled as far north as Vermont.

Lorca had a right to Surrealism as non-Spanish poets have not; his native literary tradition stems from Gongora. And the modern Spaniard has cut loose from the idea of a religious hell so recently that the private hell of the subconscious floats closer to the surface in both

Dali and Lorca than, nowadays, in artists of other nationalities. These facts must be borne in mind by the reader who, like myself, distrusts Surrealism's worth and pretensions and the worth of any poet who adheres too rigorously to its tenets. In the case of Lorca, we have proof of his poetic worth in his non-Surrealist work. The brilliant and popularly inspired *Gypsy Ballads* were published in 1928, and we have examples of them in the latter part of this book. His Surrealist period in America and Cuba followed. Later, Lorca published his "Lament for Ignacio Sanchez Mejias" (already translated into English by A. L. Lloyd as "Lament for the Death of a Bullfighter"), and in that late and superb poem we can see what the poet finally did with Surrealism. He used it as Baudelaire used "Gothic": he made it humane and the vehicle of emotion.

His ballads get at the nerve centers directly. Their oral tradition comes through at all points; we understand why this poetry is sung by illiterate people all over Spain. Objects in them move, glitter, give off heat, cold, and odor; expand and contract, glow and resound, and the heart of the reader goes through corresponding processes; is made to feel. They are grown out of the heart as wheat or grapes are grown out of the ground.

1 9 3 7 & 1 9 4 0

§ *Childhood's False Eden*

1 KATHERINE MANSFIELD

John Middleton Murry, in his preface to this collection of Mansfield miscellanea *(The Scrapbook of Katherine Mansfield),* promises a further substantial publication of unpublished letters, this year or next. The present volume of unfinished sketches, notes for stories, quotations from books read, and pieces of direct personal analysis, adds little to the Mansfield canon. It stands, it is true, as another "book," and we know that it was Katherine Mansfield's great wish to leave work of some bulk and substance. But perhaps it is not a service to her character and talents to emphasize the more fragmentary side of her work.

For the great difference between Mansfield and the Chekhov she admired and in some ways resembled was that Chekhov had more time to develop; and that he was forced, by the fact of his doctor's profession, to deal in the ordinary way with his experience and surroundings. Mansfield, on the other hand, had only the world of childhood to back her up. Whatever sorts of rough reality she had known, she repressed; or inducted only in a "sublimated" form into her writing. The everyday side of life to her was "too crude, too ugly." It was not merely childishness, but the neurotic's love of childishness which gave poignance to many of her effects. "She had the privilege," wrote her French translator, "of living in a fairyland, in the midst of a strange little phantasmagoria of which she was at once the creator and the dupe; in a little universe of her own where familiar objects . . . took on unexpected roles." And Francis Carco, in his reverent memoir, speaks of "her natural taste for the poetry of the rain, of the night, of absurd and dangerous lives . . . and false situations. . . . It amused her to frighten herself . . . to have fear and pain at the same time. . . . She was hurt by living in the midst of so much ugliness and corruption. . . . Mysteries of the [pure] heart of a child!"

It was this purity which makes her finest stories what they are. But childhood, prolonged, cannot remain a fairyland. It becomes a hell. This Mansfield came to know, and the greatness of her letters and journals is based on her efforts to escape from this prison. It was her tragedy that she saw into her situation when it was too late to do anything about it which took time. The Gurdjieff offer to waken her "will" seemed to her the quick way out, and she chose it, without hesitation. She knew exactly what she wanted to find on the other side (see the entry in the *Journal* for October 10, 1922). Isolated passages in the present book also testify to this perception and it is a pity that, broken away from a context, they often sound snappish and petty. "Peace of mind? What is peace of mind?" she asked, early. Later she sensed what it could be; and a younger generation of writers was to take from her the phrase "a change of heart" and the sentence: "To be rooted in life, that's what I want."

As an artist, it is clear that Mansfield was a forerunner, in English prose, of a new kind of sensibility which, up to our day, has been imperfectly and brokenly expressed in the prose of all European literatures. She was nearer to Lawrence and Joyce in this than she wished to admit (she disliked the cruder aesthetic explorations of both Joyce and Lawrence, and thought sensibility artificial in Turgenev). This sensibility comes through, in a distorted form, in Lewis Carroll; and has always been present in lyric poetry, folk song, and proverbs; and turns up in isolated letters and journals during the nineteenth century. To it nothing is closed; the sharpened mind and sense reflect all. "Ordinary human consciousness," says I. A. Richards in his study of Coleridge, "may not, until recently, have had a form that could thus be represented. On one interpretation of the change, Katherine Mansfield [and others] have improved the descriptive technique of prose, have caught something always present which writers in the past could not (or did not wish to) catch; on another interpretation, something new in the modes of perception had come into being for them to describe."

From this point of view, anything left by Mansfield, no matter how incomplete and disconnected, becomes important.

1 9 4 0

2 I. COMPTON-BURNETT

The novels of Ivy Compton-Burnett owe much of their
power to the fact that each of them is a nightmare into
which we are drawn by degrees but from which we
escape with reluctance. For these are high-comedy night-
mares. Miss Compton-Burnett belongs to the company
of artists who, with the aid of the comic spirit, are able
to enlarge life by imposing inexorable patterns on it.
Within a straight Victorian world—which escapes being
"period" because it lacks any scrap of fashionable orna-
mentation—her three fixed circles revolve: masters, servants, and children. And although the members of each
circle are vocal to a degree, communication among the
groups is largely indirect. Children spy on masters and
servants; servants, on masters and children; masters, on
servants, children, and one another. Situation is built up
by the intrusion of some shocking reality in the masters'
world which soon filters, by eavesdropping, into the
other two; and the only weapon available to the majority of masters is the weapon of convention. But natural
reactions, suppressed in one quarter, are allowed to the
servants and to the young. Thus, humane generosity
and simple love are allowed to break through barriers
of spite and hypocrisy; and the rigid pattern is at length
changed. Sex, in this closed universe, keeps cropping
up in terms of comedy. A prevalent background of il-
legitimacy exists; so that masters are frequently faced
with the results of their early "stumbles" in the form
of butlers who are their natural sons and housekeepers
who are their natural daughters. In *Darkness and Day*,

the world of the bastard impinges so closely upon the world of the family that one of the masters believes for a time that he has married his own cast-off child. The child's mother (a servant) proves that this is not the case. But for a moment all three circles are menaced; and the one remedy seems to be silence. "Oedipus lost no time in going the full length," someone remarks. "Anything like that would make it very public."

Miss Compton-Burnett is certainly fixed permanently at the emotional level of childhood's most "knowing" and disabused stage. This is a point of fixation which breeds a hostility to life that great gifts of intelligence and style alone can alleviate. Miss Compton-Burnett, in many ways a female Swift of our day, constantly proves her possession of these gifts.

1 9 5 1

§ *Sensibility and Luggage*

R. P. Blackmur, author of *The Expense of Greatness,* is a good critic because he is serious, and has both sensibility and intellectual subtlety. He has, it is true, in a marked degree, the faults of these virtues. His seriousness is often invalidated by the web of super-seriousness he tends to spin from it. His sensibilities are not always searching enough; he can hedge around with them, and miss the point, while using them with scientific precision. And his subtlety often enervates rather than reveals. He has, as well, extreme faults of style. It is important to deal with his virtues first, because they are the particular ones they are—rare at any time and practically extinct at the moment.

Although he can be completely wrong on matters situated on what he himself would call "the periphery," Blackmur is frequently beautifully right in matters situated at the center. He knows that a work of art is a complex product of human growth and suffering (although he does not quite manage to say this in his aphorism, "Death is the expense of life and failure the expense of greatness"). He is the direct opposite of the critic who throws off banal middle-class remarks to comfort a middle-class audience. He recognizes and admires "speed" in apprehension and expression, while he himself works with great patience and, sometimes, maddening slowness, around, above, and through his subject. He lugs in moral standards to strengthen his critical weight; but these really do not matter, because, as with all sensitive critics, his reactions are at bottom instinctive. He knows what is serious even in American art; and there has been serious American art in spite of the tendency, at present, to push it back and keep it at folk level. Blackmur, fortunately, is the sort of person who instinctively knows that there is a difference between a lyric poem written by a great lyric poet and a Mother Goose song; between wrought-iron work of a high period and a well-made doorknob or frying pan; between Bach's B Minor Mass and *Ballad for Americans*; between a song by, say, Hugo Wolf and the most beautiful folk song ever invented by anybody. He knows that the novels written by John Steinbeck, Richard Wright, Herman Melville, and Henry James differ greatly. He knows that "all things excellent are as difficult as they are rare." And he is the kind of person who would never be able to deny knowing all this.

Blackmur, however, has serious lacunae in his special knowledge. And he carries an impeding, almost crippling, amount of extra baggage in the form of a whole critical vocabulary taken over from the moral philosophy so popular in English and American universities since the last war. If Blackmur made a determined effort to throw out of his vocabulary such words as "synergical," "sordor," "anterior," "quotidian," and, most especially, "heuristic," it would be all to the good. The terms from moral philosophy, too, tend to reduce some of his passages to pure Swaheli; the result of super-imposing these terms on literary analysis is more be-fuddling than clarifying. And they are not native to Blackmur's cast of mind; when he lets himself go he tends to think in images. This philosophic apparatus, moreover, is manipulated, often, with a kind of swank unbecoming to a sincere critic.

As his perceptions, for some reason, are likely to be good or bad in alternation, his courage, too, often wavers. He can be courageously offhand and even—surprisingly—flip in dealing with obviously bad poets; on the other hand, he treads rather carefully, mincing every statement into the minutest segments, in order to get around saying something directly damning about someone who, by reason of established position or what not, is not quite attackable. Using his own methods alone, he can be triumphantly right and revealing, in the case of T. E. Lawrence (this essay, in spite of its almost impenetrable structure and style, is the best in the book), while remaining incomplete and even biased in the cases of Yeats and Hardy. He can be both wrong and right, as in the case of Emily Dickinson. Here he does stand up, with a good deal of spunk, for a decent edition of Dickinson's works. But on the other hand, because of what he does not take in, he misinterprets the reasons for her poetry; leaving out whole tracts of her circumstances, such as her psychic slavery to her father. He brings in James, Dostoevski, Gide, and Mann in discussing a novel by Frances Frost. On the other hand, he can write paragraphs of fine good sense and delicate analysis, such as the paragraph devoted to the proposition, "Assenting to experience is the basis of conviction."

A perusal of some intense, personal, non-philosophic criticism, of the sort contained, for example, in Flaubert's *Correspondance*, would do Mr. Blackmur a world of good. French criticism of all periods might help him to overcome the more annoying—to the reader—coils and tangles of his subtlety. But he is on the side of the angels, and only needs more impatience, more courage, and perhaps ten more years of varied experience and wider reading, to make him a critic of imposing stature and of the first order.

1 9 4 0

§ *The Letters of Rainer Maria Rilke*

1 THE WARTIME LETTERS

Rilke was thirty-eight years old in August, 1914, when this selection of his letters begins, and forty-six, in December, 1921, when it closes. The letters, therefore, are not exclusively "wartime." Their chief interest lies in the fact that they cover the most unproductive period of Rilke's life: the period when he was unable to write poetry and was forced, both by outer circumstances and his own spiritual state, to undergo the full experience of moral agony necessary before his final work could come into being. He had often spoken of the "heart-work" necessary before creation. In these years he was forced to experience that work anew; and it was, as is usual in great natures, great labor.

Rilke's spiritual health was precarious in 1914, as it had been for some years previously. Having accomplished an extraordinary amount of writing in the decade from 1904 to 1914, he now felt himself at a dead end: finished with one way of thinking and feeling, and not yet ready for a new phase. His nervous exhaustion was noted in 1913 by one of his close friends: "The impression he made on me was one of extreme anxiety; he talked excitedly . . . with extreme nervousness. . . . He had always given way to the feeling of other people, he said; now at last he himself was going to feel desire and love." The poet who in ten years had written down fully the account of his childhood and youthful neuroticism (in *The Notebooks of Malte Laurids Brigge*), and who in the 175 poems in the *Neue Gedichte* volumes had caught, in full complex beauty, his intuitions into nature, his own subtle mind, and the "things" created by man, might well be emptied of the impulse to create. Rilke had always known that his role was one of "openness." He was an instrument made to receive life, in all its manifestations, both monstrous and beautiful. But now, even before the outbreak of the war, he no longer functioned as this instrument; and his state of depression was so strong that he came to Munich to ask aid of a psychiatrist.

"The experience of the war was certainly the severest test of Rilke's conviction that whatever is, is right," one commentator has said. Rilke was on his way from Leipsic to Munich when war was declared. A note in the present volume suggests that what he saw on that journey across southern Germany—"the armed men, the singing, the farewells—must have swept him into the current of exalted excitement that caused him to write his only— and quickly deprecated—war poems." These poems ("Five Songs, August 1914") are truly hysterical productions. They show Rilke at his worst, and resurrect the sentimentality of the adolescent Rilke, before this for years outgrown. Their only value is that they prove no exalted poetry can ever again be written on the subject of modern war. It took Rilke only a week or so to discover their falsity; and from that time on, throughout the war, on the subject of war he was silent, except for the scathing analyses of "the whole sad man-made situation" frequently repeated in his letters.

The war, however, was not through with Rilke. Born in Prague, he had for years transferred his allegiance to Paris. Having lived in almost every country in Europe as a "guest friend," he was now forced to return to Germany in order not to be interned as an Austrian. Then, in 1915, after a military examination, he was found fit and promptly conscripted for service in the Austrian army. This conscription lasted for some months, and his service in Vienna was terminated only after the intervention of his publisher and other friends. These people have spoken of the experience, touching and terrible, of seeing Rilke in uniform.

He returned to Munich, to his own long struggle with his divided nature. The "cleft" in Rilke between "narcissism and objectivity" is nowhere clearer than in his correspondence at this time. "This cleft is common in most extreme artists, but Rilke was in danger of sheer disintegration through it." He now felt himself "a beginner," and saw the people about him in Munich as "finished" in the most invidious sense of the word. All talk of "evasion" and "escapism," applied often so glibly to Rilke in accordance with the dictates of modern jargon, seems particularly fatuous when the long slow process of his development during these years is examined. Rilke had written in 1906: "Those who live with courage . . . can never be deceived or disappointed in the essential realities of life. . . . When we accept the difficulties of life, it becomes easy (since we have enormous resources of strength within us). And we must adhere to difficulty, if we would make any claim to having

a part in life. . . . What we are to understand by courage is a valiant attitude in facing the strangest and most
inexplicable things that can happen to us." All this,
which Rilke once knew, he had to relearn. In the most
inauspicious circumstances he continued "to measure
with the carat weight of the heart, in place of the false
measure of suspicion, happiness, or luck."

These letters lead to the last poems—"because in them
the development of these greater poems develops slowly,
uninterruptedly, almost imperceptibly, through the
whole course of the correspondence." At the end, the
disoriented man has "suffered through" his problem and
in 1921 is ready with a touching eagerness "to understand and adapt himself to the needs of others, especially of those younger and perplexed by life, as he himself had often been." The later letters are sometimes
written to strangers who had written him for counsel.
And they are a corrective to the tendency to make Rilke
into a priest or prophet. His human defects show up
clearly, especially his occasional tendency toward snobbery and dependence. He was above all things a poet, of
a sensibility developed far beyond his time. He came to
a reconciliation with himself, and to a triumph in his
art, by using the most ancient wisdom combined with
the most modern insights. He was opposed to modern
brutality and, most of all, to the modern moral pretensions which cover it. He stands for the future, where "lamenting" need not cancel out "praise"; and to read him
is an antidote against the fear, hatred, and revenge of
the present. To read his poetry and his letters with understanding leads one toward a world where there are
no victories, but only "assent."

1 9 4 0

2

Rainer Maria Rilke considered his letters part of the body of his imaginative work. He stated this belief in his will (he died in 1926), no doubt remembering that he had often sent off to friends, in the freshness of recent experience, material that he later shaped into permanent form. Scholars have found omissions, confusions, and overlappings in the German editions of Rilke's letters, edited by his daughter, Ruth, and her husband, Dr. Carl Sieber. Any translation of these originals must repeat their faults in some degree. *Letters of Rainer Maria Rilke,* translated by Jane Bannard Greene and M. D. Herter Norton, is a selection from the correspondence between 1892, when Rilke was seventeen, and 1910, when he was thirty-five. It is a well-rounded collection, even though it leaves out too much of the shrewd and practical Rilke. For example, the letters to his publisher, Kippenberg, beginning in 1906, are under-represented.

Those who are familiar with the entire correspondence in its original form have pointed out the sameness of its tone, a sameness that at times seems to verge on obsession. It is true that a surface monotony exists. Rilke never plays the fool, never humorously belittles his work and aims, as less absorbed writers allow themselves to do. If he seems continually to underline the worth and dignity of his tasks, we must remember that certain lightnesses may have been edited away, and we must remember the peculiarities of his background and his time.

What is often called Rilke's "snobbery" is explained

by the correspondence. He often claimed aristocratic lineage, but he never tried to hide the facts of his childhood—the cheap flat in Prague, the neurotic mother, and the petty-official father. From his background he acquired a horror of "the little official post" in which, in the ordinary way of things, his life would probably have been spent. He early discovered that when he asked anyone for a job to carry him through difficult times, nothing whatever happened, but when he asked anyone for money outright, or for a pleasant place to write in, he almost invariably found immediate help. He was able, that is, to profit from the still-active patron system, as it existed in pre-1914 Europe. He soon discovered in just what ways this system could save him from uncreative routine and the pressure of poverty. His charm, his sensitiveness, and even the purity of his aims appealed to certain men and women who were rich, appreciative, and often titled. These people almost at once began to draw interest on their investment, in the form of exquisite works of literature composed under their roofs or on their money. The picture of Rilke advocating the simple life and unremitting labor, in the letters he sent out to his friends from a series of vast castles, great houses, and Grand Hotels, has figured in the anecdotes of his detractors. Another Rilke had to exist, and did exist. He could withdraw from any situation with gentle stubbornness. He could live as a recluse surrounded by Bohemian gaiety, as Cocteau and others have testified. He loved solitude, even when it had to be accompanied by squalor, and he was as good at getting out of castles, when need be, as he was at getting into them.

These letters show Rilke growing from the indecisive, arty, and provincial young man into the severe, civilized, completely equipped artist. They provide a background for his first great works: *New Poems* (1907 and 1908) and the prose *Notebooks of Malte Laurids Brigge* (1910). Underneath the unvarying seriousness of surface, of which I have already spoken, an incomparable variety of observation, insights, and interests slowly gathers—"the bewildering richness of his mind." I know of no other correspondence that affords so much pleasure to the sympathetic reader. Little by little the panic and the complaints of the young poet subside, and we are listening to a man who has endured all the blows his civilization can deal and has profited spiritually by them all. The tendency to make a religion out of Rilke has been strong. Reading these letters, one can understand from what sources this tendency springs. For Rilke, far ahead of his time (see, for example, his analysis of Cézanne, written in 1907), recognized certain focal points of modern neurosis and unease. He understood disintegration because he himself had very nearly disintegrated. He sought unity, insight, composure, and patience because he had seen these qualities work cures. His search corresponds to our modern search, and contemporary poets who approach Rilke in seriousness and gifts unanimously agree that it was, and is, a kind of religious hunger that activated Rilke and at present makes modern man uneasy.

1 9 4 5

§ *The Later Poetry of William Butler Yeats*

Old men mad about painting are more fortunate than old poets. With a brush strapped to their wrist, if necessary, old painters can go on with their work. But poets use words, and with words, thoughts and opinions are apt to leak in. And if they are childish opinions, or if the thoughts have stiffened, are mawkish or reactionary, the last poems become ridiculous and unreadable in a later period. Aging Wordsworth and Browning did not do the concept of the old poet as sage any good turn, but Hardy and Yeats have again proved that the old poet need not be the old fogy or the old fool.

The poems in Yeats' *Last Poems and Plays* have no "noble" or "wise" (in the Victorian sense) wrappings upon them. They are, on the contrary, the most naked and terrible he ever wrote. They call up terror; they do not soothe; they shed cold and ruthless light on man, his motives, and his works; and they keep repeating the unpalatable truth that life is horror and failure as well as joy and accomplishment, that patterns superimposed on man cannot reach his devious and cruel heart. They are concerned with lust, betrayal, wildness, and rage, and they are written in the randy measures of street ballads as often as in the purer metres of literature. At the same time, they are concerned with "beautiful lofty things"—with all that mankind knows of love, courage, and the gall that fights against stupidity, half-truths, and injustice. Sometimes, even, they are the love poems of an old poet still capable of love, as witness one of the tenderest poems in English, "John Kinsella's Lament for Mrs. Mary Moore."

Yeats, as an old man, came to reject with complete scorn all middle grounds. It was to the simplest or to the most complex he turned: to peasant songs, or to the most disinterested, useless, and gallant of man's actions and art. He has been accused of writing Fascist marching songs; it is impossible to read this last book of poems and not know that to be a slander, even if Yeats' own answer to this lie did not already exist in print. Yeats' frequent bitterness on the subject of politics is based on the political history of Ireland since the death of Parnell. It is necessary to know that history in order to understand Yeats' anger against the present situation in his native land. It is necessary only to have an ear, a heart, and some experience of living, however, in order to appreciate the power and beauty of the poems in general. The Irish poets whom Yeats exhorts to "learn their trade" have here an example of what kind of spirit poetry demands. And future generations, of whatever nationality or belief, are not likely to be stirred to pity or contempt by Yeats' stoic epitaph:

Cast a cold eye
On life, on death.
Horseman, pass by!

1 9 4 0

2

The first edition of the *Collected Poems* (1933) broke off with the volume *The Winding Stair,* published in the same year. The final collected edition adds to the earlier work the poetry written by Yeats from about 1935 to 1939, the year of his death. This additional material embodies, therefore, the last preoccupations, as well as the last stylistic development, of the great Anglo-Irishman, born in 1865, whose first book appeared in 1889. The record is thus closed of a long career spent almost exclusively in furthering the ideals of disinterested art in a period marked by triumphs of rationalism and of the machine; the cause of the individual in a time of human depersonalization; and the cause of a small nation in a period given over to various forms of imperialism. The means that Yeats chose to achieve his ends have often been derided; and it is true that his "magician" side often brought about curious shifts in his conduct and thinking. His life, moreover, does not follow any conventional pattern of peace found after conflict, of humility following after pride, of spiritual reconciliation in age. But if the last poems often present the picture of a pride-ridden old man who clings to his crankiness with an almost insane zeal, they also present an old poet continuing to explore his complicated nature and his complicated times up to the last—while extending the limits of his art with unflagging ingenuity, subtlety, and daring.

Yeats never "adjusted" to the conditions of his age or of his society. He not only constructed a religion for himself, but he spent many years "docketing the universe": building a picture of time, space, and causality which fitted the needs (and no doubt quieted the fears) of his own peculiar temperament. His ideals were both spiritual and aristocratic; he gave his allegiance to peasant and aristocrat; and he wasted neither time nor sympathy on "passive suffering" or ideas of human progress. In his universe, built in the form of a Great Wheel, man's soul went through successive incarnations—bound to an impersonal fate, but rescued by the possibility of a personal destiny. This destiny left man freedom to act and to create—to oppose the work of the spirit to the mechanisms of nature.

It was the failure of mankind in general—and of Irishmen in particular—to grasp and forward this destiny that provoked in Yeats, as time passed, an increasing bitterness and irritability. He himself had taken on discipline early; he had put off his youthful indolence and had spent years working in the more practical side of the drama, at the Abbey Theatre. But in the field of art an Irish middle class, newly come into power, let him down; and Irish politics took a turn of which he did not approve. Because of these struggles against opposition, Yeats' wit, shrewdness, and powers of intellect began, in his middle years, to develop and come into view. He began to write with ease concerning the contemporary scene, and to display his prejudices without fear. His mind became infinitely restless and ceaselessly inquisitive. He also developed, along with growing powers of invective, a kind of magnanimity—a magnanimity, it is true, which worked best in retrospect. In the poems written many years after the Easter Rebellion of 1916, he was able to celebrate the heroism of his enemies as well as of his friends; and his later work is filled with praise of human nobility, wherever found.

Around 1935, after a period spent in efforts to compromise with the Irish Free State government, under which he had served as a Senator, he came perilously near adopting ideas of undemocratic coercion and force. He quickly withdrew from this position; and the only trace of his passing belief in "marching men" comes through in the extravagant marching songs. In the years from 1936 to 1939 he experienced a tremendous renewal of poetic power. This renewal expressed itself in two definite, and opposed, poetic manners. On the one hand, he began to elaborate poems of the "Crazy Jane" variety, in which, to old broadsheet rhythms, unstinted praise of coarse human vitality is set against the powers of church, state and, indeed, every ordinary form of orderly life. At the same time he continued to produce, in his more "lofty" style, celebrations of human greatness, usually in the form of elegies to the past glories of his own generation. He flaunted "an old man's frenzy" and an old man's pride; but if he often pushed intensity toward harshness, he instinctively kept to intensity, knowing that without passion no art can live. Even in the midst of his die-hard show—which at moments verged on the theatrical—he slipped in passages of self-mockery bred of self-knowledge; and beneath his praise of crude human vitality a new note of pathos can be detected. Something stiff, divided, and hieratic drops away from the personality. The wiles of the old magician are transcended; and the final impression is one of a self-fulfilled artist using, up to the end, for selfless purposes, the unbroken spirit of an indomitable man.

1951

§ *The Gothic South*

The definite Gothic quality which characterizes so much of the work of writers from the American South has puzzled critics. Is it the left-over atmosphere of the *roman noir,* so skilfully transferred to America by Poe? Or is it a true and indigenous atmosphere of decaying feudalism? Faulkner treats the horrifying and ambiguous situations thrown up by a background which has much in common with nineteenth-century Russia in a style darkened and convoluted by, it would seem, the very character of his material. Eudora Welty, who is a native and resident of Mississippi, in the stories of this volume * has instinctively chosen another method which opens and widens the field and makes it more amenable to detached observation. She proceeds with the utmost simplicity and observes with the most delicate terseness. She does not try mystically to transform or anonymously to interpret. The parallel forced upon us, particularly by those of Miss Welty's stories which

* *A Curtain of Green,* by Eudora Welty.

are based on an oblique humor, is her likeness to Gogol.

The tramp musicians, the inhabitants of a big house (either mad, drunk, or senile), the idiots and ageless peasant women, the eccentric families tyrannized over by an arch-eccentric, the pathetic and ridiculous livers of double lives, even the Negro band leader with his sadism and delusion of grandeur—all these could come out of some broken-down medieval scene, and all could have been treated completely successfully—with humorous detachment, combined with moments of tenderness and roaring farce—by the author of *The Inspector General* and *Dead Souls*. Like Gogol, Miss Welty opens the doors and describes the setting, almost inch by inch. She adds small detail to small detail: the fillings in people's teeth, the bright mail-order shirts of little boys, the bottles of Ne-Hi, the pictures of Nelson Eddy hung up like icons. We see what happens to representatives of an alien commercial world—here, traveling salesmen: how they become entangled against their will in this scene which goes on under its own obscure decomposing laws; or dissolve back into it, symbolically enough, in delirium and death. Even the women in the beauty parlor have a basic place in the composition; they are not so much modernly vulgar as timelessly female—calculating, shrewd, and sharp. Miss Welty's method can get everything in; nothing need be scamped, because of romantic exigencies, or passed over, because of rules of taste. Temperamentally and by training she has become mistress of her material by her choice of one exactly suitable kind of treatment, and—a final test of a writer's power—as we read her, we are made to believe that she has hit upon the only possible kind. But it is a method, in Miss Welty's hands, only suitable for her Southern characters on their own ground. The one story dealing with the North, "Flowers for Marjorie," goes completely askew.

Katherine Anne Porter, in her preface, surveys with much insight the nature and scope of, as well as the dangers attendant upon, the specialized talent of the writer of short stories. She warns against "the novel," a form held up to the short-story writer as a baited trap. She does not warn against the other trap, the commercial short story, and the other tempter, "the agent." It seems impossible that Miss Welty, equipped as she is, should fall into line and produce the bloated characters and smoothed-out situations demanded by "commercial" publications. But other finely equipped persons have given in. As for the novel, she needs to introduce only the slenderest unifying device, something analogous to "a smart britchka, a light spring-carriage of the sort affected by bachelors, retired lieutenant colonels, staff captains, landowners possessed of about a hundred souls," to write one whenever she wishes.

1 9 4 1

§ *A Revolution in European Poetry*

Emery Neff's *A Revolution in European Poetry: 1660-1900* is described on its jacket as "the only short history of European poetry since the Renaissance." It is incredible that this should be true; but as one considers, it seems all too possible that it is. Dr. Neff traces the enormous influence of French literary taste, during and after Louis XIV's reign, upon the countries of Europe; and the ferments produced in this taste, in the eighteenth and nineteenth centuries, by German literature and thought, a revived interest in Greece and Rome and the Orient, and political dislocations. At the end modern poetry emerges, after the appearance in France of Baudelaire, Rimbaud, and Verlaine.

Such an account is long overdue, and one is grateful for a new emphasis, not usual in histories of literature written in English, upon the European scene as a whole, rather than upon what went on in England alone. And although it is addressed specifically to "students and teachers of comparative literature," the general reader can share in this panoramic outlook, and watch the interplay of forces which lead to increasingly complex expression in modern poetry. In America interest in these European sources was dropped when the 1930's arrived with their material difficulties. *Axel's Castle* was not followed up, as it should have been, by further detached discussion and by translations of works cited. The result has been that American poetry in the past decade, when not completely provincial, was muddled as to its derivations.

The subject, as the author states, is, of course, immense. His method, on the whole, is admirable. He condenses in a masterly way, and writes coolly and clearly. He has refused to use the tags "neo-classical," "romantic," and whatnot; and, these often academic partitions once removed, the narrative moves with breadth and sweep. J. G. Robertson has said:

There is manifest danger in the ineradicable instinct of our minds to classify and schematize. We love our antitheses: Classicism-romanticism; idealism-realism; collectivism-individualism. But with fuller knowledge comes clearness that such antitheses are inherently unreal; the evolution of thought shows no such sharp contrasts, no such hard and fast lines. Nature makes no leaps; and the progress of human idea, far from being a geometric progression, is an infinitely complicated growth, where one thought passes into its antithesis imperceptibly, like a dissolving view.

The need for these antitheses seems most real in a comparison of the arts of language. Because language is the carrier of ideas, it is easy to believe that it should be very little else than such a carrier. Comparative histories of architecture, painting, music, and even of "taste," escape bias more easily than comparative studies of the arts of language. Then it must be remembered that there are barriers in language. Linguistics are not needed in order to appreciate Palestrina, Mozart, Couperin, Purcell; or Piranese, Durer, Watteau, Constable. With poetry the ear and eye are not enough.

It cannot be said that Dr. Neff does much toward clarifying the inner qualities of the poetry with which he deals. He tends to tie up the spiritual with the turn of events and historic processes: changes of government, wars and their aftermaths, industrial changes, and alternate political enthusiasm and disillusionment. It has been said: "The critic . . . to reach the essence of poetry, must realize that he walks into a domain where the essential does not coincide with the most general, but with the most 'interior.'" But when we grant Neff's slight set toward the idea that poetry stems directly from the specific event (or in reaction against the specific event), his account of the historic background is thorough in the extreme. And when poets can be directly related to this background, he seldom makes an error, and very rarely an omission. He gives as admirably concise a description of the nature of French seventeenth-century taste as of Goethe's development and the development of *Faust*. He is also brilliantly thorough with the post-Napoleonic period: the rise of money; the struggle for civil rights and the rights of labor, in England and France; and the reactions of certain poets to these upheavals and transformations. He does a splendid job of disentangling the beginnings of modern criticism, giving Lessing and Herder their just due; and he performs another service in bringing out and relating to their age the great and neglected talents of Holderlin, Leopardi, and Vigny.

Historic events, however, can never completely explain poetry. Poetry is often generations in advance of the thought of its time. It is often a throwback. Many imponderables make up the climate of literature. The often irrational turns of taste—the almost religious currents of guilt, fear, desperation, and disillusion (or of peace and release)—must be taken into account in the study of any art. Comparisons must include differences as well as likenesses. The gaps in Dr. Neff's scholarly (and truly valuable) correlation of poetic works, important events, and sources of ideas are consistent *lacunae* where might appear the poet or thinker out of series; the man who carried the past in him unresolved, or the man, not of his time, who is to be a force in the future.

For example, the works of Vico (not mentioned) were known, according to Robertson, to both Goethe and Herder. In 1681, when Boileau's *Art Poetique* (of which Neff makes much) was being translated into English, Edward Young, the first precursor of the English Gothic Revival (of which Neff makes little) was born. Gray's enthusiasm for Ossian is put on record; but there is no mention of Gray's friend, Horace Walpole (whose *Strawberry Hill* has been described as "less an archaeological reconstruction than the expression of a state of soul"). Neff, with partial truth, traces Gothic interest to Germany and Burger's *Lenore* (1774). But Walpole was reviving Gothic in England twenty years previous to this; and certainly native English Gothic stands behind both "The Ancient Mariner" and "Christabel." (Neff does not speak of Gothic but of "Wonder"; but how much more than "Wonder" was this secularized return of medieval Catholicism into Protestantism, always accompanied by a mask of anti-Papistry!) Byron paid open tribute to William Beckford, another precursor, and to Beckford's *Vathek* and Johnson's *Rasselas,* as sources of

Eastern color. *Vathek* appeared twenty years before "Kubla Khan" was written.

It is, of course, ridiculous to push back influences too far; but should not that friend of Winckelmann, Piranesi—the "picturesque" artist who was, oddly enough, responsible for "Adam" in England and "Empire" in France—be given some notice, along with Winckelmann? And, if it is rather one-sided of Dr. Neff to emphasize the classicism in eighteenth-century England at the expense of the century's Gothic side (the two streams went on concurrently, according to good authority, from 1750 to 1830), it is certainly impossible to explain how German influence got into France without mentioning Madame de Staël. (Neff does not allow Madame de Staël in his text; merely in his appended chronology.) Madame de Staël, according to Thibaudet, smuggled Romanticism into France "through the 'gulf' of Geneva and Coppet." Again, though Dr. Neff states outright that his method is necessarily selective, it is certainly odd that so much is made of Hugo and Leconte de Lisle (both of whom, of course, bring out a great many of the points Neff stresses: the political enthusiasms of the one; the disillusion with politics, and consequent "escape" into exotic themes, of the other) while nothing whatever is said of Béranger, Gérard de Nerval, or Banville. Béranger, the most popular post-Revolution poet in France, died in the year of *Bovary* and *Les Fleurs du Mal* (how ironically these events complete one another!). Nerval was "the only French poet able to bring the actual feeling of the German ballad over into French poetry; the one French poet of the time completely open to the legend and music of Germany." Banville, admired by Baudelaire, far from being made gloomy by political events, "mocked the Empire while adoring it," and wrote of exotic subjects in the most cheerful way.

Dr. Neff ends his book with the usual sad thoughts on *fin de siècle*. But in 1900 poetry in Europe was just about to pass into a new era of brilliance: Yeats, Rilke, Valéry, Apollinaire, were alive and soon to produce modern work unmatched in depth, subtlety, and complexity. The true synthesis, of which Neff certainly has a conception, must not only range widely but plunge deeply under the surface of events. One need not be either morbid or a mystic to know that this is true; such syntheses have been accomplished time and again in histories of arts other than literature. Certainly it is in the direction of *Einfuhling* that the liberation and future of comparative literature lies. Meanwhile, Dr. Neff has written a valuable book which should serve as a rational point of reference for students and the general reader alike.

1 9 4 1

§ *War Poetry*

Awake! and Other Wartime Poems, by W. R. Rodgers, is a first book by a young Ulsterman. It has been hailed by some as the first impressive book of contemporary war poetry to come out of England. The complete lack up to now of poetry in the manner of Rupert Brooke has bothered and annoyed a portion of the English and American public. It is this public's notion that such poems as Rupert Brooke's sonnet "If I should die, think only this of me" should appear, by some process of spontaneous generation, at the beginning of any war in which England is engaged. Perhaps it would be worth while to try to puzzle out why such poetry is modernly impossible and why the Rodgers book contains the kind of poetry we are going to get, in English, from those poets who manage to remain sincere through the present upheaval.

Classically, the two high types of war poem are the battle cry (or hymn), written in the definite iambics which presuppose the march's four-four time, and the elegy. The popular types of war song are quite different (although they are almost always marches or sentimental laments) and need not be dealt with here. But one likeness between formal verse and popular poetry must be recognized: at the beginning of a war both categories are gay; at the end of a war they are terrifying, coarse, satiric, and bitter. The post-Napoleonic ballad "Johnny, I hardly knew ye" is blood brother to the poems of Sassoon, written toward the end of the First World War. What formal "war poetry" cannot be is narcissistic, sentimental, or passive. The war sonnets of Rupert Brooke and the popular elegy "In Flanders Fields" are war poetry at its very worst. They were decadent and puerile twenty years ago; they are unthinkable now. What people who yearn back to them want is the stale and dowdy moral atmosphere of the early nineteen-hundreds. In spite of ourselves, we live in a more bracing air and are made of more sincere and sterner stuff.

The First World War impaired the notion that war poetry can be written by non-combatants. The only decent 1914-1918 verse was written by young men in their early twenties who were soldiers in the trenches—Wilfred Owen, Isaac Rosenberg, Charles Sorley, and Siegfried Sassoon. The hack writing of Kipling and Noyes made no impression, then or subsequently. One attempt at war poetry was made by both Rilke and Yeats. Rilke's hysterical "Five Songs, August 1914" were repudiated by him five days after they were written. Yeats wrote the superb "An Irish Airman Foresees His Death" and then announced his withdrawal into silence in "On Being Asked for a War Poem." The silence of these two men during those years is even now more impressive than volumes of exhortation and elegy would be. It was the soldiers who impressively spoke.

English writers and the more sensitive English citizen, through the worst days of the blitz, knew that hymns of hate could do no good. To their credit, be it said that they produced nothing smugly or romantically martial. They were working with bitter reality, from which there could be no sentimental, panicky, or nostalgic flights. It was borne in upon them that the citizenry could no longer gaily send off an army of dull-witted conscripts to the tune of, say, *"Malbrough s'en va t'en guerre!"* The day of what someone has called "baby wars" was over. The involvement was now total, and a tragic insight was the first need of a writer.

W. R. Rodgers, whether or not he is a soldier poet, is not a profound thinker, but a contemporaneous and candid spirit is in him. He has at his disposal a firm, rugged idiom, since Ulster still has here and there surviving pockets of primitive speech. He uses the packed directness of the alliterative Anglo-Saxon of Hopkins' and Auden's experiments and gives it surprising Celtic turns. His unexpected and salty epithets pick out many unexpected details of what he observes, from a fountain in a park to an airman in his bomber. What is best about this poet is his glance into the future and his realization that more than a casual peace must be demanded after the end of this war.

1 9 4 2

§ *Wise After the Event*

Modern American Poetry: A Critical Anthology, edited
by Louis Untermeyer, reaches its sixth revised form in
its 1942 edition. The first edition came out unpreten-
tiously in 1919. Every few years since, a new edition has
appeared. The paper has broadened, the pages have
multiplied until they now number 712 over all. Mr.
Untermeyer has chosen poems, clipped criticism, and
"researched" biographical facts about his poets until we
have all the interesting and feasible information pertaining to poem and poet. We know not only what Mr.
Untermeyer thinks of poem and poet but what a vast
mass of other people have thought. Since 1936 this
anthology, which for years began with Emily Dickinson,
has harked back to Walt Whitman. The format is
charming if rather unwieldy, and the volume is brought
right up to the sharpest point of contemporaneity with
its closing names, Delmore Schwartz and Muriel Rukeyser, both born in 1913.

    Modern British Poetry: A Critical Anthology, edited

by the same hand, goes back to 1920 and is now in its fifth revised edition. Pruning and care have made it shrink a little since it last appeared; it is 506 pages at present. Thirty-four poets, in Mr. Untermeyer's phrase, "have been dropped"; twenty-nine, ranging from G. M. Hopkins to Sacheverell Sitwell, Auden, Spender, and MacNeice, now are "more fully represented." The volume begins with Thomas Hardy (1840-1928) and closes with Dylan Thomas (born 1914).

It is important to examine these anthologies from time to time because they stand right at the heart of "poetry appreciation" in America. The earlier editions have sold 275,000 copies all told. They appear in schools, libraries, and every center of learning and "culture." Mr. Untermeyer is the chief liaison officer between the modern corpus of British and American verse and that numerous group of American readers who wish to find out what's what in poetry but haven't the taste, enthusiasm, or time to go about digging up the material themselves or make their own choices. To such people, and to the young, fired with their first enthusiasm for the Muse but often cut off from wide sources of information, the Untermeyer anthologies give the tone and temper of their basic information. So far as American poetry is concerned, the field of anthologists is rather bare. Once there were Griswold and Stedman; now there is Untermeyer. The present editions are undoubtedly superior in every way to their predecessors. The smoke has now blown away from many poetic battles, or, to change the figure, time has now settled the poetic sediment, and Mr. Untermeyer has always been an expert at sensing in what direction the surface current of poetic fashion is moving. But as for the deeper tides, he has usually been wise after the event. He completely

missed the importance of Eliot early in Eliot's career.
He now is able to present a complete critical Eliot *dossier,* but he has needed help. He makes Robert Frost the
central figure of American poetry and tends to overesti-
mate in every instance those poets whose glibness and
conformity have today swept them to the top. I am will-
ful enough to prefer, in some ways, the good old days
between 1925 and 1936, when Mr. Untermeyer let his
taste run more freely. Then no one could predict from
edition to edition what poets would stay in or what be
tossed out. In they came for one edition; out they went
the next. It was a delightfully capricious spectacle to
watch, and many watchers appreciated it to the full.
Now much has changed. Mr. Untermeyer has read all
the books and collated all the reviews, and he doesn't
make many howlers. He sticks to some old favorites
through thick and thin (there will, for instance, always
be Nathalia Crane), but he is, on the whole, a chastened
editor. No harm will come to the taste of a nation
through these extremely popular anthologies. Mr. Untermeyer, be it remembered in spite of his faults, has a
basic love and appreciation of poetry, particularly the
lyric. If he mistakenly likes pomposity and verbalism,
he remains true to the lyric cry and simple-heartedness,
which is so dangerously near, often, to simple-minded-
ness. But he is still capable of reprinting poems which
aren't English, let alone poetry, and I, for one, would
not bet on many of his favorites for the long pull. And
to sandwich poems between great slabs of information,
quotation, appreciation, and adulation is wearing to
anyone who believes that practically nothing, as Gerald
Bullett has said, "should be interposed between the
reader and the poem." It is fine to be a liaison officer,
though combining preacher, teacher, and special

pleader with liaison officer can become rather tiresome to all concerned.

It is also fine to be an anthologist whose opinions cannot be flexed by either prejudice or false modesty. Mr. Untermeyer has accordingly included large selections from his own works. "What a pity," a poet once remarked, "that I cannot make an anthology! For then I should have to leave myself out." Such a saturnine reflection has never troubled the gentleman dealt with above.

1 9 4 2

§ *Sentimental Education Today*

The most important novel to be published in English in 1941 was the first intelligent translation into English of Flaubert's *L'Education sentimentale*. This novel, first published in 1869, was written after *Salammbo* and just before the final version of *La Tentation de Saint Antoine*. It is now generally acknowledged to be Flaubert's masterpiece. A profound and sardonic comment on Flaubert's own generation and the France of his youth, it is in every way pertinent to the human and social dilemmas of our own day.

The novel was viciously attacked by the critics and neglected by the general public, at its appearance. Only a few friends—Banville, the Goncourts, George Sand— understood Flaubert's intentions or appreciated his success in putting them through. Sand realized that Flaubert's readers were still too close to the events described, and too involved in the Second Empire point of view, to wish to appreciate the book's ruthless analysis of social change and human motives. They recognized themselves too easily. And Sand complained that Flaubert gave no overt clue to where his sympathies lay. She wanted "an expression of blame . . . to condemn the evil. People do not understand that you wanted precisely to depict a deplorable state of society which encourages bad instincts." Flaubert had run into this sort of obtuseness in the French public and government before this. It had brought about the suit against the morals of *Madame Bovary*. He was incapable of agreeing with Sand's rather sentimental moralistic demands. His idea of the relation between the individual and society was far more complicated than hers. Society warped the individual but was it not individuals who had created, and blown up to enormous proportions, the governments which symbolized this hampering agency? Perhaps the basic evil lay deeper, in the constitution of the human heart.

Flaubert was depressed by the book's failure. He wrote in 1874 to Turgenev that he was still astonished that this work had never been understood. He finally decided that the book lacked "the falseness of perspective." "Every work of art," he said, "ought to have a point, a summit, make a pyramid . . . or better, the light should strike some point of the sphere. Now, there is nothing of that sort in life. But Art is not nature!" Here Flaubert partially understands that in this novel he has created a new genre. Critics, including Henry James, have misunderstood the book's conclusions because they were in no way dealing, here, with another *Madame Bovary:* not with "realism" or "romance," but with satire of a high but hidden order.

There is no doubt that *Sentimental Education* is a difficult book to get the hang of, at a first reading. The reader must have a fair working knowledge of reaction and revolution in nineteenth-century France. To use a figure of Lowes Dickinson's, France was, throughout the century, politically in a state as though tracked by the Furies. It was a century of nervous unrest and of new and untried theory. And all theories, once applied, backfired in the most appalling way. The revolt against the Orleans line brought in the July monarchy (1830) and Louis Phillippe's dead-weight bourgeois rule. Universal suffrage, granted after 1848 and thought to be the instrument to establish the kingdom of God on earth, resulted only in Louis Bonaparte, and after three years of the Second Republic, the Second Empire. Paris fought for freedom; the provinces, fighting for the still unlaid ghosts of the old regime and Napoleon, finally voted away the newly granted franchise itself. Added to the political melee was the social one. The Industrial Revolution struck France in the '30's, in the factories of Lyons. All political parties were thrown into the rise of money, and the new concept of the right to work. The resulting confusion was severe. It is precisely this confusion, and its results, mirrored in the characters of the men and women who were at once its creators and its victims, that Flaubert here describes.

The book, written under the Second Empire, covers the period from 1840 to Louis Napoleon's *coup d'etat* of December, 1851—save for the last two chapters, which form a coda to the whole. The action, excepting a few short passages, is seen through the eyes of Frederic Moreau, of the provincial landed middle class, newly come to Paris, as the book begins, to pass his law examinations. A new spirit is in the air. The tradition of Romanticism and of the Bohemian painter, writer, and poet had worn almost completely threadbare. The period of the career based on money deals of one sort or another (*Enrichissez-vous* was said to be the counsel of Louis Philippe to his subjects) had begun. Art and industry, art and journalism, stood opposed, in spite of naive efforts to reconcile their purposes. (*Industrial Art* is the name of the magazine run by Arnoux, the husband of the woman Frederic comes to adore; the paper of the unprincipled Hussonet begins under the name *Art* and ends up entitled *The Man About Town*.) Stock-jobbing, loans, investments, and mortgages were the preoccupation of deputies and ministers. Borrowing a little money and making more, getting in with "influential" people, occupied the minds of law students, writers, painters, and hangers-on. The movement of opportunism elaborates and expands into a mounting frenzy. Notes fall due; debts pile up; the fate of men and women depends on the worth or worthlessness of shares. Bankruptcies, auctions, bailiffs finish the hopes of guilty and innocent alike. Underneath runs the theme of personal treachery. Friends betray one another; old men revenge themselves in their wills; women take it out on rivals by holding over them old debts and promissory notes.

The revolts of Republicans and the new Socialists against bourgeois rule form the book's secondary theme. The theorists make plans and hold to rigid formulas. Spontaneous outbreaks of the people link up with the planned action of the revolutionaries. Barricades go up; arms are requisitioned from the citizens. The crowd swarms into the Tuileries; grand pianos and clocks are flung out of windows. One of the book's great set-pieces describes the Paris street fighting in 1848. And the book closes with Paris again under arms; the dragoons, aided by the police, galloping against the citizens under the gaslight with sabers drawn—and the Second Empire has begun.

Senecal, the democratic dogmatist who develops by degrees into a tyrant and member of the police, is the character which has astonished modern readers by its deadly accuracy and contemporary pertinence. "Where are the labor poets?" Senecal asks, when shown a library. He wants, in literature, content and not form. He thinks *tableaux vivants* corrupting for the daughters of the proletariat. As a factory overseer, he extracts fines ruthlessly. "Democracy," he remarks "does not mean license for the individual. It means a common level under the law, the division of labor—order!" "You've left out humanity," Frederic answers. It is Senecal who kills Dussardier, "the good fellow," the honest believer in Socialist virtue "who attributed all the evil on earth to authority."

And Flaubert traces down "an insane desire for authority, of whatever kind if only it be authority," in all these people who have lost so many natural links to life. "France, feeling herself without a master [after '48] began to cry out in terror, like a blind man without a stick, or a child that has lost its nurse." And the reader continues to recognize these characters. There is something startlingly familiar in Hussonet, the journalist who prints gossip and slander as news, who "extols the fifth-rate and disparages the first-class minds." Arnoux, the intermediate type between Bohemian and businessman, infected with the failings of both—"his mind was not elevated enough to attain to art nor ordinary enough to think solely of profit, so that he was ruining himself without satisfying anyone"—is closely akin to Frederic, who feels the resemblance. Arnoux is a gourmet and gives little dinners "with ten kinds of mustard." Des-

lauriers, Frederic's friend, in the words of the Goncourts, is "with his fond envy, his intermittences of per-
fidy and friendship, his solicitor's temperament, a
perfectly drawn type of the most widespread kind of
scurvy humanity." Mlle Vatnaz, the emancipated woman,
venomous, the dupe of her passions, a literary hack and
go-between with a business head, is still not a complete
grotesque.

Then there is the gallery of "conservative humbugs,"
male and female, whom Flaubert does not spare. "Bigotry of the rich rivaled the frenzy of the starving. . . .
Property began to be confused with God, and attacks on
it . . . almost resembled cannibalism." But Flaubert
was out to show up "the bourgeois in blouses as well as
the bourgeois in coats." He examines with the same detachment social theorists, the hysterics, terrorists, and
fakes on the fringes of the Socialist movement, and the
conservative money and power jugglers and their "distinguished" circle, ready to grease the palm of any government that came into power. The stupidity of the
workers' meeting and the complicated spite of the dinner party are both analyzed. Flaubert wished to clear
the reader's mind of all "accepted ideas" concerning the
supposed nobility of either group. Suddenly, at the end
of the book, we look back and see how each category has
received its touch of clearsightedness: these liberals who
are at bottom neurotic reactionaries; these members of
a new middle class who not only "have no interest in the
things of the mind," who do not act according to motives of patience, pity, duty, love, or generosity, but actually do not know that such qualities exist. And has
Flaubert spared from his satiric justice of treatment the
supposed prototype of a lifelong love of his, Mme
Arnoux? She has been thought to stand in the book as

an unclouded exponent of womanly sweetness and virtue. Is she not, rather, a sort of Madame Bovary in reverse—a woman who rejects passion because she pietistically fears God's punishment, whose virtue brings her to the pass of offering herself, in age, to a man who suddenly recognizes the true incestuous nature of his devotion to her?

The profound psychological truth of the book's two final chapters is unequaled in modern literature. For in these two scenes Flaubert's uncanny knowledge of the pathology of modern life becomes startlingly evident. The nostalgic reminiscence of Frederic and Deslauriers, casting back to their youthful frightened visit to the prostitute's house, reveals the continuing infantilism of these two grown-up children who have never been able to lift themselves over the threshold of maturity, who cannot learn, who can only, in spite of some native decency and generosity, repeat, and flee life's consequences. The modern split between emotion and reason stands revealed. Flaubert elsewhere remarks: "You do not possess Christianity any more. What do you possess? Railroads, factories, chemists, mathematicians. Yes, the body fares better, the flesh does not suffer so much, but the heart continues to bleed. Material questions are resolved. Are the others? . . . And as you have not filled that eternal yawning gulf which every man carries in himself, I mock at your efforts, and laugh at your miserable sciences which are not worth a straw." *Sentimental Education* is a handbook to the present because the gulf of which Flaubert speaks, after seventy years, has not been filled but only widened and deepened. The thirst for some saving authority has grown stronger, the childish bigotries more complete. Let us examine our theorists, Flaubert says, and throw out their false premises.

Let us enlarge the provable human data. Have these nervous insurrections accomplished anything; are we following the "advanced notions" of a parcel of "buffoons"? Should "the government of a country be a section of the Institute, and the last section of all"?

Some partial answers lie in this novel, panoramic and profound, written in the "ivory tower" of Croisset and published one year before the inauspicious events of 1870 which ushered in the Third Republic.

1 9 4 2

§ *Isak Dinesen*

We now know Isak Dinesen to be Baroness Blixen of Denmark. It was apparent from the first that the author who published, in complete pseudonymity, *Gothic Tales* in 1934 was a woman, a native of Northern Europe, and a person whose sources were in some manner attached to the feudal tradition. *Gothic Tales,* because of their exuberance (severely regulated as it was), their civilized bitterness, their brilliantly informed fantasy, were clearly an end product of some kind. They had the quality, under the surface classicism of their style, of that sparkling improvisation contrasted with melancholy reverie so usual in Romantic music; the romance of the incompletely lighted and fantastic nineteenth-century "soul," at the end of one thing as much as at the beginning of another; caught back into nostalgia for the past and filled with premonitory anguish. But unlike Romantic music, these tales came to some sharp conclusions. Their intellectual underpinning was sturdy. They were highly conscious productions. The author behind them was not one to be taken in, least of all by herself.

Out of Africa (1938) brought the unknown author before us in the round. An autobiographical account of Baroness Blixen's life as owner of a coffee plantation in German East Africa, later Kenya Colony, it showed exactly what a feudal heritage had given this woman, and to what use she had put inherited ideas of responsibility. Her growth as an artist is also described; so that the reader, having read *Gothic Tales,* with only the information he could deduce from it, comes to any later work knowing more than one usually knows concerning a modern writer. He knows, for example, the writer's courage, both physical and moral, having watched it at work in rude and isolated surroundings. He also knows by the facts and their manner of presentation that she is as tender as she is courageous, as profoundly perceptive as she is sensitively humane.

Winter's Tales is not *Gothic Tales* repeated. The inventive extravagance has been reduced; the stories do not multiply, one within another, in the earlier manner. They share the simplicity and background, often, of the folk tale. But unlike the folk tale, they do not repeat some obsession of the simple mind—fear, desire for power or wealth, or luck, or freedom from restriction. And it is interesting to see how completely they differ from those "fairy tales" composed by Isak Dinesen's fellow-countryman, Hans Christian Andersen. In Andersen the folk tale took on, for all his charm of treatment, elements of sentiment and "rise": The Ugly Duckling is a far more bourgeois character than Cinderella. The majority of the characters in *Winter's Tales* are not going anywhere, in the success-story sense. And those who have some selfish or insolent plans for themselves are soon taken down by unforeseen small circumstance. Destiny's plans, far more noble than any they could have invented for themselves, take over (as in the case of the young wife in "The Pearls" and the writer in "The Young Man with the Carnation"). These plans of destiny often have heavy justice in them and work on two planes. The cruel feudal despot who misuses his power ("Sorrow-Acre") is baffled not only by the self-lessness of his victim but by the unfaithfulness of his wife, whose child by her lover will break the closed line of succession. And at the center of the book stands the child Jens, the pure poet and "comic fabulist" who knows his place in this world without having to be taught it; when he is transplanted from poverty to riches, he can look back on poverty with pleasure, accepting luxury the while, and remember the pleasing elements in the nature of his former friends, the rats.

The blunt and flourishing optimism of middle-class materialism could not have produced these stories. That we get them at this particular period of history is a remarkable thing in itself. They are, it is true, from time to time informed with the sharp bite of the civilized fable. But they are not fables, but parables. They deal almost entirely with inner themes of "love, hate, and reparation," with spiritual, not "practical" truths. The witty yet profound treatment of the artist and his public in terms of God and Job ("A Consolatory Story") sums up the author's view of one problem of reconciliation. Here light is thrown upon a situation by means of irony. Elsewhere Isak Dinesen prefers to irradiate mysteries of conduct by mention of other mysteries, as when, at the end of "The Invincible Slave Owners," the perplexed lover, realizing that certain human situations exist which nothing can change, contemplates the waterfall and thinks of the fugue. As in all good parables, the lines of meaning are not pulled tight. The reader is left with the threads in his own hands, and can examine and combine them according to his own experience.

The period quality is exquisitely managed. The publishers, it is true, have built up all the fustian possibilities of this atmosphere. The book is very nearly bound in seafoam and stardust; and one must grin and bear the book-jacket Surrealism which runs over onto the end-papers. The little blurbs provided by the publicity department on the jacket for each story should be ignored; their facts are sometimes wrong and their interpretation almost always queer. These are by no means special or bizarre stories. They belong to an old and great tradition and are worthy of it. That they have been written in English is our good luck, the chance of contact with European tradition at present being what it is. It is good to be able to read them early, even though they are certain to be around for a long time.

1 9 4 3

§ *Stefan George*

A selection of poems by Stefan George, translated from
the German by Ernst Morwitz, a friend of his later
years, and Carol North Valhope, has finally appeared
in English. George has held the position, in some enlightened opinion, of being the greatest European poet
of the start of the century and of our own times. Interest
in his work, however, has lagged far behind interest in
Rilke's, a fact which would have caused George himself
(he died in 1933), and has caused surviving members
of his circle, considerable anguish. George consistently
ignored Rilke, and George's followers have on occasion
been ruthless and unfair to Rilke's achievement and
ideas. George had, it is certain, a streak of the megalo-
maniac in his nature, and that Rilke's poetry should
have insinuated itself into the hearts of English, French,
and American readers was a development that he could
not foresee.

Mr. Morwitz and Miss Valhope have chosen work
from seven George volumes, beginning with *Hymns*

(1890), published in his twenty-second year, and ending with *The Kingdom Come* (1929), published in his sixtieth. The original poems stand on pages facing the translations. The full sweep of a career extraordinary in its nature is rather fully recorded. Mr. Morwitz, in a long preface, attempts to give American readers some inkling of the reasons for George's impressive life and art. This exegesis partly fails, as have so many explanations written by men who knew the poet. The addition of a portrait would have been enlightening. It is always a shock to the student who has begun the study of George without knowing what he looked like to be confronted with the almost brutal planes of the poet's skull and jaw, the thin, ascetic mouth, and the ecclesiastical costume he affected. Americans have seen this sort of face before, but usually it is the face of a prizefighter or an impresario, rarely of a creative man. There is something rather fake, moreover, to my view, in this clerical getup. The rigorous, serious, completely dedicated hierarchic figure and the consistently ordered and almost stage-managed life we do not understand because in America we do not yet produce such people (at least in the field of literature) or such careers.

Rilke is on record as making a kind and sympathetic explanation of the high-priest act George indulged in. "When a great poet is born into a time inimical to him," Rilke said, "he must protect himself." It is still a puzzle just where the George protective mask ended and his vanity and power drive began. Underneath all this rigidity, strangely enough, existed not a particularly complex nature but a rather simple one. "A simple soul," as a disciple has called George, certainly produced those lyrics of which the expression alone is complex. What saved George and what made him powerful, apart from the impression his very looks must have made on the beholder, is the manifest sincerity and profound depth of his emotions. George drew everything into himself, but his temperament changed the world he so seriously absorbed into verse ranging from the most lucid songs to poems glittering with the religious pronouncements of the seer. It is his magnificent language combined with his simple heart which save him in the end.

Born in 1868 of peasant and petty-bourgeois Rhineland stock, George was given a good formal education and soon left Germany to study with Mallarmé. Naturalism was in full swing in Germany and throughout Europe, and George made a determined stand against the ideals of the society in which he found himself. As he grew older, he felt a traditional German pull away from lyricism toward seership, ethical ideas, and religion-making. He has been accused by some of thinking Hitlerian thoughts before Hitler. His friends, however, including the present translators, have cleared him of any views even remotely National Socialist. It is true that the Third Reich tried to claim him, both in life and after his death. He died in self-imposed exile at Locarno, but I have seen a volume of his selected poems published of late years in Germany in which the place of his death is given as Munich. Many facts will become available after the war ends. Meanwhile, anyone interested in the comparative literature which is becoming so important in our day should try to understand George while remembering to enjoy him.

1 9 4 3

§ *Some Notes on Popular and Unpopular Art*

Will folk art save us from creative and moral aridity if we can find and use it? The reiterated insinuation that formal art is fraudulent because it is difficult to understand and makes no effort to appeal to the majority— that it is, in fact, somehow treasonable to mankind's higher purposes and aims—is a typical bourgeois notion that has been around for a long time. That formal art cannot be put to any immediate use also lays it open to materialist denigration. The conviction that the simple is straight and pure and true, while the complex is concocted and double-dealing, is a partially moral one. It is a conviction which shares room, in the minds and emotions of many people, with an unconscious yearning for a lost rural world. In America, just enough time has elapsed since real urbanization set in for this yearning to roll up to its present proportions and to have acquired its present rationalizations. In spite of these desires and beliefs of the middle-class subconscious, the fact remains that no civilization has ever produced a literature out of folk (either current or revived) alone. The formal artist cannot be outlawed. The whole question is muddled in the extreme. Let us examine it with as much detachment as possible.

It is true that the formal artist, at least twice within living memory, has succeeded in getting past modern barriers to a real folk tradition, and that remarkable literature has resulted in both cases from the intersection of the formal with the folk line. Lorca's genius was ignited in the most brilliant way by Flamenco tradition, and Yeats was fortified and refreshed from the beginning by his close knowledge of the Irish peasant. Both these poets received the experience of poetry still attached to music, at the improvisatory stage; and of an audience creatively involved (actually listeners, as distinguished from mere readers) in what they as poets produced.

But the fact is that only the most abnormal situations, political or otherwise, kept these two folk traditions alive so late in an industrial and urbanized Europe. The turning toward the folk, at the end of the eighteenth century, was not only preindustrial but prerevolutionary; and the same sort of ferments were present in Yeats' Ireland and Lorca's Spain. The current attempts in America to get back to primitive material are natural enough, but they are different. They are the desire of a far from revolutionary population to get back to some earlier fun, as well as some earlier integrity. Certainly the material is there. We can trace the line of the American folk song through the ballads of English, Irish, and Scotch origin (broken away from their original scene and transformed) through the work songs of all kinds (sea chanteys, songs of the plantation and the cattle-range), the hymns and spirituals, up to the beginning of town life. Then the culmination of the American folk song appears. Stephen Foster, the untrained and greatly gifted writer of "popular songs," managed to express fully the emotions common during this period of transition. On the one hand, through him the loneliness as well as the rough gaiety of a primitive society found its voice. On the other, Foster gave expression to something quite new: an emotion which was to become increasingly persistent in the American spirit—the sense of profound nostalgia for an already disappearing nonurban way of life. The strong sentimentalization of Foster by his modern audience proceeds from the holdover of this crucial though hidden nostalgia into our own time. Clearly, he was the end of one kind of American folk, the point beyond which no unadulterated development of his kind of material was possible.

We begin to get the production of the urbanized folk after the hymns and marching songs of the Civil War. The railroads building and having been built, we get the railroad songs. The cities once made, we get the hybrid genteel, and the barber-shop ballads, and, what is more vivid and interesting, the songs of the "underworld": brothel, saloon, dope-joint, and prison. The earlier tradition fell into neglect as the way back to the farm became more and more closed. It was rediscovered and refurbished, along with hooked rugs and pine blanket chests, when the 1914 War broke up American Victorian and aroused, in some not quite understandable fashion, the middle-class enthusiasm for the American antique. The folk tradition, as a result, has become thoroughly "bourgeoizified." At present there is no way for the artist to get at it, for it has been dragged into a region where nothing living or nutritious for his purposes exists. It can be looked at and listened to, admired and imitated; but it cannot at the present time be called upon to do any truly important task. Only a writer thoroughly immersed in middle-class values, and soaked through and through with the sentimentality of the middle, could for a moment believe that this mummified and genteelized folk could contribute any spark of life to his purposes.

The English and French tradition of town-folk (with a head start of some forty or fifty years of true industrialism over the United States) channeled itself into the music hall. "The supreme embodiment of the surviving character of the English working people," writes one chronicler of the English nineteenth-century scene, "was the music hall. . . . Springing spontaneously out of the sing-song of the upper tavern room and the old out-of-door gardens of the artisans of the pastoral past, it became for a space of time a British institution. Its morality was to make the best of a bad job; its purpose to make everyone free and easy. . . ." The authenticity of this institution, created by the first articulate development of urban folk for its own enjoyment, soon impressed itself on the artists and writers of the time. Through it, they were able to skirt the middle, find excitement and restorative energy, and make a point of contact with "life." But the music hall decayed. It was based on that period of "proletarian" existence when the workers were stiffly encased in the tradition of knowing their place and imitating their betters. This tradition exploded in 1918; and we hear Eliot making a final tribute to Marie Lloyd, with added gloomy prognostications for the future:

. . . It was her capacity for expressing the soul of a people that made her unique. . . . It was her understanding of the people and sympathy with them, and the people's recognition of the fact that she embodied the virtues that they most genuinely respected in private life, that raised her to the position she occupied at her death. I have called her the expressive figure of the lower classes. There is no such expressive figure for any other classes. The middle classes have no such idol: the middle classes are morally corrupt . . .

Eliot then goes on to express his fear that, with the disappearance of the music hall, and "the encroachment of the cheap and rapid-breeding cinema, the lower classes will drop to the same state of protoplasm as the bourgeoisie," and, moreover, when this state has overcome them, that they may die off from sheer boredom! This essay, written in 1923, closes with words of deep dismay as to the possibility of the hastening of this general disintegration by the development of another mechanical device for transmitting entertainment—the radio.

Eliot underestimated his "lower classes." The music hall disappeared only after it had reached a high point of breadth and elegance. Folk expression continually runs toward this elegance, contrary to the *idée reçue* of its being by necessity clumsy and "vulgar." (And this elegance is not to be confused with the empty slickness of the *revue* kind.) But as a rather stuffy set of prewar conventions broke, the urban crowd shifted toward a freer, less imitative and reverent habit of mind and manner. Something new began immediately; persistent energy released itself into new forms and new media.

The energy is now at a more primitive level than formerly; these shifts go back and forth, as this current of urban life or that is released and breaks; many reasons requiring specialized attention are here involved. But the fact remains that American folk has never been more vigorous than at this moment. In "hot jazz," words are attached to music, as in all primitive states of poetry and music. Improvisation (the "lick") is in every talented performer's power. The rhythm is the important matter; the music has all the harmonic tricks under control with which to surround and embellish the beat. The various mechanical devices which Eliot feared and deplored have served, as a matter of fact, to aid the development and dissemination of this folk art. The folk now gets exactly what it wants to listen to. If the radio does not give it what it needs in sufficient quantity, people have their records and juke boxes, and, of course, the live performers. The vigor of folk at present is shown by its tendency to raid over into "classical" and bring back whatever tunes please it. The juke-box repertoire is a thing in itself: there the hymn tune (disguised) shares popularity with the crooned ballad and with certain holdovers from the open spaces of the past. Compared to the songs of the upright piano and sheet music era, even the most naive songs are less awkward and saccharine, more vitalized. And the imitation "folk song," such as the really remarkable "Blues in the Night," has taken on a finish which always characterizes folk in a good creative period *of its own*.

It is interesting to note that at this particular stage, "popular" interest in accident, sudden death, and the morbid in general (unlike American songs of an earlier day) has very nearly disappeared, along with the "topical song," that sister to the broadsheet.

A proposition could be drawn up:

Folk crosses formal art:

1. When folk has reached a moment of comparative breadth and elegance (when it can express anything, from the grotesque through emotion and satire, well).

2. When formal art has become easy and secular

enough to recognize just where folk lies; and having located folk, understands what is happening
there.

A long period of time must elapse before, in America,
the demands of this proposition can be fulfilled. But
Eliot's fears were unjustified; just as the present middle-
class hope that L. Stokowski can be crossed with Disney,
or some genteel poet with the songs of pioneering back-
woodsmen, is at once previous and misplaced.

Let us now take a brief glance at the American intellectual. The intellectual is a middle-class product; if
he is not born into the class he must soon insert himself into it, in order to exist. He is the fine nervous
flower of the bourgeoisie. His task, ideally, would be
the close critical observation of the field in which he
stands, while keeping his attention alert for new movement in the landscape as a whole. That the intellectual
fails in this job is one reason for the wholesale mixture
of genres, the unrebuked mistakes of prize committees,
publishers, etc., the general insolence of entrepreneurs
—in fact the general failure to understand what is going
on which marks the small remaining section of American life still interested in literature.

The intellectual, being nervous, is subject to all the
floating airs of modern religion (present in quantity, no
matter how fogged and misted into the semblance of
something else). One must not forget that religious enthusiasm (and intolerance) has always been inextricably
mixed with every materialist idea; has been a concomi-
tant of all material push since Calvin. Intellectuals
range through the finest gradations of kind and quality:
from those who are merely educated neurotics, usually
with strong hidden reactionary tendencies, through me-

diocrities of all kinds, to men of real brains and sensibility, more or less stiffened into various respectabilities or substitutes for respectability. The number of Ignorant Specialists is large. The number of hysterics and compulsives is also large. It is natural that the truly sensitive intellectual should have spiritual needs; for such a person the necessity for those moments in life when one is forced to see reality without wraps and unrationalized is strong. This necessity leads to a real breakthrough into maturity on the part of some individuals. For the less sensitive, the spiritual necessity hardly exists; they require not steadying insight but emotional outlet. It is in this class that we find the hot-gospellers, the morally pretentious, the reformers, and the seekers of closed systems of salvation. These men and women are not entirely the products of an imperfect culture (for the type appeared in quantity in France in the nineteenth century) but of a culture somehow blocked and mixed; and of the impact of this curious situation upon natures more simply constituted than they themselves suppose. Flaubert wrote down an approximation of the type in *Bouvard et Pécuchet*. He gave the two simple-minded copyists a set of manias which is still complete for the dislocated middle-class mind of our time; manias ranging from the collecting of antiques to an absorption in various forms of science and politics. These two prototypes of the middle-class yearner with a few retouches could represent not only the modern lecture-listening audience, but many of "the experts who tend the complicated machinery of modern civilization."

One characteristic of the Bouvard-Pécuchet sort of enthusiasm is the violent repudiation after violent interest of one craze after another when the satiation point is reached. The revulsion shown by the intellectual toward the artist, during recent years, resembles this sort of compensating tendency. The too-great emphasis of emotion and hope placed upon the artist in the preceding period is lifted and placed at an opposite point. The D. H. Lawrence, Proust, Hart Crane kind of semi-worship went over, for a time, to Malraux; and then became transformed into something else. The very complexity of the artist's equipment became as much a target for the subsequent badgering and denigration as the nonmaterial quality of his aims. It is moral blame of the most childish kind that we find most frequently expressed; and real puzzlement, also at a childish level. The atmosphere of former religious paroxysms and squabblings returns; the old fights between established religion and the sects and between the sects themselves; the old tiresome yet dangerous extremes of the persecutory centuries.

Now, one would think that the unstable intellectual should stand out against all these moral acrobatics and tergiversations: if not as judge, at least as arbiter. If he cannot remain firm, he should at least be in another part of the field, out of the melee and ahead of it. But as things turn out, he is either squarely in the mix-up, name-calling with the best or making motions of advancing, the while he has managed rapidly to retreat into something truly comforting in the way of pre-Copernican scholasticism, or has made a full flight back to Aristotle. And if he is of no real use in reconciling embattled sects, perhaps he could do a little simple journeyman's work in keeping entrepreneurism in its place. But here he rather fails us, too.

At this point it is necessary to remember that the middle class has produced, at the expense of much time and effort, a whole literature of its own. Its own writers, bred out of its own bone and flesh, educated in its own schools and amenable to its own scheme of manners and custom, have fanned out into the middle region; adapted in every way to express the middle intellect, temperament, grasp of reality, powers of analysis and emotion. Some of these poets, novelists, critics, biographers, and belletrists were born middle; some either rose or sank to where they at length find themselves. The complicated but smoothly oiled machinery of the publishing business, the general run of reviewers, the committees giving out literary awards, the more benumbed mass of academics: all these agents function, for the most part (and changing the figure), inside the same structure. During certain short periods, certain wild individuals stay outside and throw rocks, but since these intransigents tend to disappear for long intervals, the easiest supposition is that they are absorbed. And the periods of almost complete absorption present a very amusing spectacle indeed. These are the times when the book sections produce, week after week, month after month, serious judgments on books, but when everything judged and the judges themselves are cut out of the same piece of medium material. The commodity books are being dealt with by the commodity critics— a spectacle which would be purely funny if there were not elements of rather tragic irony in it.

The intellectual should at least know the difference between kinds, and have the courage to speak up when matters get really out of hand. He should make some admonishing gesture when a particularly startling piece of mutual aid comes through. He should know how the literary mechanism works: the way blurb-writing and prize-giving, journalists and literary impresarios engage with each other. He should be able to sense, watching the open pulls and twitches given reputations, all the subterranean maneuvering which must go on so that certain effects are produced at eye-level. What about the distinguished specialists who write blurbs for dust-jackets? Is this a harmless bit of fun, or a plan to get around the subsequent remarks of the book reviewer? What about the American prize committee (situated rather disadvantageously, one might suppose, for any-one not a journalist, in a school of journalism) which, having ignored brilliant talent, young and old, falls back ever again upon old standbys? What about the extra-literary influences which manage, from time to time, to bring to laudatory view a book of gibberish? What about certain anthologists who teeter on the verge of being members of the vanity press: are all their con-tributors paid? Who is to deal with these matters but the intellectual?

Meanwhile, the cry rises that poetry has disappeared. This plaint often comes from the dead center, say from the core of the Sunday book section. It rises with par-ticular sharpness during times of cataclysm. The middle wishes poetry to throb, as it were, under the historic processes without a break; to light up ambiguous terrain with continual succeeding flashes of "inspiration." But poetry cannot be counted upon to act as a sort of com-bination faith-healing and artificial thunder and light-ning. Poetry of the lyric order disappears for a century at a time. It shifts. And when the formal line has in some manner been exhausted, the vigor goes back to the base. The middle must put up with what it has: their flabby little songs, their attempts at reviving the "golden" American past; and their more ambitious flights: those attempts to combine autobiography with *post hoc ergo propter hoc* comment on the world situation.

"The function of the great individual is to take up and transform what has been communally produced." For this function one must wait, when the folk material is in a transitional phase—unmalleable and too full of its own rough vigor to be handled, and when "great individuals" seem to be lacking. Even the artist may misjudge the time. In Eliot's "Sweeney Agonistes" and "Fragment of an Agon" the two lines—of formal treatment and "rough" material—are somehow artificially combined; the result cannot really move us. But there are times when the poet can deal with whatever comes to hand. And folk will not always remain ungraspable.

A few notes on the future direction of the poet:

The true hierarchic attitude as exemplified by some "inheritors of Symbolism" (Stefan George and to a lesser degree Valéry and Yeats) seems to be exhausted. George's "willed rationalism toward the antique, his aesthetic and individualist humanism . . . which seeks in the universe the exaltation of man"—this line we have seen warped and corrupted; it now leads nowhere. The lesser task of the poet at present is satire. But satire cannot be asked to bear all of the weight of the diversified and subtle modern spirit. There is another development of this century's early period of aesthetic experiment and moral explanation. This proceeds from Rilke. "In Rilke (as opposed to George)," writes Genevieve Bianquis, already quoted above, "exists the most absolute abandonment to the laws of the inanimate; the need to unknot, to detach the bonds of the individual; the need to love everything, to absorb everything into himself and to absorb himself in all; to channel toward God or toward things all happiness, all sorrow and all emotion." This is the contrast between the will which builds Ages of Faith and the act of faith itself; between compulsion and serenity; arrogance and humility; between the raw act of force and the more complex refusal of force but openness to spiritual power.

The foundation-material is ready for this tendency. The only really usable and incontrovertible modern discoveries are in the spiritual field; and these have their everyday diagnostic and therapeutic uses. Truth has been told, experience undergone, and movement undertaken—"forward" as Eliot says; but this forward has not its old "progressive" connotation. The number of individuals engaged in writing poetry of this order will not be large, and, as is so often the case, may be unseen by their generation. The forms will be kept clear and the tone uninflated. No more rhetoric; no more verbalizing; no more exhortations or elegies or eulogies. No more conscious and affected investigations of dark corridors and deserted strands; no more use of the universe as a backdrop against which one acts out hope or despair. No more dejected sitting about. No more searching nature for an answering mood. . . .

This exploration and movement can go on without having to search out the folk for refreshment. The more complex tasks have been neglected for a long time; attention to them is overdue. Compared to these at once subtle and difficult necessities the reiterated standardized demands of the bourgeois yearner sound incredibly stupid and outdated.

Is it possible that despite our discoveries and progress, despite our culture, religion and world-wisdom, we still remain on the surface of life? Is it possible that we have even covered this surface which might still have been something, with an incredibly uninteresting stuff which makes it look like drawing-room furniture during the summer holidays?

Yes, it is possible . . .

But if all this is possible . . . then surely, for all the world's sake, something must be done. The first comer, he who has had these disturbing thoughts, must begin to do some of the neglected things; even if he be just anybody, by no means the most suitable person: there is no one else at hand. This young insignificant foreigner, Brigge, will have to sit down in his room five flights up, and write, day and night. Yes, he will have to write; that will be the end of it.

This was written at the beginning of the century; but nothing much seems to have been accomplished. Now that a good deal of the drawing-room furniture lies in ruins, there may be another beginning.

1 9 4 3

§ *Marianne Moore*

1

Marianne Moore's fifth book of poetry, *Nevertheless,*
is her best. It contains six poems of no great length.
The small format is delightful—a proof that a commercial publisher need not badger a poet to pad a
volume with second-rate material in order that some
outmoded publishing tradition be kept up. This little,
firm, profoundly beautiful set of poems is an event for
which a country more conscious of the importance of
the good artist would crown Miss Moore with official
laurels. As it is, officialdom has never seen fit to give her
the Pulitzer Prize.*

Many of the facts about Miss Moore's quality and importance have already been set forth in T. S. Eliot's
preface to her *Selected Poems* (1935). Eliot speaks of
her service to the living language "in maintaining its
strength and subtlety and preserving its quality of feeling"; of her appreciation of the individual word; of her
success in startling us into an unusual awareness of

* This oversight has since been corrected (1952).

visual patterns with something like the fascination of
a high-powered microscope; of her elegance and form.
Eliot also speaks of two characteristics of Miss Moore's
earlier work which have baffled many readers in the
past—her lack of out-and-out poetic "music" (her rhythm
is basically that of good prose) and her intellectual detachment, which sometimes seemed to stiffen into actual
coldness. During the nine years which have passed since
Eliot's preface, Miss Moore has become both more
"musical" and more openly warm-hearted. The warmth
was always there, but it is now more noticeable because
it is more personal, tender, and even playful. It is
a humane, humorous, imaginative warmth that satisfies
the heart and mind equally. Neither wistfulness nor that
self-pity which often attacks women writers when they
let down their guard has invaded these self-possessed
poems.

Miss Moore's love of animals, fruit, flowers, and
beautiful artifacts, once shown rather obliquely, at present touches her subjects with a subdued but penetrating
light. The poems are like fables, giving new point and
meaning to certain necessary virtues of mankind. The
fortitude bred by mutilation or deprivation ("Nevertheless"), the tragic bases of equanimity ("Elephants"),
the beauties of stalwartness and skill ("A Carriage from
Sweden"), the need for every man to search out, in time
of war, the arrogance and division in his own heart
("In Distrust of Merits")—these are the things Miss
Moore brings before us—few, but of terrible importance.
Added to these is her charming poem on the ordinarily
comic skunk ("The Wood-Weasel"). This little animal,
suddenly detached from cheap jokes, is restored to its
dignified place in Nature by a few words from the imaginative and kind heart and by a merciful look from

the just eyes of Miss Moore. Marianne Moore acts according to the rule she herself has demanded in art—that it should be "lit with piercing glances into the life of things . . . acknowledge the spiritual forces which have made it."

Marianne Moore is now our most distinguished contemporary American poet. Her talents should be guarded and encouraged, so that we can expect from her a long career, rich with the superb poetry she is able to compose.

1 9 4 4

2

Impressionist critics, because they have attributed to Miss Moore many of their own manias and virtues, have left her actual virtue—her "secret"—untouched. She belongs to a lineage against which the impressionist and the "modernist" have for so long rebelled that by now they are forgetful that it ever existed. In Miss Moore two traditions that modernism tends to ignore meet. She is, on the one hand, a nearly pure example of that inquisitive, receptive kind of civilized human being which began to flourish during the high Renaissance: the disciple of the "new" as opposed to the "old" learning, the connoisseur, the humane scholar—to whom nothing was alien, and for whom man was the measure of all. Her method, in her "observations," has been compared, and rightly, to that of Francis Bacon and Sir Thomas Browne. But we soon come upon in her work another, angularly intersecting, line. Miss Moore, child of Erasmus, cousin to Evelyn, and certainly close kin to the Mozart who refracted *Don Giovanni* as though from a dark crystal, does not develop, as we might expect, toward full Baroque exuberance. She shows—and not to her demerit—a definite influence derived from that Protestantism against whose vigor the vigor of the Baroque was actively opposed. Miss Moore is a descendant not of Swiss or Scotch, but of Irish presbyters. She is, therefore, a moralist (though a gentle one) and a stern—though flexible—technician.

It is not an infrequent American miracle, this combination of civilized European characteristics in one gifted nature. Miss Moore, American to her backbone, is a striking example of a reversion toward two distinct kinds of heritage; of an atavism which does not in any degree imply declension or degeneration of the original types involved. She does not write *à la manière de* . . . ; she produces originals. She does not resemble certain seventeenth-century writers; she might be one of them. She stands at the confluence of two great traditions, as they once existed, and as they no longer exist. "Sentiment" and the shams of the *pasticheur* cannot touch her, since she ends where they begin.

Examine her passion for miscellany: it is a seventeenth-century passion. "Academic feeling, or prejudice possibly, in favor of continuity and completion," she wrote in 1927, "is opposed to miscellany—to music programs, composite picture exhibitions, newspapers, magazines, and anthologies. Any zoo, aquarium, library, garden, or volume of letters, however, is an anthology, and certain of these selected findings are highly satisfactory. . . . The selective nomenclature—the chameleon's eye as we might call it so—of the connoisseur, expresses a genius for difference." There speaks a sensibility unmarked by the flattening pressures of an industrial age. Alive to the meaning of variation, Miss Moore can examine what the modern world displays, with an unmodern eye. This is her value to us. She sees as a specialist trained and bred sees. She is never, therefore, indifferent to what might strike her contemporaries as either precious or rubbish. Advertisements, travel folders, yesterday's newspaper, the corner movie, the daily shop and street, the fashion magazine, the photograph and the map— these phenomena are gathered into her art with the same care with which she "observes" small mammals, birds, reptiles; or with which she microscopically examines details of human artificats: "sharkskin, camellia-leaf, orange-peel, semi-eggshell or *sang-de-boeuf* glaze" in Chinese porcelain, for example. Unlike a magpie, she is not attracted by any kind of glittering swag. She is never in danger for a moment of appearing either a dilettante or a snob. She is occupied with the set task of imaginatively correlating the world's goods, natural and artificial, as a physician correlates "cases," or a naturalist, specimens.

The tone of her poems often derives from her "other," Protestant inheritance. Are not many of her poems sermons in little, preached in the "plain style" but with overtones of a grander eloquence? Are not many of them discourses which are introduced, or subsumed, by a text? Note the frequent cool moral that she extracts from her poems' complexities; and the dexterity with which, from disparate and often heavy facts, she produces a synthesis as transparent and as inclusive as air. Her sensibilities are Counter-Reformation; her emotion and intellect, Protestant.

She has immensely widened the field of modern poetry. She takes the museum piece out of its glass case, and sets it against living animals. She relates the refresh-

ing oddities of art to the shocking oddities of life. The
ephemeral and the provincial become durable and civilized under her hands. She is a delayed product of long
processes. She is at once a contemporary American, a
seventeenth-century survival, and a native of those timeless and pure spiritual regions

where there is no dust, and life is like a lemon leaf,
a green piece of tough translucent parchment.

1 9 4 7

§ *The Time of the Assassins*

The modern detective novel originated in times physically, and perhaps spiritually, darker than our own. The *roman policier* was based on the invention, new and terrible to the French, of the political police, under Fouché and Napoleon. Later, Vidocq, an adventurer born under the Old Régime, managed under the new dispensation to make a transformation in which the chaos of the period is summed up: he became Chef de la Sureté and used his criminal career as a basis for his position on the other side of the law. His *Memoirs,* published in Paris in 1829, intersected the legend of the Byronic hero. Here was something new, a product of another social situation, the beginning of a new legend. Vidocq appears almost immediately in literature as Balzac's Vautrin. Meanwhile, and following closely in the steps of actual spies and *agents provocateurs,* Eugène Sue began to produce, in the '30's, his series of *romans-feuilletons,* which included *Les Mystères de Paris* and *Le Juif errant.* Jean Cassou has stated that the development of the *roman-feuilleton* and the creation of the social sciences is parallel. The secrets of "sordid and terrible Paris" were sought out, in the first, under the cover of darkness. The rich and the poor, the intriguer and his victim, were linked together. "The poor adventurer, the pariah, the *carbonaro,* the artist, the regenerator, the adversary of the Jesuits . . . these were the phantasmagoria projected by [the beginning of] the nineteenth century." They were symbolic of the strange desire that had manifested itself in the midst of chaos: "to pass beyond the political to the social revolution."

The earliest detectives worked by mystery and ruse rather than rapidity and force. Roger Caillois, in his intelligent study of the genre, *Le Roman Policier,** says that the detective is at first successful not through his logic but because of his disguises. He is, at the beginning, an inheritor of Fenimore Cooper, the infallible observer of the forest. The great city has become a new jungle, more dangerous than the solitudes of Canada. This pattern was soon abandoned, but it has returned in the spy and secret-agent stories of the present. But let us watch the closing in of the form, the development of "deduction," which at one point made the detective novel into an almost pure play of the logical faculties, a detached *jeu d'esprit.*

This tendency toward rules was observed in the detective novel while rules elsewhere in nineteenth-century literature were being progressively rejected. The detective novel splits off from the surrounding anarchy of form. And within its closed universe Poe further limits its locale by inventing the convention of the

---

* I have followed the analysis of M. Caillois' *Le Roman Policier* (Editions des Lettres Françaises, SUR, Buenos Aires, 1941) very closely. I am also indebted to *Quarante-Huit,* by Jean Cassou (Gallimard, Paris, 1939).

locked room. The detective now has completely rejected his bloodhound role. He becomes the scientist "coordinating indices," the artist-priest astounding the world at large as well as his rather stupid human foil. The crime becomes as isolated from life as a chemical experiment. Rules to protect the reader emerge: "Give the reader an equal right with the detective . . . no supernatural or scientific marvels . . . no tricky architecture . . . no factors brought in at the last moment." And the *acte gratuit,* the motiveless impulse, cannot function at this point; the diabolical machinery must work on the basis of accepted motives. Now, "the detective story must take from existence nothing but a frame. . . . It is not interested in passions or emotions except as a force to set the mechanism in motion. It is only interested in forming a complete and simple figure from incomprehensible and partial fragments. The novel attaches itself to the nature of man. This nature is a bother to the detective story, at this stage, and it supports it only unwillingly."

M. Caillois' analysis now reaches a crucial fact. Here is this new form, coldly opposed to everything literature stands for. But the pure exercise of the intellectual faculty, the detachment from emotion, the devotion of the detective to the penetration of "an artificial miracle"— all this is brought up against the unalterable convention that a detective novel must be based on a corpse. It demands a murderer—a person who has killed and risks capital punishment; no other sort of malefactor will do. And because of this anomaly between crude subject and skilled method, the detective story cannot remain a pure puzzle for long. "The cards must be shuffled." Suddenly "neither the murderers are real bandits nor the searchers real police." Variations multiply; here, in a late development, is Simenon's Maigret, a detective with a compassionate heart. "An obscure necessity obliges these policemen to make reservations in their role. They have a liberal attitude or a liberal profession. . . . They occupy a marginal place in regard to society, in the manner of the sorcerer or devil in the ancient tales who appears in the guise of a stranger, a horse dealer, a doctor, an itinerant merchant."

The closed circle begins to break. The puzzle begins to widen back toward the novel proper. Now the criminal has become anyone. "The most unexpected person" is now any man or woman, of whatever age or condition. And the elaboration of the setting becomes inexhaustible. *Everywhere* has become the scene of the crime. No situation, however sacred or cut off from life by money, power, or prestige, has been omitted. As in a fox hunt, every modern type and modern locale has been "blooded" by the detective novel. But the detective story has not by any means merged with the novel. It has, instead, drained off from the other form many of its residues of "sensation." While apparently working with the most icy logical detachment, the narrative breaks off "complaisantly to recount scabrous scenes of cruelty or eroticism. The ambition of the intelligence is flattered while the appetite for sensation is satisfied."

The mention of death and dissolution has almost disappeared from modern middle-class and "folk" literature. The detective novel does not reject one detail of the macabre. And it openly accommodates fear and aggression, open or disguised. Certain authors specialize in the frozen will of the nightmare—or the neurotic symptom; their characters may not escape even if they could. The rat-in-the-trap, the spider-and-the-fly motifs recur. The baseless fears of the folk tale or the psychi-

atric clinic are endlessly repeated. And the inveterate
reader of detective stories can soon classify his reading
into stories written by and for sadists, by and for masoch-
ists; into stories in which someone, under a pseudonym,
is working off some obsession or perversion or fear that
is sure to link up with similar aberrations in some
reader. On a higher level we get a complete picture of
paranoia in Kafka's *The Trial*.

The obscure religious undercurrent in these dramas
of sin and retribution cannot be overlooked. "One of
the strange phenomena of the nineteenth century"—I
quote a modern clergyman—"is the spectacle of religion
dropping the appeal to fear while other human interests
have picked it up." The Gothic novel that began in the
late eighteenth century bore the marks of a broken-
down, secularized, floating religion. It is the supernatural that intervenes. The trappings are Catholicism's
ruined abbeys; the fumes are those of a Protestant personal hell. Ritual has dissolved. The detective story, on
the other hand, has all the marks of a live cult, developing from primitivism toward complexity. The victim is
always there, whether the sign of a brutal sacrifice or a
more human oblation. And the priest-like character of
the detective was once very clear: Sherlock Holmes, in
whose human reality many people believed, is the supreme example of this type.

"The present-day individual," writes a psychiatrist,
"is more and more called upon to give up his aggres-
sions. The repressed and therefore unconscious criminality of the normal man finds few socially harmless
outlets: dream and fantasy life, the neurotic symptom,
and some transitional forms of behavior. . . ." The
break-through of the submerged unconscious, the symbolic struggle between good and evil—in the detective

story we find a re-enactment of these struggles. And the
flight motif has returned, along with the tracking-down-
of-the-fugitive role of the official or unofficial police.
Graham Greene, one of the most intelligent and exciting writers of the modern "thriller"—because his imagination seems peculiarly sensitive to archetypal subconscious themes—has recognized the role of the conscience
in these dramas; he gives one book in its English edition
a title extracted from Francis Thompson's poem "The
Hound of Heaven"—*The Labyrinthine Ways.* And it is
Greene who has stated that the history of contemporary
society is being written "in hundreds of volumes, most
of them sold in cheap editions—the detective novels."
The great and perceptive writers of the nineteenth century from George Eliot through Henry James accepted
the material and announced the themes, in a period devoted to ideals of "progress" and bourgeois complacency.
At the moment, continuous and sharp attention should
be paid to this vehicle, in which every rejected and denied
human impulse can be accommodated, from the petty
but terrible *Schadenfreude* (joy in another's misfor-
tune), bred from the poorer native qualities of the human heart as well as from the pressures of a competitive
society, to larger evil schemes of power and ambition.
The detective novel, now snobbishly cut off from the
main stream of literature, reviewed flippantly if at all,
may at this moment have within it secrets of what we
are and shall be. And the future may look back to it, as
it now exists, through great works engendered by it, as
we look back through Baudelaire's poems to Sue's Paris,
and back through Shakespeare to the crude horrors of
the Tragedy of Blood.

1 9 4 4

§ *The Silver Clue*

F. O. Matthiessen's intelligent study of James' later period, *Henry James: The Later Phase,* appearing one year after the rather neglected James centenary, presages, it is to be hoped, other criticism directed toward the Works and produced by critics who do not hate James or misprise good writing. Matthiessen mentions at one point the present interest in the international scene as having some relation to a new interest in James. It would be one more queer twist of circumstance if Americans now come to an interest in their great compatriot because of reasons quite separate from the central values in James. What James really was—a great "poet" and a profound psychologist—and what he actually accomplished, is beyond any interest of a "timely" kind, no matter how pressing and serious such an interest may seem or be.

James' reputation has been affected by the turns of fashion before this. He has been earlier than his time, later than his time, and his work has fallen into neglect between "periods." He has been thought outmoded, when his modernity was notable; genteel, when he had become the sharpest critic of "gentility"; a dull expatriate, when his books flashed with incisive American wit; "fine drawn," when, at the end of his life, his writing was loaded with almost an excessive weight of insight and experience. He lost one audience at the end of the '80's. He gained a younger one in 1918, only to have it almost completely fall away during the experimental and eclectic decade of the '20's. The Parrington-Van Wyck Brooks sort of attack appealed to exactly the type of reader who, by nature and training, would decry James in any case: the middle-class mind dead set against anything it cannot "use" or "understand." James, being a shining mark, drew to himself all the concentrated vituperation such minds are capable of producing. Every dictum of Flaubert's—and there are many—concerning the hatred of the artist felt by the rank and file of the bourgeoisie was proved as a deadly truth by the attacks made, and the misinterpretations thought up, by such critics, on the subject of James.

Matthiessen has made a choice among the works, and deals at length with the three last novels—*The Ambassadors, The Wings of the Dove,* and *The Golden Bowl* —published during James' lifetime; together with, in passing, *The American Scene* and the two posthumous and unfinished novels, *The Ivory Tower* and *The Sense of the Past.* This phase Matthiessen calls "major." It might better be called the "past-master" period, for James had been "major" for twenty years or more before he entered into his last and greatest powers of thought and expression. A period of mature experimentation—with the theater, with the strict dramatic form as applied to the novel, and with various special viewpoints (notably those of the child and the neurotic)—intervened, in the '90's, between the middle and late James. The later novels have often been singled out for special praise—or blame; they have never, however, been analyzed with the thoroughness they deserve, and we must be grateful to Matthiessen for the attention he has paid to their subtleties, and the care he has taken not to split their form and content into two unnatural divisions. He is out to shed light, and to direct attention not only toward the master's "pattern" but also toward the magician's enchantment surrounding that pattern and the fine mind's relentless insight into it. This is the James, Matthiessen with tacit irony reminds the reader, who has been accused of identifying himself with his characters. This is the "snob" who was taken in by the European scene. This is the dim-witted old man drawing out a tangle of conclusions from desperately small premises. We see, instead, the deliberate, immensely skillful artist in his sixties adding to his effects; the clear-eyed man who can penetrate, to the point of clairvoyance, almost every human obscurity. We see James writing these last novels with a speed incommensurate with their complexity. During the three years of their composition James also produced the life of William Wetmore Story, the American sculptor, and several short pieces. The delightful Story biography, revealing James' perfect grasp of the American artist's problems during the period with which he deals, is a Jamesian success too little known. It is a pity that Matthiessen does not include a detailed estimate of it in his treatment of the last phase, where it belongs. Matthiessen had access to eight working notebooks, running from 1878 to 1914. Not a great deal of clarification of James' intentions is, however, drawn from this source.

One or two matters not accented by Matthiessen come to mind, together with what seems to me a real underestimation, based on imperfect analysis, of *The Golden Bowl*. Matthiessen believes that James' twenty years' absence from America, during a period of crucial American social change, made him uneasy with the "multimillionaire" Adam Verver. Do we not see, instead, in Mr. Verver, as well as in Maggie, James' recognition of a new American type? Surely some kind of maiming and distorting force, as well as increased powers of specialization acting upon basic American romanticism, aggressiveness, and naïveté, reverberate through *The Golden Bowl*. Mr. Verver and Maggie are at first grotesques. They are at once far too powerful and far too infantile. Maggie must learn that love and "help" cannot be bought, or called in, and later neglected; that these things turn out to be dangers to face up to. Matthiessen states that the dynamics of the book are provided entirely by Maggie. The exact opposite is true. Maggie is reduced to impotence and fear when she tries to "go it" alone; to run everyone. It is only when Charlotte steps out on the terrace with her silent offer of help that Maggie is deflected from her crass, childish, and neurotic course. And behind Charlotte is the Prince's "humility" and delicate sense of balance and form. In this book it is the Europeans who "save" the Americans; it is the Americans who have become corrupted by power, and by "taste" pushed too far. Note should be made of Mrs. Assingham's extraordinary analysis, at the end of the novel's first part, of the relation between the four principal characters—an analysis securely based on the truth of modern psychology, and all done without benefit of Freud or Jung. James, in *The Golden Bowl*, had come to the point where he could hear aright, in spite of "stock" pretenses, the whole hidden story of the human heart, including its minor "intermittences." The reader is led, through small truths, toward stern, prodigious human facts. He experiences, not minor interpretation, but comprehensive wisdom.

From one point of view, *The Golden Bowl,* written in the same year (1905) as Debussy's *La Mer,* is one of Impressionism's triumphs. Both works are formal accomplishments "of magnificent scope" of that school. And the later James must be approached in the same way as one approaches music. Soon any surface stylistic oddity disappears. The center continually shifts, but the development of theme never stops for a moment and never errs. As in great music and in tragic life, the shifts are always toward the larger and unsuspected capacity, modulation, event; and toward a final major resolution.

James knew that democracy was diversity. To step into his world of Americans, Europeans, and every international combination of the two, is to find oneself in developing diversity. To read James we must follow "the silver clue . . . to the whole labyrinth of the artist's consciousness: his active sense of life." To understand James we must be the opposite of his "awful Mona Brigstock, who is *all* will, without the smallest leak of force into taste or tenderness or vision, into any sense of shades or relations or proportions—the thriftily constructed Mona, able at any moment to bear the whole of her dead weight at once on any given inch of resisting surface." The Mona Brigstocks, American or "international," should leave James alone. The non-Monas should go toward him without fear, if they have not already found him.

1 9 4 4

§ *Yvor Winters*

Yvor Winters, whose selected poems, *The Giant Weapon,* have recently appeared in the New Directions series "The Poets of the Year," has held to unpopular modes of expression in poetry and criticism for a long time. He has clung to what often seemed crotchets, in a time particularly unfriendly, really, to displays of determined individuality. His poetry, which at the start adhered to the severest tenets of Imagism, refused to break up and deliquesce when Imagism went into a decline. It turned back, instead, to the stylistic severities of the seventeenth century. There it settled and there it developed, slowly and very nearly without listeners, let alone friends and admirers. The fashion for what Winters himself has called "chaotic reverie" spread on all sides, but Winters went on writing and translating, and in 1940 he printed, on his own press, all of his work he had decided he wished to keep, some hundred poems in all. The new volume is much smaller; it contains thirty-three poems, written in the past fifteen years. "It clearly shows Winters to be one of the really significant poets of conservative tendency now writing in America," his publisher says. That this conservative tendency has become so rare nowadays that it is again almost *avant garde* is an interesting fact in itself.

How stern and dry, how sharp and narrow these poems look on the page. Some readers, to whom the looseness of modern verse has become a norm, will be ready and waiting to pin the word "neo-classic" to Winters' style and attitude. But when we examine this close-grained, coolly detached writing, we come upon many delicate yet firm effects which elude this small classification. Winters' general form and tone lend themselves to the didactic, and elegiac poems are here, but with a difference. This poetry's light, undercutting observation, its tenderness, which keeps it on the side of life and joy even when it seems most grave, its total avoidance of cliché, its lack of sentimentality, its deep interest in themes of truth and justice—these elements separate it completely from dead formality and generalized emptiness. Gradually we realize that Winters is revealing to us imaginative flashes into the relationship between man, nature, and man's artifacts (between, for example, the airplane and the night sky and the human watcher who experiences them both)—flashes so unexpected that we understand rather tardily that what we are reading gives us more of the future than of the past.

Several poems have a power of evoking atmosphere and tension that more "romantic" poets might well envy. "By the Road to the Air-Base" is one of these, and "Before Disaster, 1932-3" is another. Winters teaches English at Leland Stanford, and his subjects are often drawn from his professional life. The limp and leaden academic tone has not touched these subjects, however.

His passion for integrity comes to have a searchlight intensity. He loves the classic bases of life; he suffers when he finds these bases absent or broken. His interests appear to be limited only because he has made choices; his treatment of his material makes up in height and depth for what it has abandoned in breadth. But are his subjects actually so limited? We examine them a second time and find them surprisingly numerous. And the problems he deals with, whether abstract, as his insistence upon the worth of learning and discipline, or concrete, as his defense of a friend on trial for murder, are real problems. Winters has that rare sense: the cool power to appraise evil. He does not reject evil, or try to laugh it off, or attempt to streamline it into acceptable form. He looks it in the eye and brings a sober sense of compassionate justice to bear upon it.

His poem "To a Military Rifle, 1942," I feel, turns out to be one of the fine poems produced by the war. It is as far removed from ordinary war verse as a poem can possibly be and still deal with its subject. That Winters should have written this poem, which is a poem of the future, that he should continue to exist at all, that he should have persisted in his way of writing until the turn of the wheel brought him back as "modern"—these facts should delight us. They are proof that as a people we can produce untouchable probity and distilled power in the most unlikely times.

1 9 4 4

§ *The Prophet Job: Yankee Style*

A Masque of Reason, by Robert Frost, is published
near the occasion of Frost's seventieth birthday. This
short verse play deals with the Job story in a spirit
of good middle-of-the-road grassroots conservatism;
Frost speaks in the language, and with much of the
point of view, of the "dry" cracker-box philosopher.
Job, a reasonable farmer at heart, has never been really
satisfied with the elaborate explanation of the reason for
his misfortunes given to him, on an unforgettable occasion, by God out of the whirlwind. Now safely dead,
and granted the company of his beautiful but sleepy
wife, Job decides, when God appears in the desert of the
afterworld, to get down to facts, to face up to Mystery
with Reason. Job's wife, too, has a few questions. God
hems and haws but finally comes out with the explanation familiar to us all along: He did it to show off to the
Devil. Satan's lieutenants act only for hire, but God
counted on Job's free will and Job did not fail him.
Job's integrity, it is true, leads to near despair and per-

manent puzzlement, but Job holds out, and a great moral turn occurs in the affairs of both God and Man. In the course of this little drama, many asides on present-day matters appear, and a charming ending, that will not puzzle, shock, or bemuse anyone (that will, indeed, bring down the house in a gathering of, say, the Ladies' Aid Society), gives Mrs. Job the last word, as she lines up God, Satan, and her husband for a photograph to commemorate the occasion—a photograph in which she will not appear but for which she asks them to smile.

We cannot bear down heavily upon this little divertissement. Frost, bringing us up against the problem of Pain and Evil, adds nothing to our insight into the subject. But it would not be in character for Frost to startle us with some new concept or to throw dangerous light into the shadowy corners of his scene. It is interesting to note, by the way, that Frost deletes Elihu. Rereading the original story, one is struck by the modern wisdom of this enthusiastic and invigorating young son of Barachel the Buzite. Here is a character for a modern poet to take hold of. Elihu's remarks would delight T. S. Eliot: Elihu's insight into the power of dreams, no doubt, long ago delighted that student of religions, Jung. Elihu urges Job to give up and give in, to forget about his stiff civic righteousness and his sense of moral pride. Frost, like Yeats and Stefan George, has a strong belief in Job's kind of individualism. Elihu is on the side of Rilke, Eliot, and (at present) Auden. Frost's God is thrifty, crafty, and nonexperimental. (He wagers only on a sure thing.) God according to Elihu brings briefly before us Imaginative Immanence, which deals out, with one hand, mystery and suffering and, with the other, instruction and grace. Frost, too, reduces Satan to what he calls a "sapphire wasp," and an emaciated one at that.

He makes Evil a rather slight and annoying malicious force, whereas certain modern poets, from Baudelaire on, have magnified the power of Evil. It is interesting to trace the line of reasonable conformity in Frost's little *jeu d'esprit* and to recognize how difficult it is, even in an era of the utmost tragedy, for a poet who has chosen the middle road to be serious in tone and searching in intent.

1 9 4 5

§ *The Quest of W. H. Auden*

1

W. H. Auden has emerged rapidly from the soliloquy darkened by private associations, a form that might have hampered him for a longer time. His first dramatic efforts, "Paid on Both Sides" and "The Dance of Death," were founded on the feeblest possible dramatic framework: the charade. He has written, in *The Dog Beneath the Skin, or, Where Is Francis?*, with the competent aid of Christopher Isherwood, a long, highly amusing revue, whose satire is so deft that it may stand, without cutting a sorry figure, beside the early Gilbert. Along with the satirist's wit, the imagination of a poet and the broad humor of a sane young man are also involved.

Auden's play is closer to the original music-hall entertainment so admired, in the nineties, as a refuge from the torpid, affected art and literature current at that time, than Eliot's "Sweeney Agonistes" or Cocteau's "Orphée," derived from the same source. It is less dependent on pure oddity than Cocteau's play, and it is not heavily symbolic, like Eliot's. It is a light-hearted yet fundamentally grave parable of the noble youth who descends from his class to give humanity in general a hard and unprejudiced stare.

The hero, Alan, accompanied by a comic dog called, after its quarry, Francis, sets out from the ideal English village in search of the lost noble heir. The two make their progress through the symptomatic institutions of a debased and lunatic society in the leisurely but erratic manner of all innocent pilgrims steered by an author's moral indignation, from Christian and Gulliver on. They are accompanied on certain stages of their journey by the press in the person of two journalists who comment, aid, abet, prod, rescue, sympathize, and interpret. They take boat and train journeys; they invade a tottering monarchy, a night-town, a Fascist insane asylum, a rest-cure for self-poisoned egotists, an operating theatre, and a de luxe hotel. The Dog, in spite of a lamentable taste for double whiskies, served in a bowl, shows remarkable cleverness and devotion throughout. He proves his true valor when the simple-hearted Alan falls into the clutches of a night-club entertainer; he casts his skin and stands up from it revealed as Sir Francis Crewe, the object of Alan's search. The two, in their roles of the seeker and the found, return to the village as comrades. Alan sees all in a new light and the one-time Dog sums up, in public, his general feelings about the world seen from below:

As a dog, I learnt with what a mixture of fear, bullying and condescending kindness you treat those whom you consider your inferiors, but on whom you depend for your pleasures. It's an awful shock to start seeing people from underneath. . . . You are units in an immense army: most of you will die without ever knowing what your leaders are fighting for or even that you are fighting at all. Well, I am going to be a unit in the army of the other side.

Auden and Isherwood are by no means the first young members of the English upper class who have pilloried their caste. Even the rather unsettled Sitwells have put down, in terms far from uncertain, the grotesque antics of members of the three estates. The most noticeable ingredient in Auden's attitude is his lack of hatred; he has much pity and strong anger, but he is not bloodthirsty and he does not blame. He surveys the scene from above and below; he gives it elevation, section and plan, but he does not rant against it. The hysterical, the gloomy, the portentously righteous and solemn note is missing, yet the power of his indictment is not diminished because of its absence. And there is a hint given from time to time that it is man's present (and perhaps future) partial capacity for sense and for good, his defective and divided nature, that helps to distort the scene.

To men of action, pity is sentimental and insight into the human heart unnecessary. To a poet, pity and insight may also kindle the fire of action and sharpen the pen in the hand. Auden fearlessly incites to action, after he has shown that what must be fought are not only the outer horrors but also the flesh on the bones and the stupidity in the veins:

You have wonderful hospitals and a few good schools;
Repent.
The precision of your instruments and the skill of your
    designers is unparalleled:
Unite.
Your knowledge and your power are capable of infinite
    extension.
Act.

[1] 9 3 5

2

New life can come into an art only when that art becomes more casual in tone. A shift in emphasis or a change in subject matter does no good. A stuffy state of mind and a bigwig style will stifle a poem about sharecroppers as quickly as a poem about peacocks in the twilight. Once rigidity or efflorescence has set in, it is useless to try to escape the effects. Something else, completely different, must be done. Change must be sharp; the whole encumbered ground must be cleared, and this clearing can only be the direct result of an examination of conscience which brings humility.

Obscured as modern poetry has been by every kind of rhetorical curlicue, intellectual pretension, and spiritual gloom, the reaction had to be fundamental. W. H. Auden, in his new book, *The Double Man,* has cleared a lot away, including much of his former self. He returns to the nice, crisp, open beat of four-stress iambic lines and to the couplets of the letter in rhyme, and he has reduced modern wisdom (of which there is some) to the simple proposition that man is not perfect, or perhaps even perfectible; he must, however, keep going and try to do the best he can. Expecting the impossible of himself, and failing to achieve it, leads to dangerous self-contempt, panic, and despair.

In a rhymed letter to a trusted friend one can tell the truth, bring in many things not accessible otherwise to poetry, make a running comment upon the world and one's own soul without becoming pompous, examine the surroundings without pedantry. Auden does all these things in the "New Year Letter (1940)," of some seventeen hundred lines, addressed to Elizabeth Mayer. The poem is followed by a series of notes taking up more pages than the poem itself. These notes will undoubtedly irritate readers eager for a smooth flow of poetry as such, especially since some of the notes are irreverent. Believers in man's sublimity and the social optimists alike are in for a few jolts here. Auden ranges over embryology, psychiatry, anthropology, history, metaphysics, sociology, and modern views on the nature of the universe. He quotes Chekhov, Henry James, Margaret Mead, the authors of *Middletown,* Soren Kierkegaard, Kafka, Rilke, Wolfgang Köhler, Thucydides, and Carl Jung, among others. That it is a real enjoyment to read these notes and relate them to Auden's text will not count, perhaps, to outraged specialists in the various fields. Other people will not care for the thought of the poet as student, notebook in hand, and not wrapped in a prophetic garment.

Quite apart from its sources and philosophy, "New Year Letter" is a pleasure to read. It is full of the aphorisms proper to, and charming in, the rhymed couplet. It runs to straight, unadorned nouns and verbs, so that the occasional epithet comes as an accent and surprise. The poem has two climaxes of real power. One of these is a lyric burst, an actual emotional passage of a kind Auden has not up to now been given to.

A group, chiefly of sonnets, "The Quest," follows. It is in Auden's former manner and sounds a little composed. A short epilogue and prologue to the volume continue the cool, reticent sincerity into which Auden seems steadily to be working.

1 9 4 1

3

W. H. Auden's new volume, *For the Time Being*, appears three years after his last, *The Double Man*. Even before *The Double Man*, Auden had changed from a closed dogmatic materialist belief toward an open moral faith. The general effect of the two long poems in his new book—"The Sea and the Mirror: A Commentary on Shakespeare's *The Tempest*," and the title poem, written in the form of a Christmas oratorio—is one of restlessness under control, of talent steadied and enlarged. The two poems, taken together, constitute the most minute dissection of the spiritual illness of our day that any modern poet, not excluding Eliot, has given us.

We are unfortunately used to writers who repeat their pattern, from youth to age, without deviation. They begin as young sheep or young goats and end up as old sheep or old goats. Americans are suspicious of "conversions." In a country where the strongest religious coloring is that of romantic Evangelicalism, we associate conversion with revivalism and expect a spiritual change to be an emotional reaction, slightly hysterical in character. Auden's change occurred on a non-Romantic level, in a region where the beliefs of Christianity and the proofs of modern psychological knowledge meet. Auden has taken less time than Eliot, indulged in fewer gestures, put less emphasis on ritual, in his search for a religious attitude. A streak of Yorkshire common sense, underneath his complexity, has kept the younger man on the side of simple feeling and away from elaborate orthodoxy.

"The Sea and the Mirror" deals with Shakespeare's *Tempest* characters after the ending of their play. Each character finds himself, but only according to his original capacity. Nothing whatever happens to the truly evil or silly people. As it turns out, the thoughts of the reformed intriguer, Alonso, King of Naples, are more interesting and more poignantly expressed than the thoughts of the reformed magician, Prospero. Alonso's letter to Ferdinand, on the delights and dangers of power, is one of the high points in Auden. The speeches are a little museum of form: one in terza rima is followed by a sestina, a sonnet, and a ballade. The long concluding speech of Caliban to the audience, written in a prose which combines certain characteristics of the later Henry James with baroque periods comparable to the prose of Donne and Bossuet, has an eloquence that one would have supposed a modern poet incapable of producing; and the analysis, in this speech, of the modern spiritual *malaise* restores to literature a subject long neglected under the present-day pressure of "rational" thought. The lengthy, exact, intricate, and many times terrifying recital is a perfect answer to those advocates of "useful" poetry who would reduce all expression to a mechanical base. There appear to be qualities in the human spirit, even now, that require a full rhetorical diapason for complete expression.

The oratorio, "For the Time Being," deals in a different way with the problem of modern spiritual estrangement and offers a way out through faith and suffering. Auden here has undertaken a technical problem of large proportions. He is trying to get formal poetry working on a larger than usual scale and to link it to music and the human voice, from both of which it has been long alienated. He has gone back to the one big musical form where English poetry has been successfully employed. The oratorio, under Handel, succeeded in enlarging the English song into choral magnificence. Auden gets much variety and dramatic contrast into his own work. Its lyric passages are moving, its satire (as in the Herod speech) sharp, its philosophic passages (the Simeon meditation) articulate, its humor sometimes lively and sometimes appropriately horrifying. We again realize how limited and barren the field of modern poetry has become when we are presented with such a number of human thoughts and emotions, boldly designed and arranged to set one another off. This elaborate work has an interest, an intellectual validity, an emotional range so rare that it should be read with the seriousness and attention it deserves. That it has been seriously composed, as opposed to being thrown together for effect, is as evident after a tenth reading as after a first.

1 9 4 4

4

A moment occurs (or should occur) when the growing artist is able to bequeath his tricks to his imitators. The mature writer rejects the treasured "originality" and the darling virtuosities of his apprenticeship in art, as well as the showy sorrows and joys of his apprenticeship to life, often just in time. "How they live at home in their cozy poems and make long stays in narrow comparisons!" Rilke once said, speaking of the run of versifiers, who never change or grow. Once youth's embroidered coat is cast aside, what is left? Only imagination, ripened insight, experience, and the trained sense of language, which are usually enough.

The Collected Poetry of W. H. Auden is a sizable volume for a poet born in 1907 to have credited to him in 1945. Auden, it has for some time been apparent, has succeeded Eliot as the strongest influence in American and British poetry. And he has managed, in this collection, by skillful arrangement and deletion, to present himself to the reader as he exists at this moment. He does not draw attention to his growing pains or take us step by step through stage after stage of his development. He begins the book with one of those poems ("Musée des Beaux Arts") which announced, a few years ago, the beginnings of his maturity—a poem that seems as simply composed as a passage in conversation. It is not filled with Anglo-Saxon compression, or clogged with modern apparatuses and machines, or trimmed with off-rhymes. Earlier poems on his favorite subjects and in the special manner of his youth are included in the book. But they never leap out at us. The general tone is one of composure and simplicity, of that ease wherein, for a time, a young master can rest.

The collection gathers up, fortunately, poems that have so far been scattered in plays or books of prose. The sonnet to E. M. Forster once served as the dedication for *Journey to a War,* written in collaboration with Christopher Isherwood. Other sonnets and a verse commentary come from the same volume. The fine "Journey to Iceland" is out of *Letters from Iceland,* written in collaboration with Louis MacNeice. Some choruses from plays turn up as separate poems, now with titles. The volume also contains two prose passages —the early "Letter to a Wound" and a new "sermon" entitled "Depravity." Last autumn's *For the Time Being* is reprinted complete, and there are several new poems.

What is the particular thread that runs through this collection, the clue to Auden's importance and power? In what way is his great gift different from Eliot's, and in what way is it of importance to Auden's contemporaries? Auden shares with Eliot a sense of his time. He is, however, much more exuberant, restless, sanguine, and unselfconscious than the older poet. And he is a natural dramatist in a degree surpassing Eliot. Eliot can dramatize his lyrics but rarely projects dramatic action with force. Auden dramatizes everything he touches. He is wonderfully effective with that most dramatic of lyric forms, the ballad. At the same time, his purely lyrical endowment is so deep and so natural that many of his songs sound as though they had been worked up at a moment's notice as improvisations. He can sing about as many things as the Elizabethans, and with the same disregard for the demands of the high literary line and the "refined" literary tone.

Eliot's importance is based on the fact that he had the sensitiveness and the melancholy foreboding to sense the general tragedy of his period when that tragedy had not yet impressed other observers. Auden, nearly twenty years Eliot's junior, stands farther from the shadow of the nineteenth and early twentieth centuries; he is more able, therefore, to deal with particulars. He is conscious of his physical surroundings down to the last contraption of "light alloys and glass"; conscious of his spiritual scene down to the last sob of modern self-pity, down to modern brutality's last threat. He has smashed the "taboo against tenderness," as someone has said; he is not afraid or ashamed either to laugh or weep. (How gloomy everyone was, after Eliot!) He knows what Rilke felt and foresaw, what Kierkegaard rebelled against, what modern psychiatry has plumbed. He is not ignorant of facts or clumsy in dealing with them. He is able to absorb and speak of any item in the extraordinary crowd of objects and techniques he finds on all sides. He is able to define and present a range of ideas, passions, compulsions, manias, anxieties, fears, and intuitions that at present float about, only half-perceived by many people and most poets, in our intellectual and emotional climate. He is at once able to act and to imagine, to formulate and interpret.

Behind him stand exemplars he acknowledges—Rilke and Henry James, Freud, the Symbolists and post-Symbolists, and Surrealism at its most effective. Part of the excitement in reading the volume through derives from the fact that we are dealing with a poet one of whose inner urges will always be to transcend himself, that we are reading the work of one who is still a young man, so that there will be more to come.

1 9 4 5

5

A healthy and civilized poetry should be able to express anything. It should be varied, comprehensive, and flexible. Experiments in the larger poetic forms have in our period lagged far behind experiments in poetic texture —experiments, that is, in language as such. Modern poets have been haunted by the now completely outdated formal poetic play. Shakespearean drama has cast a particularly strong spell over poets writing in English. The nagging belief that somehow the poetic drama could be restored to its former immense prestige has hampered the most gifted of contemporaries. Even Eliot and Auden have succumbed to the temptation to tinker with decrepit dramatic machines. Recently, however, Auden has given up these attempts and has applied himself, singlehanded, to the task of creating new semi-dramatic structures. He has already written an oratorio. His new work, *The Age of Anxiety,* bears the subtitle "A Baroque Eclogue." In this long poem, a series of conversations, dramatic monologues, and occasional songs, he tries to crystallize to some degree the fluidity and complexity of modern character, and at the same time, as a dramatic poet should, to stylize the commonplace, everyday scene and event.

The dilemmas of the romantic hero, fighting it out against Fate, are no longer fully satisfying or evocative to a modern audience. In a period when values are uneven, when motives are warped and masked, when the citizenry does not know exactly who it is or where it is, a poetic form is called for that combines short surveys of the situation at large with detailed inquiries into individual human types. An eclogue, as any professor will tell you, is a pastoral poem in the form of a conversation—pastoral and primitive in the time of Theocritus, and highly sophisticated during the eighteenth century. Auden's adjective "baroque" suggests the fanciful. His eclogue, far from being pastoral, starts with a conversation in a city bar, goes off into a dream sequence, proceeds (with dialogue, monologue, and song) to the apartment of the single female character, and finally frays out in the subway and the city streets. Practically nothing happens, yet a good many matters are analyzed by means of that poetic "reason" in which the happy guesses of the imagination, as well as the oddest suggestions of fancy, play a part. While his characters occupy themselves in giving various answers to their own questions (Why do I feel so queer? Is it the general situation or is it I? Who are all these other people, and are they baffled in the same way that I am baffled?), Auden takes on a subsidiary task—to point up and freshen the language with which they communicate with one another. Avoiding the more threadbare English metres, he works in a closely stressed line reminiscent of Anglo-Saxon prosody. He also uses alliteration with great vigor and freedom, exploring its more elegant as well as its massive and powerful possibilities. Again, he makes use, when the occasion requires, of archaic and obsolete words, not as a casual affectation but in order to weight, diversify, and amuse, and he deals easily with the American vernacular: witness his superb stylization of the radio commercial. Here experimental language, rescued from the useless doldrums into which the Surrealists have forced it, is restored as a useful tool in the serious poet's equipment.

This modern eclogue is clearly transitional, but by intention, not by chance. And the characters never lapse into the dullness of allegory. They are symbols, but with enough admixture of human reality to make them interesting and plausible. The general tone of the poem is that of high comedy. Auden is not attempting to plumb the deepest labyrinths of the heart and mind. He is making a survey of contemporary manners and morals on the basis of what he considers the highest sort of ideal—the Christian. But he allows crosslights from other ideals to fall upon his scene: see Rosetta's speech on Israel, for example.

Auden has now reached a middle period, in which it is difficult for any poet not to indulge in self-repetition or self-parody. He has largely managed to dodge both these traps. His inventive powers, both in language and form, are still enormous, and it is delightful to watch him go about the task of revivifying old rules. Assonance, consonance, alliteration, an ancient, closely stressed rhythm—all these poetic procedures he frees from the books of rhetoric, so that they again function in living poetry.

1 9 4 7

§ *The Summers of Hesperides Are Long*

The legend of Emily Dickinson has grown in America since 1890, when the first series of her posthumously published poems appeared. And this legend has not been confined to the literary field. The shadow of the spirited little figure, self-secluded in her father's "mansion" in Amherst, is known and loved by many people for whom the quality of her poetry would have little or no appeal. She has become a kind of secular saint. For she has redeemed and justified that former American type: the lonely and eccentric Old Maid. The Old Maid, formerly a character more comic than pathetic, became, in the person of "Emily," a mysterious and transcendent being. The desire to hunt up a definite lover for Emily, noticeable in several rather fanciful biographies written in the 1920's, was perhaps due to romantic hope that the legend could be fully rounded out in a conventional way. All old maids are disappointed in love. Who, then, disappointed Emily Dickinson?

The peculiar manner in which her works came before the public helped not only to promulgate mystery but

to prevent the poems themselves from being closely attached to the life. Mrs. Todd, Emily's first editor, presented the poems under the headings, "Life," "Nature,"
"Love," and "Time and Eternity" (how we feel the
breath of the '90's here!). Mrs. Martha Dickinson
Bianchi, Emily's niece, taking over the role of editor in
1912, continued this classification in all subsequent "collected" volumes. Moreover, an underlying drama of
family feuds and split allegiances kept the material itself in an incomplete state. *Ancestors' Brocades: The
Literary Debut of Emily Dickinson,* written by Mrs.
Todd's daughter, Millicent Todd Bingham, now brings
before us for the first time a full account of the circumstances connected with the appearance of the first three
books of poems (1890, 1891, 1896), and with Mrs. Todd's
edition of the *Letters* (1894). Mrs. Todd copied and collated hundreds of poems from the difficult and cryptic
manuscripts, she gathered in letters from crotchety and
non-cooperative correspondents. Her version of Emily's
life is still a sensible piece of narration. She did not know
everything and she did not understand everything; but
neither did she throw dust in the reader's eyes, or make
any effort to build up the facts into "romance."

Amherst, in the early and middle nineteenth century,
far from being a community in which "revolutionary"
Transcendental and Unitarian ideas could take root,
was a provincial, principally Congregationalist town
where Puritan emotions were passing over into Evangel-
ical ones. Edward Dickinson, Emily's father, was a product of this stern and unyielding background: a man, as
Emily said, who stepped like Cromwell when he went
to gather the kindling. He was, it is becoming evident,
a character of pathological harshness whose word in his
family was law.

"I never had a mother," the poet remarked to Colonel

Higginson. Edward's wife was allowed, it would seem, little voice in the management of her three children, Austin, Lavinia, and Emily. Austin, after making some futile early gestures of escape to the West, finally settled down in a house adjoining his father's and subordinated his career to his father's wishes. He married outside the clan—a witty and "worldly" woman called Sue—but this marriage was not a success. A coolness grew up between husband and wife and Austin spent more time in his father's house than in his own. Emily and Lavinia were from the first subdued by the paternal will. And Emily adored her father. She was always her brother's friend, although her friendship with her brother's wife was, it now appears, soon broken. Lavinia, in later years, guarded and protected Emily. It was to Lavinia that Emily tacitly entrusted her manuscripts; what now seem to be thousands of these turned up in the Dickinson house after Emily's death.

Mrs. Todd, pretty and disarming, managed to break through the poet's later reserve. It was natural, then, that Lavinia should come to Mrs. Todd for help in the matter of the manuscripts. Mrs. Todd was to devote years of her time to deciphering the material entrusted to her. The poems, and later the letters, once printed, had a certain success, and Mrs. Todd took to lecturing on the poet. Lavinia, to whom all the profits from the published poems accrued, saw her beloved Emily slipping from her. Austin, on the other hand, wished to reward Mrs. Todd in some way. He deeded to her a strip of land adjoining the Dickinson estate. After his death, Lavinia, now an eccentric and rather appalling spinster, brought suit for the land, and won her suit. Mrs. Todd at once stopped work on the manuscripts, locked them in a box, and never referred to the incident in her lifetime. After some years, Mrs. Bianchi began to publish poems from the original manuscripts, which had now fallen into her hands.

Mrs. Todd realized that the poems could be classified, according to handwriting, into three distinct periods. Mrs. Bianchi never admitted that these distinctions existed. Thus Mrs. Bianchi's collections, brought out in a haphazard way as the years went on, were notable for their carelessness and inaccuracy. Even the most cursory reader could not help being baffled by poems that did not make any kind of sense. This sort of presentation was unfair to Emily Dickinson. Whatever her oddities of style, she had the firmest notion of what she wanted to say and how she wanted to say it. The poems are never the babblings of a broken heart or the ravings of a broken mind. They show, even in their present disordered arrangement, a clear line of development: a classic line, rising through early sentiment and experiment to a middle ground of technical and spiritual control. Beyond this middle period the "great" expression begins. The compressed, direct force of the later work points to a spirit freed, as well as to a technique mastered.

So much can be puzzled out. Fortunately, the mass of published material is now so large that certain rough conclusions can be drawn as to both the life and the work. The newest collection, *Bolts of Melody* (more than six hundred and fifty "new" poems), is edited by Mrs. Bingham from the manuscript copied by Mrs. Todd. It is now perfectly apparent that there were two personalities involved in the work and in the life: the poet whose courage and spiritual fiber developed into a massive and imperturbable maturity, and "Emily," the child who never developed at all, but lived, even after her father's death, in her father's shadow.

The letters show that this division was the result of some shock undergone by the poet in her early twenties. The earliest letters are gay and outgoing. Some shattering blow (which Mrs. Bianchi glosses over) was then dealt. "It is extraordinary," Colonel Higginson wrote Mrs. Todd, "how the mystic and bizarre Emily is born between two pages [of letters]—as Thoreau says, summer passes to autumn in an instant." Whatever happened, the eager young girl disappears, and a child and a "bizarre" woman take her place. Both of these personalities became "poets." So that, in 1862, when Emily Dickinson wrote to Higginson, asking for literary criticism, we are rather repelled by the "child's" coyness of approach, but amazed at the maturing woman's already considerable powers.

The "roughness" of rhyme and obscurity of meaning, so troubling to Mrs. Todd and Colonel Higginson, fall with perfect naturalness on modern ears. The wheel of taste turned; and "Emily's" sentimental verses, concerned with fainting robins, waltzing butterflies, and the like, began to show up for the childish utterances they actually are. But now another layer of her work came into view; and a new generation, with subtler ears, and a sterner sense of poetic values, found this poetry exactly suited to its taste. The influence of Emily Dickinson's "great" period on the generation of Auden, if not that of Eliot, is inestimable. She had instinctively, on her own, "wrung the neck of rhetoric"; cleared out the trash from her versification; condensed her observation to a sharp focus. She became one of the "ancestors" of the young; her poetry, in recent anthologies, stands side by side with the poetry of Blake, George Herbert, Donne, Thomas Hardy, Hopkins, and Yeats—with Shakespeare's songs and the Border ballads. She is able to face up to Edith Sitwell as well as to Christina Rossetti; and her influence is not yet wholly absorbed; she still stands open toward the future.

Mrs. Bingham does not hope for a complete and competently edited *Works* for at least fifty years. The original manuscripts are still not available. For scholars, a grueling task lies ahead. Meanwhile, we probably have the heart of the work already in print. And now that the legendary, romantic side of Emily Dickinson's life has been pretty thoroughly canvassed, it is surely time for her readers to consider her as a writer and to assess her powers on the highest level of mystical poetry, where they should be assessed. Her insights are equaled in intensity only by the intuitions of the greatest mystics and visionaries. Her wit (as opposed to her "fun") is of a "metaphysical" kind. Her range is wider than the fragmentary manner in which her poetry has been presented would lead us to suppose. Her mature work, as a matter of fact, passes, in an amazing way, beyond the mystic poetry with which we are familiar; it is something quite new; it has infinite weight and infinite reverberation. Beside her triumphs, her habit of childish play with the idea of "littleness" and helplessness, her coy tricks and affected airs show up for what they are— some compensating or compulsive game. The quality of the great lyric poet continually enlarges and will not shrink as fashions change. When the myth of the saintly American spinster no longer has any appeal, the works of the poet Dickinson—the woman who possessed "the disenchanting and re-enchanting faculty of seeing the world in its simple truth"—will continue to attest to the one-time existence in America of a heroine, an artist and a seer. "The summers of Hesperides are long."

1 9 4 5

§ *The Portrait of New England*

The Bostonians, evidently written sometime between James' fortieth and forty-second years, serialized in the *Century Magazine* in 1885, published in both England and America in 1886, has never until now been reprinted in an American edition. Its non-appearance in the *Collected Edition* (1907-1917) has raised various questions, chiefly concerned with James' apparent later squeamishness toward the frank insight of his early work. Whatever the reason, James never rewrote the book, as he did some others. It stands, therefore, as perfect "early James." That it has not become, and will never become, a "period piece"—a novel irremediably of its time, an outmoded lump of costume drama—can be put down to the fact that James, even in his early forties, "knew the world." *The Bostonians* is shot through with the lights of humor, with the satire of a detached, experienced, civilized intelligence. Far away from the milieu he presented, James drew the picture of Boston in the '70's with the greatest variety of detail, the utmost vivacity of presentation. He is grinding no ax, shedding no tears, driving through points without fanaticism. His separation from his material gives him a freedom that is almost the freedom of an expert in some sport; James often, here, plays a wide, high, and handsome kind of game. The underlying tone of the book is gay—the tone of high comedy.

The title is not to be applied to the inhabitants of Boston in the large. James makes it clear that his "Bostonians" are two young women—Olive Chancellor, of a certain position and means, "a spinster, as Shelley was a lyric poet or as the month of August is sultry," living on the water side of Charles Street; and Verena Tarrant, the daughter of a mesmerist and all-round charlatan, who lives in a wooden cottage "with a little naked piazza," on an unpaved "place" in Cambridge. Verena has a "gift"—the gift of eloquence. She is able to move audiences, speaking inanities in a voice that James compares to both silver and gold. She is a kind of reductio ad absurdum of that influential American figure, the platform orator. Gotten up in a costume resembling that of a circus rider, she opens her pretty mouth and exerts her fresh and genuine charm upon a variety of audiences in the cause of women's rights. Olive is, by contrast, a far more complicated character. A woman of distinction (James insists on this throughout), no fool, completely in earnest in her desire to establish some contact with "the toilers"—the workers who, she senses, touch reality beyond and "beneath" the layer of middle-class vulgarians she despises—Olive is yet sterilized by an aridity of spirit, baffled by genteel prejudices, and warped by a nervous constitution. Set against James' portrait of a woman reformer of an earlier period—the warmhearted, eccentric, but touching Miss Birdseye—

Olive Chancellor is a rather terrifying resultant of Puritanism gone to seed, a female organism driven by a masculine will, without the saving graces of masculine intelligence or feminine tenderness and insight.

These two young women move in a tepid atmosphere of post-Abolition idealism. It is an atmosphere still peopled by the cranks, faddists, cultists, evangelists, revolutionaries, and dogmatists so usual in America in the '40's and '50's—the intellectual and emotional débris of the breakdown of faith, the beginning of the "scientific view," of the general ethos of still crude industrial and moral revolutions. James knew these visionaries, of all shades of sincerity and sanity, well; his father's New York home had been a sort of clearinghouse for them. It is James' background of plain experience and accurate youthful observation which makes the revolutionaries in *The Princess Casamassima* so modernly recognizable and the cranks of *The Bostonians* so sharply alive. In these two books, written almost concurrently, James pays these characters his clear-sighted and ironic *devoirs,* and leaves them for good.

The "outside observer" in *The Bostonians* is, insolently and cleverly enough, a young man from the recently "conquered" South. Of first-rate intelligence, completely "unreconstructed," holding "unprogressive" ideals of manliness, courage, and chivalry, Basil Ransom, introduced into the midst of these, to him, vaporous ideas expressed by these decaying, except for Verena, personalities, has a civilized set of principles to fall back upon—principles that seem "medieval" to his cousin Olive and her "set." James' artistic and moral courage in contrasting, at the time, Ransom's "prejudices," Ransom's humorous and "feeling" nature, Ransom's underlying flexibility of outlook with the eerie and run-down New England prophets of "progress" and "change," cannot be underestimated. James had, it is true, Turgenev's example. Turgenev, earlier, had bent an artist's eye on the follies committed in the name of "progress" by the romantic Russian reformers and their allies in the middle class (he invented the term "nihilist"). *The Bostonians* loses nothing by being read along with *On the Eve* and *Rudin,* and Verena Tarrant often resembles a Turgenev heroine. But James, in describing her surroundings and giving her motives, is solidly on his own ground.

Ransom's pin-point sharpness of eye results in a sort of continual sparkle in the first part of the book. The young Mississippian does not hesitate to put a name to things; he sorts out the real from the artificial instantly. He spots the self-sufficient sincerity of the little woman doctor with the same swiftness with which he puts down Verena's father as a "carpetbagger" and a "varlet." He sees through the pretentiousness of Mrs. Luna; and he does not fail to see true discrimination and an actual passion for justice in Olive, in spite of his quick recognition of her manias. James succeeds in keeping Ransom free from a romantic emphasis. As Philip Rahv, in his preface to this edition, says, "In the figure of Ransom [James] created with remarkable prescience a type of intellectual who has only in the last few decades come to the fore in the English-speaking world . . . a type, exemplified in writers like T. S. Eliot or the school of Southern agrarians, whose criticism of modern civilization is rooted in traditionalist principles. Thus James anticipated . . . one of the major tendencies in twentieth-century thinking."

Behind the central figures—and how masterly is the introduction and first grouping of these—James has painted in with complete verisimilitude, combined with his own peculiar kind of poetic light and coloring, the New England social, spiritual, and physical scene as it has never been rendered before or since. Anyone who has grown up in New England during the last fifty years can vouch for the truth of these delineations of New England social and spiritual tremors. Here is the top layer shot through and through with the humanitarian feeling which must, rather guiltily, accompany utilitarian push and compromise—seeking for "roots" and reality. Here is the entire middle class yearning upward, toward "the fragrance of Beacon Street." James bares the many thin layers of provincial snobbery with scalpel nicety. Turns of both vulgar and affected speech; wrong entrances regretted; all sorts of little affronts taken as "liberties"; shabby genteel uneasiness; upper-class *idées fixes* and brutalities of placement ("it is as though [I] had struck up an intimacy with the daughter of [my] chiropodist"); the beginning of newspaper curiosity into private lives; the pushing tactics of the vigorous outsider—the whole brittle, energetic, shifting scene, filled with cruelty, uncertainty, nervousness, and "nerve"; here it stands in James as in our memory.

Nor does he scamp the scene's *décor* and backdrop. Note the poignant description of the period's American bleakness, seen in "the red sunsets of winter" from Olive's drawing-room windows. Remark the details of another Boston dusk, as Ransom walks the Boston streets before Verena's "big" lecture. Consider the exquisite description of the Cape—the background James puts behind the bitter struggle between Ransom and Olive for the "possession" of Verena. One sentence, beginning, "There were certain afternoons in August, long, beautiful, and terrible, when one felt that the summer was rounding its curve," can be set, for sheer power of evocation, against anything in Emily Dickinson.

I have always associated the little "Square," Union Park, in Boston, with *The Bostonians*. Set between two busy and now run-down avenues, it takes the form of a flattened oval—that shape dear to the nineteenth century. Great trees shade it, around a grass plot running its length, decorated by two small cast-iron fountains. The red brick houses, with their "salient" bulging fronts running from top to bottom of the facades, exemplify the first Boston architecture purely American-nineteenth-century in character. The naive assumption, usual at the beginning of a period of technological and political triumphs, that anything sufficiently bold and powerful must last forever, is built into these "fronts" along with their brick and mortar. It was in such a house that Miss Birdseye lived, and that Ransom first saw Verena. But things change. Today—and for the last forty years or so—these houses have been shabby boardinghouses or "light-housekeeping" rooms. The roomers, armed with their paper bags of food and their milk bottles, return to them at night under the shadow of the gracious trees, mount the steps beside the flourish of scrolled iron railings, and enter the big doors under obsolete, elaborate "gasoliers." The materialist spirit that thought to build enduring mansions built, instead, the most solid and dismal furnished lodgings.

In *The Bostonians* James fixes the crudities and misapprehensions of that spirit. Far from identifying himself with Ransom, he uses this character to throw uncompromising light on a humanitarianism itself grown harsh, proud, and aggressive, cut off from the humility and the realism which must be charity's true base. He shows us perfectionists blind to their own imperfections, liberals neutralized by their "liberality," radicals bound by unyielding dogma to callousness; as well as the "moist, emotional" yearners and the hysterics of both sexes, unconsciously seeking a ritual and a master that they consciously reject. *The Bostonians* is happily again available to those who have overlooked one of the greatest of American novels, which has existed, as it were, in the shadow of the very culture upon which it sheds light, since 1886.

[1] 9 4 5

§ *The Modern Syndrome*

In *Medea: Freely Adapted from the Medea of Euripides,*
Robinson Jeffers works for the first time within the
actual frame of Greek drama. Jeffers has adapted Greek
legend before this, and in 1935 he used the Medea theme
in the poetic narrative *Solstice,* setting it against his
California landscape. Now, keeping both his Romantic-
Nihilist attitude toward life and his overblown rhetorical tendencies intact, he adopts a classic mold. Curious
results naturally occur. Jeffers has chosen, it is true, a
Greek tragedy which seems to call for his kind of shock-
dealing hand, for the *Medea* is by no means a stiff and
formal vehicle of classic "pity and terror." An early
work of the highly original Euripides, it seems at moments to accumulate and to release only terror. As critics
have pointed out, there is no tragic interlock between
character and situation. Medea, the Asiatic princess and
sorceress, brought to the Greek city of Corinth by the
wily Jason and there abandoned with her children,
reacts to the situation as she reacted to earlier events in

her career—with vengeful guile and frightful cruelty. "If the only profit in the *Medea*," says a modern British scholar, "is the news that barbarian magicians who are passionate and villainously treated do villainous things, the demands on our tolerance cannot be met."

In the Jeffers version, very little in addition to Medea's villainous side comes through. Euripides, on the other hand, in this study of oppression and revenge, treats the dreadful story with the sharpness of psychological insight, the compassionate and truth-loving skepticism, the striking combination of realism and imagination, which characterize his work. He not only keeps before us, by exquisitely managed implication, the fact that "the passions and unreason to which humanity is subject are its greatest scourge"; he suggests as well the presence in the universe of implacable forces to which the wild nature of Medea is related. She is, of course, the granddaughter of Helios, the sun god, and it is the double potentiality—at once benign and destructive—of natural powers that Euripides stresses in the ambiguous final episode, in which Medea escapes by supernatural aid.

Jeffers ignores these implications. He changes Medea, by a process partly of cutting and partly of expansion, and by abrupt shifts in emphasis, from a woman who has some degree of control and some power of awakening our sympathy into a creature so obsessed by jealousy, pride, and a paranoid fear of ridicule that she passes from the normal world into the regions of insanity. From her first cry of inordinate rage, she is in an extreme of sadism. Euripides' Medea, however, is capable of a long, tender, relenting speech, in which we feel the current of human love, and she is surrounded by the poetry of the great choruses, in which, in spite of everything, love, and not fury, is the dominant theme. His Medea outlines her ghastly plans, is admonished, and plays out her frenzy against a background of understanding wisdom.

Jeffers, following the Romantic tradition, depends upon suspense for his big effects. And to the Euripidean horror, calculated with great nicety by a master in the field, he adds all manner of overwrought frightfulness. His Medea's mania for grinding, mashing, slicing, pulverizing, and beating her enemies into a bloody froth soon paralyzes and numbs our sensibilities. Jeffers' nightmare world, in which reality is squeezed and beaten into the shape of a brutal adolescent's dream, is, however, more relevant to our present situation than it was when it burst upon us, twenty years or so ago. If Jeffers now pitches his tone so high that it becomes a shriek of hysteria, he is only screwing up to their utmost the tensions of our scene. To compare this "free adaptation" of his with Euripides in a straight translation is to be brought up against the most shocking symptoms in our literature and life.

1 9 4 6

§ *The Secular Hell*

Was von Menschen nicht gewusst
Oder nicht bedacht
Durch das Labyrinth der Brust
Wandelt bei der Nacht.
       —Goethe: *An den Mond*

The "classic" myth is fresh, subtle, and varied. Its variety
is the result of a long process of accretion, stratification,
and absorption. Its subtlety is the crystallization of
"mankind's deepest emotions." It is saturated with
meaning; no matter how deeply we explore it, an irreducible residue of unconscious allusiveness remains
inexplicable in any terms but the original legendary
ones. The luminous primordial scene surrounds it; in
a light that is still large, mankind's earliest awe before,
and pleasure in, natural phenomena appears. The details are often, to use the Victorian term often applied
to them, "repulsive" in the extreme. We can still re-
spond, however, in spite of our modern knowledge of
the myth's darkest sources, to Schlegel's definition: "The

myth is a hieroglyphic expression of environing nature
under the transfiguration of imagination and love."

Even a partial listing of the labors of Herakles, for
example, shows the broadness and richness of the imaginative forces involved. "The capture of the Cerynean
hind; the procuring of the girdle of Hippolyte; the
cleaning of the Augean stables . . . the fetching of the
red cattle of Geryon"; and then, with "the procuring of
the golden apples of the Hesperides," we are transported
into a climate of pristine beauty. The labors are translated into a region outside the material world, and the
material world is exquisitely changed thereby.

The Hero as Transcendent Breaker of the Taboo
stands at the center of many myths. But the taboo is not
broken at once, or without previous bafflement. Before
the hero takes on full responsibility, full guilt, he must
at least once face up to insoluble mystery, be completely
humiliated, or be changed into a compelling "opposite."
The myth does not set up a series of material barriers
only. One test is never actually passed; through and
around it we hear the laughter of the Powers. It is
when we see Herakles a prisoner of Lydian Omphale
(who wears his lion-skin) that the story begins to vibrate
with mystery and passes over into the "truth" of the
dream. Beyond the crisis—and it is always great and
compelling—of the final assumption of guilt, lies the
irreducible strangeness of strength face to face with a
spiritual or physical Force it cannot move, change, or
understand. Oedipus before the Sphinx, Christ in the
Wilderness and in the Garden, Herakles among the
women: it is at these points that the myth opens another
dimension to our view—a dimension to which we can as

yet give no name, with which religion and poetry themselves can deal only tentatively and in part.

It is the rite which enables the individual to participate directly in the myth. The myth always moves toward the rite. It can only be *lived* through the rite. Religious ritual codifies, stiffens, and rationalizes. But the rite also reassures and shares; sometimes, it would seem, its operation is almost entirely fear-dissolving in character. But, as Roger Caillois has pointed out, in his interesting survey of the "sacred" (*L'Homme et le Sacré,* 1939), a religion at a high point of health and effectiveness often allows, within whatever culture it operates, the occasional functioning of "permitted license" of an extreme kind. The institution of the festival (the feast-day, the holiday, the *fête*)—during which rules are broken, sacrilege is at least ritually allowed, the profane is permitted to break into the stronghold of the holy, and authority is mocked—brings into a religion bound by the strictness of rules, not only a relief for pent-up energies, but a refreshment based on a return to older, and otherwise disguised, rites of fertility and "creation."

When a religion begins to lose health, it is always the releasing rites which are the first to disappear. The threatened organization puts increasing pressure upon rituals of *atonement,* and begins actively to persecute "the heretic." The ideas of the Sublime and the Numinous dwindle into superstitions ever proliferating into smaller details. Meanwhile, the dammed-up energies of "the faithful," once provided for by the ritually controlled "festival," break out in a persecutory manner toward any activity which seems to duplicate "the festival." The "myth" begins to float freely in the culture into which it has been loosed. It turns up in unexpected places—not only in literature and art, but in the general ethos of the society. And it is always "Hell" which breaks loose, as "Heaven" fades out. The magic which religion straitens and controls for its own purposes; the "will" that religion tames; the fear and guilt which religious practice resolves and accommodates—all these escape into "the profane." The magician and sorcerer (who "wish to coerce nature, instead of allying themselves with it") take up the priest's power. The individual conscience, meanwhile, is asked to bear the full weight of the individual's transgressions.

The dispossessed festival and the fertility rites now become obsessions. Malice and envy walk freely abroad. No force is available to confront Evil but more Evil. It is the Time of Demons, as well as of new—unrecognized —"mythmaking" power.

The witch and the warlock stand as twin "mythical" figures at the beginning of the modern world. A "white-witch" Jeanne d'Arc is burned at the stake in 1431; but it is the figure of her comrade-in-arms, Gilles de Rais— the child-killing "Bluebeard"—that continues to fascinate the popular mind. And soon the terror and fascinated dread of sorcery and witchcraft is codified and fixed in the *Malleus Maleficarum* (1486 or a little later): a work which "spread widely and became for centuries the great formulation of the Catholic attack on sorcery." And now the figures of the witch and the heretic merge. The repetitive pattern of the witch-coven rituals is faced by the repetitive pattern of the witch trials. When, late in the seventeenth century, after prolonged and multiplied horror, the belief in witchcraft died out, it was more from pure exhaustion than because of the light of reason newly shed upon it. The last English witchcraft trials occur in 1717; the last Scottish trial in 1722; and finally we hear Tam O'Shanter's healthy drunken laughter as he watches the still-feared witch revels "through the Gothic window in the ruins of Kirk-Alloway."

Lines of origin of the witch myth reach back to the Old Testament and the Greek and Roman worlds; yet there is little doubt that its later European manifestations were rooted in the post-medieval breakdown of religion. The persecutions in England, for example, reached their height after Elizabeth. It is when a myth of this kind seizes the imagination, and affords an outlet for the passions of a whole society, that dangerous things happen. "Historic and social facts" then cease to be "the envelope in which the myth lies" and become instead the bases of power on which it feeds.

At the heart of an "age of reason," look for a counter-development of irrationality. It is interesting to consider the character and career of John Wesley in this connection. Wesley's life roughly coincided with the years of the eighteenth century. He succeeded in channeling the religious "enthusiasm" present in England since the Reformation, in one form and degree of intensity or another, into a compelling "personal" religious movement: the Methodist Revival. This "great, practical religious manifestation" was considered by Leslie Stephen to be the most important event of the eighteenth century in England. Methodism took into account the deprivations, spiritual and material, of the English lower classes. It gave them an outlet, in the revival meeting, for their emotions; and, if not a ritual, at least a new kind of permitted license. This, too, was the great age of the English hymn. Wesley, a practical man and a great organizer, was, on one side, according to the records, a witch-hunter *manqué*. "A firm believer in ghosts and apparitions," he was opposed to the repeal of the witchcraft statutes (1735) and he wrote, when over eighty, an account of the haunting of his father's Parsonage at Epworth by a "noisy ghost," or *poltergeist,* ascribing these peculiar disturbances to witchcraft. He thus sums up, as a transitional figure, many of the floating myths of a transitional age.

"The word *enthusiasm* was anathema to the polite in the eighteenth century." The English upper classes were totally immune to the revivalism of the poor. Yet from the middle of the century through Napoleonic times the class which, in Gibbon and Hume, had thrown up extreme examples of "the skeptic and infidel" was swept into an "enthusiasm" of its own—an interest which became a mania: the passion for "Gothic" and particularly for the "Gothic romances." The "graveyard poets" opened the path for Bishop Hurd's *Letters on Chivalry and Romance* (1762) and Walpole's *Castle of Otranto* (1764). At the end of the century the flood of Gothic novels was in full spate. The preoccupation of these productions with the "trappings" of an outlawed Catholic ritual was marked. The cloister, abbots, monks, nuns, friars, convents, priories, and anchorite's retreat crowded out other wild and gloomy preoccupations, such as bandits, robbers, and spectres. *The Confessor, The Haunted Priory, The Horror of Oakendale Abbey, The Hermit's Cave, The Children of the Abbey,* and the tremendously successful *The Monk,* by Matthew Gregory Lewis; ruins, underground passages, midnight—all these expressed "the triumph of chaos versus order" in the fiction of the period.

The thoroughness with which the Gothic romance— in a time when the feeling against superstition ran high and anti-Papist riots broke loose—canvassed every smallest detail of a former religiously-based age, indicates that some life-giving forces had been omitted from "enlightenment." The imagination alone knew what had been lost. From the ruined halls, the broken monastery arches, the toppling and devastated churches, a life-giving breath of hell arose, and the reasonable man turned again and again to his brother, the fallen angel and the proud fiend.

"The liberal ideal," says Croce in his *History of Europe in the Nineteenth Century,* "contains what is essential and intrinsic in every religion: a concept of reality and an ethic that conforms to this concept. It excludes the mythological element, which constitutes only *a secondary differentiation between religion and philosophy.* The concept of reality and the conforming ethics of liberalism are generated . . . by modern thought, dialectical and historical. Nothing more was needed to give them a religious character, since personifications, myths, legends, dogmas, rites, propitiations, expiations, priestly classes, pontifical robes and the like *do not belong to the intrinsic* [italics mine]. . . . But the religion of liberalism showed itself to be essentially religious in its forms and institutions, and, since it was born, and not made, was no cold and deliberate device."

Let us oppose to this rather shallow misconception of the nature of "liberalism" and the modern worthlessness of the myth, a passage by Jung (*Psychology and Religion,* 1938): "In the last two thousand years we find the Christian Church assuming a mediating and protective function between 'supernatural' influences, and man. Protestantism, having pulled away many a wall that had been carefully erected by the Church, began immediately to experience the disintegrating and schismatic effect of individual revelation. . . . As soon as the dogmatic fence was broken down and as soon as ritual lost its efficiency, man was confronted with an inner experience, without the protection and guidance of a dogma and a ritual which are the unparalleled quintessence of Christian as well as of pagan religious experience. . . ."

"The hero as implicated in mythical situations is he who finds a solution: an upshot, an issue, fortunate or unfortunate. For the individual suffers above all from not being able to get out from the conflict of which he is the prey." The role of active hero comes to a point of stasis in Hamlet. The chosen breaker of the taboo is now baffled by the taboo. Beyond Hamlet, Faust begins a new role, a role which, in the modern "liberal" world, has become usual and "archetypal." Faust acts; but he must be split in order to act. "In Faust the crisis of modern thought is very clearly reflected," says Croce (with more insight), "when, having shaken off traditional beliefs, it began to perceive the emptiness of the rationalistic philosophy which had taken their place. . . . Two souls dwell in Faust, and the one wishes to separate itself from the other. His condition is the condition of a sick man."

A refinement of this splitting of the hero's "soul" occurs when the opposing forces begin a grim action of flight on the part of one, and pursuit on the part of the other. This theme is as old as the myth of Orestes. But from the beginning of the nineteenth century to our own day, this pattern begins to absorb other myths in great variety. And as the modern myth becomes less "repulsive" in detail, it becomes increasingly ambiguous, and weighted with both guilt and fear. Caleb Williams, in Godwin's cautionary tale, is *pursued by the murderer*. The shift in roles between Jean Valjean and Javert (who finally is pursuer or pursued; who at last is hero or hunted?) fixes a symptomatic situation from which the modern mind does not seem able to escape.

Society has been seen ostensibly to move in one direction toward certain "ideals" and goals, when actually it was unconsciously being drawn in a totally opposite direction. The birth of a new myth lets free new springs of energy. "The passions are good": this was the truth, spoken in "the language of Satan," that the nineteenth century, through the ferment of the Romantic Movement, was finally forced to learn. For the myth is never completely contemporaneous. As we have seen, it can regress, in order to gather up suppressed material needed for new life. It is also supremely capable of shooting ahead. It may point toward the region wherein some enlargement of the human consciousness is about to occur. Even the "Gothic" exploration of the "night-side of Nature" and the Romantic emphasis upon an (at the time) outmoded demonic, fatal, "insatiable" hero, pointed inexorably to unconscious complexities and needs which only a later century was equipped to face, and find analytical means to explain and resolve.

It is now mainly to literature and art that we must look for clues to the unconscious processes. Does our need for "the numinous"—"the fearful, the uncanny, the dauntingly 'other'"—become fixed, and, as it were, trapped, in our crime novels and "murder" stories? "It is curious," says a contemporary observer, "how the great Victorian writers moved instinctively toward a tale of scandal and spiritual corruption. . . . The preoccupation grows stronger as the great bourgeois period becomes self-confident." Compared with the richness, fullness and solidity of the Romantic and the Victorian imaginative productions, we are currently presented with dryness, thinness, fixity, and attenuation. Where is the valuable and revivifying darkness in the glaring seashores, the empty horizons of Chirico, Dali, and the Surrealists? Nature is dead; we are pushed to an extreme verge of the physical and spiritual world, our only companions a litter of half-human furniture, of wrecked bare forms, of amorphous abstractions.

By attending with intense and detached interest to what the imagination (at all levels) presents to us, we may hope to catch at times a hint concerning the myth that is forming at the heart of our world. The hero, for example, reaches crucial modern expression in Kafka. *The Castle* and *The Trial* show to us a nearly unbearable extreme of powerlessness in the face of the unknown. Here everything "means something"; we share the obsessive suspicions of the insane; everything whispers, cunningly cajoles, and promises hollowly; accuses and waits. In "crime novels" we are continually confronted with the "victim." Are we building up a symbolical kind of *printed* bloodless shedding of blood (a sacrifice being defined as "the giving of life to promote and preserve life, to establish union between the individual and the unseen forces that surround him")? What quiver of meaning, present and future, stirs in the hunting and "detecting" malice, in the fugitive's panic and guile with which our "popular" (and unpopular) literature is saturated?

Dread, in literature, has now shifted from the outer to the inner scene. Terrible events now take place in the most usual surroundings to the most ordinary people. Here is the suppressed personality as antagonist (in Conan Doyle, John Buchan, and countless others). And from time to time we see the myth, formed and whole, in a piece of fiction whose surface and conscious intention is rational or didactic: a birth-myth in a fantasy concerned with orthodox religion; the "father-found-and-murdered-underground," in a novel on a "social theme." And in Graham Greene we encounter the hero conscious of inner guilt, who draws to himself the outer guilty situations as a magnet draws iron.

Instinctively, "liberal" man has built around himself half-formed ritual, and occasions for vicarious expiations and propitiations. He has turned toward healing mystery and "the shudder."

Das Schaudern ist der Menschheit bester Teil.
Wie auch die Welt ihm das Gefühl verteuere,
Ergriffen fühlt er tief das Ungeheuere.

It is Goethe who speaks these words, to explain the possible virtue inherent in our modern compulsive patterns of panic, terror, and flight.

1 9 4 6

§ *Satire and Sentimentality*

"I write poems for poets and satires or grotesques for wits," says the English poet Robert Graves in an uncompromising short foreword to *Poems, 1938-1945*. "For people in general I write prose and am content that they should be unaware that I do anything else. . . . To write poems for other than poets is wasteful."

Let us allow for some satire and grotesques in Mr. Graves' pronouncement. Modern poets, nagged and harried as they frequently are by critics, often fall into a self-deprecatory manner; they run for cover and mumble apologies and fumble for explanations. Some, however, like Mr. Graves, stand their ground and refuse suggestions that they distrust their gifts, hate their art, and denigrate their colleagues. In the same week that Mr. Graves' book appears, Mr. Norman Rosten, a younger man and an American, reiterates his conviction that poetry for poets is no go. "I do not belong," Mr. Rosten says, on a slip of paper tucked into the review copies of his long narrative poem *The Big Road*, "to that school which holds to the curious belief that poetry is written for poets and should be as difficult and obscure as possible. Poetry should neither exhaust nor confuse, but invigorate and clarify."

Now, it would be easy to place Mr. Graves' and Mr. Rosten's books beside one another and proceed to run one down in terms of the other. Because the two men are working in completely different genres, it is more important to get beneath their dissimilarity of form and aim to what they share in common. And it is more important, in view of their opposed poetic positions, to try to estimate the clarifying and invigorating qualities in each, for the present and for the future.

Mr. Rosten's narrative deals with the building, during the war, of the Alcan Highway, from Dawson Creek to Fairbanks, by forces of United States Army Engineers. "Here in tremendous reading," says the book's jacket blurb, "is a poet's challenge born out of bold yesterday and the roaring techniques of today." The narrative's own technique owes a good deal, let us say at once, to W. H. Auden and T. S. Eliot, two poets; Mr. Rosten may not have written for *them,* but they certainly wrote for *him.* The overwhelming influence is that of radio (sections of the story have been presented over national and armed-forces networks). And how Mr. Rosten loves power! Strong men succeed strong men: Roman empire builders, Spanish conquistadors, American pioneers, and Russian navigators. Power conquers and regenerates; by rough methods alone are slaves transformed into free men. Clean, true-hearted, tender-hearted toughness, which breaks into folk music and psalm-singing from time to time—there's an ideal for you, fit for any radio network at any hour. "All things vanish but the road," says Mr. Rosten, thus summing up the entire contribution made to civilization by the Roman world.

It is fatally easy to make fun of such a tale, and, at this point, one could seriously begin to extoll Graves' exquisite small effects and deplore the splash of Rosten's large ones, to praise Graves' wit and note Rosten's lack of humor, to point out the older man's quiet complexities as opposed to the younger's loud simplicities. But the real difference between the two men, and between their respective works, does not lie in detail; it centers in the large underlying fact that while one is wrapped up in his time, the other is outside it, observing it in a detached and chilling way. Rosten is giving "the public," during a transitional period, what he and that public believe it needs: romantic braggadocio to comfort it (for it is sad), to reassure it (for it is bewildered), and to needle it (for it is exhausted). Graves is merely using a trained ear and eye and a mature set of emotions to note certain striking features in the strange set of circumstances in which he has found himself; to set down in musical language the unusual turns of thought that come, in crisis, into a sardonic mind. Graves uses the sharp edge of satire to cut toward the future through a mass of accretions that belong to the past. History, the facts of which Rosten sentimentalizes with so much vigor, has its distilled truths, and one of these is that satirists alone see through confused, transitional times. It is difficult to hear them—or to believe them, once heard—but they are there, and it is their insight which marks out lines as definitive and lasting as any wilderness road.

1 9 4 6

§ *The Head and the Heart*

It is a good omen that the first book to come through
from France, in translation, after a silence that gripped
that country from the 1940 invasion on, is a piece of literature—and one so fresh and vigorous that it might
have been written by a man in his vigorous prime. It
was written, as a matter of fact, by a man in his early
seventies. André Gide was born in 1869, a date difficult
to credit in this connection. Malcolm Cowley, who has
done an excellent job of translation with these nineteen
dialogues, two short essays, and a brief journal written
at the fall of Tunis, brings out in his introduction to
Imaginary Interviews the presence of certain passages
concealing hidden fire to smoke out treachery. These
passages exist, it is true, and no one can bring off such
subtleties with the same ease and *brio* as Gide. At the
same time, it would be a mistake to take this book as a
piece of writing whose value lies solely in its hidden
polemic. The remarkable thing about it is its openness.
By comparison, much of the writing to which we have

been accustomed in an uncensored American literature, these last heavy years, seems closed and stifling. It is the final answer to those opponents of Gide—and how numerous and vocal they once were—who prophesied for him final sterility. It is the final proof that his "Christianity without dogma," his belief in harmony and joy, his determined belief in individuality, had firm bases. It is also a proof, as Cowley says, that a wholehearted devotion to the literary art may in itself constitute political action. The *Interviews* appeared regularly from November, 1941, to the spring of 1942 in the literary supplement of *Le Figaro*, one outlet for serious writers in the unoccupied zone.

The works of André Gide have been presented to American readers in the most haphazard way. *The Counterfeiters* came out rather promptly after its French publication; but detached completely from Gide's career as a whole, it could not but puzzle many readers. *Si le grain ne meurt . . .* , the key book to Gide and one of literature's great confessions, appeared in its first French public edition in 1924; it was published here in an expensive limited edition (*If It Die*) in 1935. The two lives of Gide in English to which Mr. Cowley refers in his preface are valuable, but nothing is so valuable as reading Gide himself, from beginning to end, in his proper order. He has, from the first, possessed the rare faculty of being able to make more or less disguised autobiographical material a continuing basis for his writing. This accomplishment—for autobiography is the most dangerous, and can be the dullest, material in the world—proves an actual underlying development. His vivid grasp of his own experience has been put into the service, moreover, of his moral ideas.

This man, whom readers without French will have to

piece together from the scattered books available to them—they have his *Dostoevski,* his African travel notes, his books on Russia, and *The Counterfeiters,* as well as certain short pieces of prose—became a center of influence only after 1918. He had purposely kept his early productions small and varied, in what his opponents considered a perversely baffling manner. His opponents were intelligent and formidable. To Catholics especially he came to represent corruption and secret-keeping: the result of a truly demoniac possession. What was manifesting itself in Gide was showing up in several isolated individuals at the time—Freud, Havelock Ellis, Shaw. The fact of the unconscious was breaking through European thought. Gide's basic tenets, upon which he acted with, to others, an infuriating tenacity, were actually rather simple. Combining in himself opposing elements of the most irreconcilable kind—a Protestant upbringing and a passionate nature the sexual organization of which differed from the "normal"—he early broke, through action, from the illness and misery imposed upon him by seemingly implacable forces. He refused to continue the endless and sterile struggle "against a conformity to which all nature was in contradiction." "It dawned upon me at last that this discordant duality might be resolved into harmony. And then I saw that harmony must be my supreme object, and the endeavor to acquire it the express reason of my life." Many years later he repeats his conviction—the conviction that defeated, for him, the anxiety which so afflicts modern man: "When I made the discovery that joy was rarer and more difficult and more beautiful than sadness, joy became for me not only (which it is) a natural need but even more a moral obligation."

In order to give his "dangerous thoughts" some kind

of circulation in the heavy pre-1914 world in which he found himself, Gide resorted to ruses. He wrote his books under the protection of the myth. It is difficult fully to understand Gide without a knowledge of these small early works. They are filled with a diffused wit, gaiety, and freedom. They brought into French literature something completely opposed to the heavy work of Barrès—in its own way "mythical." They gave release from deadly compromise and pervasive hidden or open pressure. They "decompressed," in the phrase of one modern French critic.

It is this faculty for "decompression" which gives life and vigor to everything Gide writes. It is present in his criticism—in France the criticism which comes nearest to the warm humanism of Montaigne. It is a releasing touch that operates under the cool and pure classic style that Gide has made flexible, while keeping about it "an odor both resinous and dry." Under this serene surface exists an intellectual and emotional organization fully conscious of "the winds from the abyss." Gide has never allowed his need for reconciliation to blind or deafen him to the terrible contradictions of life, to the often insane tensions functioning in the human spirit. It is the appreciation of the force of these terrors that has drawn him to Dostoevski, Blake, Flaubert, and Shakespeare. He believes in the validity of the extreme, of the sincere, of intense limitation.

The crucial importance of Gide's thought at present is that he has discovered, and long acted upon, the fact of each man's personal responsibility for evil.

What a sad need for hatred [he wrote in his *Journal* in 1937] I see on all sides today! . . . the need to oppose all that should be understood, completed, enriched, united. These conflicts I have felt working in myself, before having come upon them in the outer world. I know them; and by this personal experience I know how one uses oneself up in the struggle. . . . [A day came] when I said: What good does it do? when I began to look, not for struggle and partial triumph, but for accord: to understand that the more separate and different are the parts composing this accord, the richer the harmony. And in the same way in a state—it is a somber kind of Utopia, this dream of smashing one part by another: this dream of a totalitarian state where the subjugated minorities cannot make themselves heard: or, what is worse, where each and all think the same. It cannot be a question of harmony when the choir sings in unison.

It is inevitable that this translation of *Interviews imaginaires* should bear some marks of being printed for an immediate use; of being enlisted to a hard-hitting purpose, with a special target in view. This sharp direction of appeal has resulted in one or two faults. The first translation into English of a set of Gide's essays should be more fully annotated. Some footnotes exist, but not enough. Such annotation would tie these essays firmly into a background of reference, as well as stand as a reassurance that the time will come when literature will again move freely over long open spaces, without fear of traps or ambushes.

The sly, the sinuous, the demoniac Gide: can his opponents find him in this book? I do not think so, any more than his admirers can find an infallible guide; for Gide can make mistakes in literary judgment. The important thing is that they are never mistakes of sympathy. He can be wrong about American writers, but for interesting reasons. And we search in vain for the stiff old figure, loaded with years and evil—the end his enemies prophesied for Gide long since. This man who, during the fighting in Tunis, walks the streets happy in the radiant spring weather, who falls into a happy conversation concerning the respective merits of George and Rilke with the first British staff officer he meets, who lies at night with his window open on "a field of stars," is an aged man. It is impossible to remember this as we read him. His trust in life has not been an empty hope; he is free; and he hands an unambiguous key to freedom to us all.

1 9 4 4

2

The publication of this first of a projected three-volume American translation of Gide's *Journal: 1889-1939* should mark a fresh start, rather than a continuation, of Gide's reputation in the United States. The *Journals* draw Gide's other works into focus; but do many people now read the scattered American translations of Gide? The latest work published in America was Malcolm Cowley's translation of *Interviews imaginaires,* in 1944.

The *Journals* provide a firm basis for judgments of Gide's character and place in letters. For they are the central pier upon which the imposing edifice of his work is built. Gide from the beginning of his career has been a diarist. The regular, often daily record of thought and event has provided him with a form at once exigent and large, wherein his desire for stability as well as for movement and change, his detailed inquisitiveness as well as his wider curiosity, could be satisfied. Bored with the "big machines" of French literary form, incapable of filling-in conventional backgrounds or of inventing stock figures, wary of technical tricks not based on actual emotion, happy to change his mind concerning the worth and direction of his material while that material was still in the process of composition, Gide has always preferred the short form, where effects can be brought off with full spontaneity, before the impelling emotion is exhausted.

Gide's most unfriendly critics have never been able to attack him in respect to his style. The present volume of the *Journals* shows us that style in the making, from the days when the young Symbolist had not yet decided to write "without metaphors," to 1913, when the accomplished man of letters had evolved a manner of writing so clear and flexible that it was a matter of pride to himself and of emulation to his disciples. The youthful admirer of Chateaubriand has "sharpened his beak" upon Stendhal. The *Journals* soon come to be based upon sincerity of feeling. In this way they never become a mere record of events. Neither do they fall into the errors and *longueurs* of the *journal intime,* since Gide effectually skirts the endless introspective self-indulgences of the intimate diarist. Experience and interest continually enliven the record: books read, music played (Gide is an "intellectual" who can use his hands with precision and speed), journeys undertaken, gardens planted, friends met, meals eaten, daylight walks and midnight prowls described, methods of work delineated with the same care as the most obscure of passing moods, the weather, and the scenery enjoyed. Gide's advance into maturity is by no means in a straight line, without forced detours or periods of circuitous progress. But he soon found his pace and his road. He writes, in 1905: "I escaped early from that world in which, to appear proper, I had to watch myself too closely."

Gide's courageous moral stand, which had so much

influence on the post-1918 generation, is not indicated very clearly here: he has written his "confessions" elsewhere. The first exposition of his moral theories appeared in *Les Nourritures terrestres* in 1897, in the last decade of the nineteenth century, at a time when, in French intellectual life, all that was not "determinist" or "finalist" was suspect. A rigid positivism had penetrated French thought to an excessive degree. The only escape for "sensitive souls" was into the refuge of an equally strict and confining religious dogma. In this situation, through bitter personal suffering, after a stay in North Africa and a friendship with Wilde, Gide dared to reconcile irreconcilables. He brought emotion over into the moral realm, declaring the experiences of the flesh to be of equal value to those of the mind and the spirit; and he affirmed that spiritual values could operate in a life-giving manner outside the rituals of religion. Always claiming a basic Christianity, he began his meditations on the figure of a Savior who stood for man's joy rather than for man's tragic and deforming frustration.

As the world of affairs begins to claim more of his attention, Gide meets people and events head-on; he does not take anyone's opinion as his own; he analyzes character and motive with a penetrating combination of intuition and acumen. His dislike of virtuosity in art parallels his impatience with the deviousness and pretentiousness of human beings. The tension between the oppositions within himself continues; perfect balance between impulse and scruple, asceticism and sensuality is never entirely achieved. There are breakdowns, nervous crises, and capitulations, as well as spiritual and physical convalescences and reanimations. By keeping the poles of the tension clear, however, Gide escapes most of the enticements of self-deception. His life and relationships must be kept, so far as possible, vital and necessitous. All must be natural in the area of the senses while at the same time the will must function with a kind of "supple obstinacy." Gide's dealings with his colleagues and friends never lack an edge of critical sharpness; but shows of ambition, jealousy, rancor, and spite never occur, and small gossip and downright malice are relatively rare. His chief desire is to have friends who "exist behind and beyond what [they] reveal to us." He does not neglect "the insulted and injured."

Take upon oneself as much humanity as possible. That is the correct formula . . . Absence of sympathy equals lack of imagination. The most gifted natures are perhaps the most trembling . . . As soon as an emotion decreases, the pen should stop; when it continues to run on just the same —and it runs on all the more easily—writing becomes detestable . . . The wonderful thing on this earth is that we are forced to feel more than to think.

These are the words of a man and an artist who has detached himself from killing and "glacial" abstractions and moved into a world where the modern divided spirit is at least partially healed, where there are provable and classic linkages between the timeless and the time-bound.

Nothing has been spared—neither good-quality large paper nor an intelligent and meticulous editor—to make this American edition, to be complete by 1950, impressive. The French *Pleiade* edition (1939 and 1940) on which it is based still retains a peculiar charm, however. Complete in one volume, printed on thin paper, its 1,352 pages compactly yet flexibly bound, this French edition resembles some object delightful and usable: a

convenient missile, let us say, against "the Philistine";
or a concentrated form of nourishment, on which one
could maintain life over a long period.

                                                      1 9 4 7

3

The reader who advances into the second volume of
Gide's *Journals* in English translation can be sure of a
very nearly complete record of sincerity on all levels.
The style takes its tone of truth from the material; the
material is clarified by the style. In spite of our roman-
ticisms the classic ring of absolute sincerity in writing is
happily recognized by modern ears. The broad, generalized biographical work, as well as the emotional "confession," now leaves us more or less unmoved. We can
easily detect that false smoothness and serenity which
echoes a "maturity" achieved through the repression of
a whole side of the personality. We also suspect, as Gide
points out, the finicky style, as in Amiel, or the self-
satisfied style, as in the Goncourts. Gide's *Journals* are
one biographical work of our period where modern
"truths" are discovered, and then openly presented in a
manner equal to their complex demands.

The second part of the *Journals* also disproves the as-
sertion of Gide's enemies that he is always ready with a
specious formula that might at any moment be trans-
posed into its opposite. We see only too clearly in the
entries between 1914 and 1917 how Gide, harassed by
the paradoxes of his own nature, as well as by the historical situation in which he found himself, and the object of critical attacks from all sides, was often compelled

to improvise some way of life, and some means of spiritual survival, from day to day. It is one of the virtues of the *Journals* that these desperate improvisations have not been deleted from it. Gide often allows himself to sound like a lost soul—or like an ordinary human being whose control is snapping and whose will is petrified.

The search for equilibrium in a highly organized modern man, the theme which runs through the long work, is particularly apparent in this second section. Gide, at the beginning of the 1914-18 war, was able to envisage his own worth and the moral and aesthetic tasks which lay before him, but only intermittently and in a partial way. He was forty-five, an age when the spiritual nature is impelled toward some comfortable orthodoxy, when the physical being begins to lose energy, and when the creative mind is assailed by fears of depletion and dryness. It is a period, moreover, when manias and compulsions may seize hold of the personality and force its acts into some repetitive pattern. It is an age when one must learn patience, without losing drive. "I cling desperately to this notebook; it is part of my patience; it keeps me from going under" (February 1916).

The *Journals* at this time of doubt and loss become confused and begin to stammer. Long periods are filled with entries that are empty and dull. Gide finally consents to their mediocrity. He also consents to any diversion which will give him a little peace; piano practice, reading and translating, pets, botany, household tasks, and gardening. This is a time of the sharpest analysis of people. Whatever "life offers must be scrutinized with care"; and Bourget, Cocteau, Valéry, Proust, Maritain, alive and in the flesh, are so examined along with crowds of the nonillustrious. We now recognize in these activities the attempts at "therapy" of a man whose more minatory side has taken the upper hand, and who is convinced that part of his nature is "abominable." Later Gide could write: "Arrogance and boredom are the two most authentic products of hell. I have done everything to defend myself against them and have not always succeeded in keeping them at a distance. They are the two great provinces of romanticism."

Gide finally made two decisions, with what difficulty the contemporary entries show. First, he rejected any sort of orthodox religion, in spite of his belief in God and the proselytizing efforts of his converted friends. Second, he decided to put down his "childhood recollections," in the first person singular, with as much frankness as possible. He also decided that the time had come to publish his study of the place and importance of homosexuality (*Corydon*) in a signed commercial edition. His dissatisfaction with his work continues (". . . it all lacks tremor, elasticity, and richness . . ."); but soon the days of real desperation are over, even though the necessity for constant self-discipline continues. "I must go right on even if I have to write in the margin: to be re-written." By 1917 Gide has made himself capable again of love and joy. The periods "when my mind [is] much concerned with ridiculous anxieties that fatigue and dim it" lessen and then almost totally disappear.

The Gide who in 1921 begins *The Counterfeiters* has come into that state of equipoise where original, because unfrightened, assessments of human nature and morals can be made. *The Counterfeiters,* published in 1926, begins where most novels leave off. The conventional theme of adultery becomes only an ironic detail in this survey of the neglected sides of human existence: the tragedy of senility, the sadism of childhood, the latent or real criminality of adolescence, the irresponsibility of the romantic. By 1927 all Gide's secrets were out. The man who had for a long time projected his ideas in the form of parables was now able to step forward with open statements.

This volume ends with Gide convinced, as one of his best critics has said, "that evil is a force which can become a factor of progress"; that "the real value is hardly ever the apparent value"; that "life destroys individuals, but, on the other hand, individuals bungle life." At fifty-eight Gide tells us that self-satisfaction on the anxiety level is both stupid and a waste of time. There is a world elsewhere. If he has not formulated the approaches to that world in neat metaphysical language—which he abhors—he has allowed us to watch the full spectacle of himself living them through.

1 9 4 8

§ Baudelaire Revisited

A new translation, by Geoffrey Wagner, of a selection of Baudelaire's poetry, called *Flowers of Evil,* has recently appeared. Enid Starkie, the English Baudelaire scholar, contributes an excellent short introduction to the volume. But the disparity in quality between Miss Starkie's prose and Mr. Wagner's verse is so great that it is a puzzle how the two came together into book form. Granted that certain insuperable obstacles to a feasible translation of Baudelaire into any language exist, it is still a disappointment to find Mr. Wagner making the most elementary blunders in choice, in tone, and in detail. The volume is, moreover, oddly lacking in the ordinary aids to the reader; it has no pagination, no table of contents, no notes, and no index.

Baudelaire's vocabulary and atmosphere constitute, without question, problems for translators. The vocabulary is filled with those splendid French abstract nouns and substantives that tend to come through into English sounding rather silly, and the atmosphere, particularly that of his early work, is rather repellent to Anglo-Saxon taste. It is the atmosphere of French Second-Empire luxury, morbidity, and eroticism. Baudelaire was a master of a whole rhetorical apparatus for evoking effects of horror and lubricity. The workings of this stylistic machine are now outmoded. And nothing is more tiresome than the reiterated subject—so usual in the early Baudelaire—of woman as puppet, as sinister idol of the alcove, or as erotic mannequin. Translators are attracted, however, to Baudelaire's more overheated and dated productions, and Mr. Wagner, no less than Arthur Symons and other searchers in the field, has chosen proportionately more poems from this side of Baudelaire's work than from any other. Yet, as Miss Starkie points out, the figure of Baudelaire as dandy and decadent has steadily diminished in this present century, to be replaced by the concept of a man whose insights were profound and valuable for a complex set of reasons. We now recognize Baudelaire as the first poet who saw through the overweening pretensions of his time. He stripped man's nature to its essentials, and he discovered, in an era when his contemporaries were still occupied with "rationalism" or with "romance," urban mankind's bitter loneliness and spiritual isolation. Baudelaire, as T. S. Eliot has said, learned everything for himself. He went from the confines of his early physical excesses into the streets of Paris; he drew portraits of the poor, the debauched, the senile, the obsessed, and the mad in a manner as uncompromising as Daumier's. He depicted the houses, the rooms, the roofs, the shuttered windows, and the chimney pots, and beyond this he recreated the look and the feeling of those times of day and of those turns of the seasons when the city's sadness is, as it were, distilled and the full, cold mystery of existence leaks through into our consciousness. These poems have the power to hit us like a blow. They are scattered through his work, and the beginner in Baudelaire needs guides to them. Mr. Wagner, in making his choices, has merely gone through the collected work and picked out a poem here and there, seemingly at random. The thirty-eight selections in this volume represent less than a quarter of Baudelaire's poetic output. To appropriate the title *Flowers of Evil* for it seems odd to anyone who remembers Baudelaire's careful sense of arrangement—"the inner architecture"—in his *Fleurs du Mal,* in both its editions published during his lifetime. Miss Starkie's biographical summary and her short but penetrating analysis of the poet's present place in French letters, combined with the French texts (here included) of the poems, give this compilation a certain value, but the day when Baudelaire's translators match his critics in sensitiveness and understanding is yet to come.

1 9 4 7

§ *The Heart and the Lyre*

The record of the verse written by women in the United States is remarkably full, for a variety of reasons. In the first place, the country became an independent republic, well equipped with printing presses and paper, during the period when American women began to write in earnest. Then, a new and eager periodical and newspaper audience, with the sort of pioneering background which holds women in high esteem, awaited bits of feminine sentiment and moralizing dressed up in meter and rhyme. Finally, the critical standard of the country remained for a long time rather lax and easygoing. A great mass of verse, good, bad, and indifferent, therefore managed to get published. Through this prolific feminine production we can trace, with much accuracy, every slight shift in American literary fashion, as well as the larger changes of an emotional and moral kind. An examination of the rise and development of female poetic talent over a period of more than one hundred and fifty years in a society which, on the whole, encouraged that talent to function freely and in the open, brings to light various truths concerning the worth and scope of women's poetic gifts.

Before we survey the interesting, colorful, and frequently comic array of American women "poetesses" from Lydia Huntley Sigourney (1791-1865) through the youngest feminine contemporaries, let us look at some of the assumptions and prejudices that have long lodged in people's minds on the subject of women as poets. One rather hoary idea is that women put emotion before form and are likely to be indifferent technicians. Do they not usually, as well, imitate closely the poetic productions of men? A third dark suspicion concerning women's poetic powers troubled even the highly intelligent and ardently feminist mind of Virginia Woolf. Mrs. Woolf, in her delightful series of lectures published in 1929 under the title *A Room of One's Own,* is continually bothered by the thought that in spite of material and moral emancipations women may never write a work of wide and compelling force comparable, for example, to Shakespeare's plays. To exorcise this spectral doubt, Mrs. Woolf canvasses fully the history of woman's difficulties in the role of artist.

Women have always been busy and poor, Mrs. Woolf's argument runs; busy, because they are physically responsible for the production and early care of specimens of the human race; and poor because it seems that men's laws are often framed to keep them in that condition. Lack of education, the tyranny of families, the ridicule of society, as well as lack of independent means, have been factors which, perhaps, kept women from writing epic poems or long poetic plays. Mrs. Woolf gives every credit to the anonymous women who had a hand in composing folk tales, folk songs, adages, proverbs, and nursery rhymes (for it is, after all, Mother Goose, and *Ma Mère l'Oie*). And she is happy to note that, when new freedoms arrived in Europe and England at the end of the eighteenth century, women novelists, at least, appeared in numbers and with brilliance. But what of Shakespeare's supposititious sister—ignorant, penniless, and fearful of masculine jeers, had she tried to carve out a career for herself in the sixteenth century? It is at this point in her argument that Mrs. Woolf begins to stumble against the doubt that no woman is ever going to write a great poetic tragedy in five acts. Perhaps after a hundred years or so this goal will be realized, if the creative woman is given five hundred pounds per annum and, behind a door with a lock on it, a room of her own.

It was a little old-fashioned even in 1929 for Mrs. Woolf to choose a five-act poetic play as the final test of a woman poet's powers. Her vision was somewhat clouded by an Anglo-Saxon literary point of view. Why should women, past, present, or future, remain fixed in the determination to out-Shakespeare Shakespeare? Can it be that there is no basic reason for women to excel in the art of poetry by producing the same sort of poetic structures as men? Men, as a matter of fact, stayed with the five-act poetic tragedy far too long. Perhaps women have more sense than to linger over an obsessing form of this kind.

We turn to the full and complete annals of American women poets hoping that we may discover facts that will lead to a new estimate of the poetic gift in women, as well as hints about its present and future direction. The first women versifiers who appear on the American scene were, it must be confessed, unendowed, grim, pious, and lachrymose. Mrs. Sigourney was provincial and naive enough to glory in two titles: the "American

Hemans" and the "Sweet Singer of Hartford." She reigned, however, over a long period as the head of American female letters—from shortly after Washington's second term as president until just after the death of Lincoln, to be exact. She was fluent, industrious, and rather pushing; but she managed to put feminine verse-writing on a paying basis, and give it prestige; even Poe did not quite dare to handle her work too roughly. She gave simple men and women along the eastern seaboard and in the backwoods of the West something to be proud of; it is pleasant for a young nation to have a vocal tutelary goddess.

During Mrs. Sigourney's lifetime the choir of female singers enlarged. Soon a series of anthologies began to appear, exclusively devoted to "songstresses." *The Ladies' Wreath* (1837), edited by Mrs. Sarah Josepha Hale, who also edited *Godey's Lady's Book,* was the first of these. Others followed; and by 1849 Rufus Griswold was able to make good profits with his collection entitled *The Female Poets of America.* This collection went through several editions and, after Griswold's death, turned up in the seventies with a new editor. We are now in a new world. The more depressing ante-bellum aspects of female piety and melancholy have worn off, and we are presented with the spectacle of women becoming ever more ardent and airy. The ardors of Poe's women friends, Fanny Osgood and Mrs. Whitman, are now surpassed by their successors. When we come to Edmund Clarence Stedman's *An American Anthology* (1900), an often unbroken phalanx of women with three (and sometimes four) invincibly Yankee names advances down the table of contents, and their work is now startlingly filled with evidence of culture, with whimsicality, self-preening, and affectation.

But although women's literary manners and, it would seem, their affections became ever more wayward and free, their grasp upon basic conventions remained firm. Even the Wisconsin farm girl, Ella Wheeler, who spiced her stanzas with hints of sin in *Poems of Passion* (1883) soon quiets down into marriage and respectability with a Mr. Wilcox. The list of these late-nineteenth-century women in Stedman, with their multiple names printed in chaste Gothic type, tends to become a blur. But if we search carefully for even the smallest sincerity and talent, personalities begin to emerge. Alice and Phoebe Cary; Celia Thaxter; the mill girl, Lucy Larcom, protégée of Whittier; Julia Ward Howe; Emma Lazarus, who was Jewish, and Louise Imogen Guiney, who was an "Irish Catholic"; Lizette Woodworth Reese of Baltimore and Harriet Monroe of Chicago; and, farther back, crowded in with Mrs. Spofford, Mrs. Moulton, Thomas Bailey Aldrich, Joaquin Miller, and Edward Rowland Sill, we come upon an unpretentious name, easily overlooked, of a woman born in 1830 and dead in 1886: Emily Dickinson. Emily Dickinson represents the final flowering of a long Puritan tradition. Her genius has a hard, bitter, but real kind of civilization behind it; women poets share with men the need for some sort of civilized ground from which to draw sustenance. But it is apparently more difficult for women to throw off the more superficial fashions of any society in which they find themselves. The earlier history of women poets in America should stand as a warning to modern young women of talent. The special virtues of women are clear, in the same record. Women are forced to become adult. They must soon abandon sustained play, in art or life. They are not good at abstractions and their sense of structure is not large; but they often have the direct courage to be themselves. They are practical, intense, and (usually) both generous and magnanimous. They often have a true contemplative gift; and they are natural singers. They are capable of originality and breadth of emotional and intellectual reference as soon as their background opens to any breadth and variety. They are often forced to waste their powers in an inadequate milieu, in social improvisation; to tack back and forth between revolt and conservatism. Far from imitating men to an untoward degree, they often experiment boldly with form and language. Early in the twentieth century, Gertrude Stein, working indefatigably and alone, begins to examine words with the detached interest of the scientist and arrange them in abstract patterns. A little later H. D. gives back to Greek themes some of the pure severity of Greek poetry in the original. Marianne Moore applies a naturalist's eye to objects of art and of nature, describing "with an extraordinary magnificence of phraseology" unlooked-for combinations and harmonies between matter and the spirit. These women have had their male, as well as their female, followers.

Young women writing poetry at present are likely to consider the figure of the woman poet as romantic rebel rather ridiculous and outmoded. The youngest generation of women poets is, in fact, moving toward an imitation of certain masculine "trends" in contemporary poetry. They are imitating, moreover, the work of male verbalizers and poetic logicians, rather than the work of men who have carried through, out of a profound urgency, major poetic investigations; there are few feminine disciples of either Eliot or Auden, in these poets' later phases. Even the greatly gifted Elizabeth Bishop, whose first book recently appeared, places emphasis more upon anecdote than upon ardor. The fear of some regression into typical romantic attitudes is, at present, operating upon feminine talent; and this is not a wholly healthy impulse, for it negates too strongly a living and valuable side of woman's character. In women, more than in men, the intensity of their emotions is the key to the treasures of their spirit. The cluster of women lyric poets that appeared on the American scene just before and after 1918 restored genuine and frank feeling to a literary situation which had become genteel, artificial, and dry. Sara Teasdale's later verse; the best of Edna Millay's early rebellious songs and meditations; Elinor Wylie's ability to fuse thought and passion into the most admirable and complex forms; the sensitive, intellectual poetry of Léonie Adams—all these poetic productions helped to resolve hampering attitudes of the period.

The great importance of keeping the emotional channels of a literature open has frequently been overlooked. The need of the refreshment and the restitution of feeling, in all its warmth and depth, has never been more apparent than it is today, when cruelty and fright often seem about to overwhelm man and his world. For women to abandon their contact with, and their expression of, deep and powerful emotional streams, because of contemporary pressures or mistaken self-consciousness, would result in an impoverishment not only of their own inner resources but of mankind's at large. Certainly it is not a regression to romanticism to remember that women are capable of perfect and poignant song; and that when this song comes through in its high and rare form, the result has always been regarded not only with delight but with a kind of awe. It is a good thing for young women to bring to mind the fact that lost fragments of the work of certain women poets—of Emily Dickinson no less than of the Sappho quoted by Longinus as an example of "the sublime"—are searched for less with the care and eagerness of the scholar looking for bits of shattered human art, than with the hungry eyes of the treasure hunter, looking for some last grain of a destroyed jewel. Though she may never compose an epic or a tragic drama in five acts, the woman poet has her singular role and precious destiny. And, at the moment, in a time lacking in truth and certainty and filled with anguish and despair, no woman should be shamefaced in attempting to give back to the world, through her work, a portion of its lost heart.

1 9 4 7

§ *John Betjeman*

John Betjeman's *Slick But Not Streamlined* brings the reader up against some unexpectedly weighty considerations. Modern poetry, although filled with nostalgia of various kinds and degrees, is notably lacking in pathos. Pathos, it might be said, is an emotion derived from contemporary objects or contemporary experiences; it is not a yearning for the past. Modern poets have so firmly eliminated pathos from their work that the suspicion sometimes arises that they are incapable of experiencing it, that the modern sensibility has become so hardened and abstract that entire areas of emotional response are outside its range. We would not wish, certainly, for a return to the sentimental repining of early and middle Romanticism. Yet this lack of true pathos deprives modern verse of a whole set of emotional effects and reverberations. Betjeman has nevertheless made a serious and emotional contribution to the modern lyric, all the more surprising since every effort has been made by his American publishers to em-

phasize his lighter side. Even W. H. Auden, who has
written an introduction to Betjeman's book, dwells
lengthily on the poet's skill as a satirist and on his "theatrical" manner of presenting things. Satirist and wit
Betjeman surely is, but a special kind of gravity underlies a good deal of his work. Nothing is farther from
pathos than parody, which is Betjeman's manner of
projection, and it is an unexpected experience to find
him now and again pushing parody over into the region
of pure feeling. (Gide observes somewhere in his *Journal* that aesthetic problems that will not yield to a
frontal attack may sometimes be solved by oblique or
outflanking methods.) Betjeman brings off his effects
with the greatest deftness. He is capable of writing in
the most glittering way about British middle-class
mores; he is capable, too, of abruptly stepping into another dimension, where sensibility is all. Suddenly, we
are in the midst of pathos before we realize what response is being demanded of us. Because Betjeman's interests are basically topographical and architectural, he
goes directly toward visible and concrete symbols of
middle-class pretensions and yearnings: churches and
chapels, parsonages, suburbs, provincial gaslit towns and
seaside lodgings, railways, viaducts, factories, tearooms,
and hotels. He involves these various locales and structures in perfect replicas of nineteenth-century verse
forms, not forgetting the hymn. But he matches form to
feeling, rather than the other way around. So, instead
of getting a stream of sly jokes and satirical cuts, we get
poems whose high spirits and sharp observation are continually breaking off to admit the spirit of place and of
character, the sadness of human beings and of things.
The dangers in Betjeman's method are obvious. Some
of his poems hang in a hair's-breadth balance between

the success of sincerity and the failure of smartness. The tone of "The Arrest of Oscar Wilde at the Cadogan Hotel" is not quite a success. On the other hand, "Parliament Hill Fields" (a note of nostalgia, it must be admitted), "Death in Leamington," "Sudden Illness at the Bus-Stop," and the exquisitely satirical "Bristol and Clifton" are perfect examples of how emotion may be smuggled into the modern lyric without restricting its freedom or dulling its finish and point.

1 9 4 7

§ *The Poet Lawrence*

New Directions has done a real service to English and American letters by bringing out, in its "New Classics Series," a small book of D. H. Lawrence's verse, *Selected Poems,* an excellent job of editing by Kenneth Rexroth. Lawrence's poetry has been rather poorly treated by English and American publishers. All the single volumes, both early and late, are out of print, and the collected edition, in two volumes, published in America in 1929, is also unobtainable. It is, therefore, extremely difficult for anyone who has not, as it were, grown up with the poems to get a comprehensive view of Lawrence's poetry, of his development of poetic thought and feeling, or of the progressive refinement of his literary methods. Mr. Rexroth, in his introduction, analyzes Lawrence's purely poetic contribution, a contribution that can now be recognized as one of the most important, in any language, of our time.

The most striking characteristic of Lawrence's poetry, from the beginning to the end of his career, was, as someone has said, its extraordinary power of "intense, direct, personal, mystical apprehension of reality." He began to write poetry in a period when English poets were afraid of approaching Nature in any but the most sentimental and shamefaced way, and when human problems, unless they were of the most naive order, were omitted from verse entirely. Lawrence's early work bears a few marks of the constricting conditions that prevailed at the beginning of his career. In an astonishingly short period of time, however, his burning curiosity and his insatiable taste for the compelling experience had lifted him far out of the ruck of his more timid contemporaries. Rexroth traces this rapid development with great insight. The early poems show the progress of a bewildered young man writing within the scope of "nice" values, whose worth he has not yet learned to suspect; of the "common" young man slicked up to look like a provincial schoolteacher, whose likeness, with a stubborn chin jutting out over a high white collar, we have seen in an early photograph. This conformity disappears when we come upon the tragic poems on his mother's death. In them, he pours out his grief so violently that it almost never again recurs. Thereafter, Lawrence is able to get at reality in his own way. He gets at it by direct contact with, and by sympathy for, Nature. Nature, to Lawrence, comprises more than "birds, beasts, and flowers." It includes the most complex human relationships. Lawrence makes a difficult and complicated marriage, and he writes down the steps of this mature love relationship (many of which had to be taken in the dark, for lack of adequate knowledge in the society around him) in the magnificent poems of "Look! We Have All Come Through!" a title that makes unself-conscious use of the exclamation mark, from which modern taste tends to shy. These poems, written between 1912 and 1917, accomplished in English literature what Gide had accomplished some twenty years earlier in French literature; they affirmed the importance of human joy. "Feel grief," they say, "but give over guilt and anxiety. Only the materialist and madman is afraid of happiness."

Lawrence's insight into the "secrecy" of man and of things grew steadily deeper; because he was continually exploring new fields, he succeeded in keeping the barrier between his unconscious forces and his consciousness extremely thin. European history opened up before him; he reconstituted the ancient Etrurian domain and way of life. He gave us a prophetic vignette of modern Europe in ruins, and he gave us warnings against the "police State" and "spy government everywhere." His technical ease increased. Over two hundred short lyrics, aphorisms, and satires were gathered together in the volume called *Pansies*, published in 1929, the year before his death. In these, Lawrence had advanced so far into a future he saw with the utmost clarity that many of his more sentimental and dogmatic followers fell away from him in a state of shock.

Not enough poems from *Pansies* appear in the present volume. Mr. Rexroth has, however, on the whole done his sampling with a sense of proportion. What is needed, of course, is a complete collection of Lawrence's poetry. The importance of his later work will then stand out. This work, for various reasons, has been not only neglected but maligned. The young English poets who trod hard on Lawrence's heels learned some of their most valuable lessons from it. Lawrence taught them to be sensible, to be at ease, to be good-natured, to be sane.

He taught them that no subject is closed to the poet who
is himself truthful and free:

Give, and it shall be given unto you
   is still the truth about life.

But giving life is not so easy.

It doesn't mean handing it out to some
   mean fool, or letting the living dead eat
   you up.

It means kindling the life quality where it
   was not, even if it's only in the whiteness
   of a washed pocket handkerchief.

1 9 4 8

§ *The Creative Experiment*

The scholar cannot always be trusted to be fair to a poet's outer work or inner aspirations, particularly when scholar and poet are contemporaries. For although the percentage among Ph.D.s (or their equivalent) of those who hate, despise, and distrust imaginative literature is surely small, there is, nevertheless, a large proportion of scholarly critics who would twist and transform the poet's work or intention into something nearer to a doctorate's desire. Condemnation of the poet on rational grounds is fairly common, and learned writers, at their most meddling and obtuse, will even step into the poet's place and rewrite his poem. The poet is, therefore, at times as badly served by the scholar as by the man in the street, and this is a pity, because the scholar, however unimaginative, at least knows history and can remember how crudely poets have been served by their contemporaries in the past, whereas the ordinary citizen, as he recoils from a work of the imagination, believes he does it for the first time and credits himself not only with tremendous common sense but with tremendous originality.

C. M. Bowra, whose new volume of essays concerned with modern poetry is entitled *The Creative Experiment,* is a scholar—Warden of Wadham College, Oxford, since 1938, and Oxford's Professor of Poetry since 1946. The book is a sequel to *The Heritage of Symbolism* (1943), wherein Bowra discussed, with much learning and liberality of approach, the post-Symbolist poets Valéry, Rilke, Aleksandr Blok, and William Butler Yeats. In the new volume, he deals with men whose experiments with form, content, and language belong to a later period—the first half of the twentieth century. Two elements are outstanding in Bowra's treatment of his subjects. In the first place, he is so sympathetic to their aims that he often becomes belligerent about the essential rightness of their methods. In the second place, he is a linguist, with a broad knowledge of European literature in a variety of languages. Because of this breadth of choice, he is non-provincial and fitted to combat the suspicion, widely held in America, that modern poetry is a conspiracy composed entirely of writers who are members of the English-speaking world. The poets whom Bowra here presents as fruitful innovators are Constantine Cavafy, an Alexandrian Greek born in 1868; Guillaume Apollinaire (de Kostrowitsky), of polyglot origin but a Parisian by choice; the Russians Mayakovsky and Boris Pasternak; the Andalusians Garcia Lorca and Rafael Alberti; and T. S. Eliot, British subject but an American by birth.

Bowra understands both the historic and the poetic processes. That action brings on reaction, that a stiffened convention immediately creates the need for the breaching of that convention are the facts that hold true in history as well as in aesthetics. Poetry must continually change, since it is close to the stream of life, which cannot for a moment remain stagnant, and it must change with increasing swiftness, and with a complete disregard for the past, in periods—like our own—of unceasing and shifting pressures. Light alloys have replaced cast iron; people no longer decorate their rooms (except in fun) with copperplate engravings of Landseer's dogs; young ladies no longer play "A Maiden's Prayer" on cottage pianos. Modern art is firmly based on a new sensibility. The aim of modern poetry, as of the other arts of our time, is, Bowra says, not to simplify or explain, not to soothe, console, or "give an ultimate sense of harmony," not to teach or exhort, but simply "to present." And this problem of presentation, he points out, is one that must be settled not theoretically but according to the circumstances in which the individual poet finds himself.

Conservative poets cannot cope with the situations of a period in which codes are breaking down, and experimental poets, too, sometimes make mistakes—Marinetti, for example, with his worship of power as embodied in the machine. But for the last fifty years there has been a flow of modern vitality only in the experimentalists. Whether or not an experimenter manages to keep to his chosen track or is catastrophically derailed by his temperament or his times depends upon a thousand contributing factors, ponderable and imponderable. Bowra follows the revolutionary and tragic career of Mayakovsky with the same understanding that he gives to the more pliable Pasternak. He emphasizes Apollinaire's rare power to absorb the modern world with joy instead of rejecting it with loathing, and he brings out two virtues often overlooked in Eliot—his exquisite ear, and his insistence upon dramatic balance as well as intellectual content. Bowra's exegesis of *The Waste Land,* by the way, is the most nearly complete and rewarding of any written by Eliot's contemporaries.

Bowra is a good critic because he understands not only the aesthetic process (what the poet sets out to do, and how he does it), insofar as it can be understood, but also the aesthetic experience (what the sympathetic reader receives from the poem). And he is on the poet's side, since he realizes what infinite and inexhaustible vitality, spiritual and mental, is required in order that, in our time, as in any other, "the maximum of truth and of poetical effect" may be secured.

1 9 4 9

§ *Goethe Two Hundred Years After*

A general eagerness to wring some usable wisdom from Goethe, preferably in condensed form, on the two-hundredth anniversary of his birth, has pushed the great man from the company of the poets into the company of the philosophers, for the twin barriers of language and of time do not matter so much in the realm of philosophy. Metaphysics, by reason of its airiness, can seep from one period to another, and when one deals in abstractions, the partitions of language are fairly thin and yielding. But poetry, and particularly lyric poetry, is forever stuck fast in its original tongue. And although Goethe from youth on was surrounded by philosophers and knew them as close friends and as correspondents, and although his liking for abstractions, symbols, and enigmas steadily increased, he remained a poet *pur sang*. Schiller, who, Goethe said, "cared more for speculation than for the direct vision of things," found him but an indifferent Kantian, and if Goethe showed a strong sympathy for certain portions of Spinoza's thought, it is doubtful that he followed through to the end Spinoza's complicated and geometric arguments.

Being a poet, Goethe thought in images, trusted his intuition, and, in his own words, dwelt "in the truth of the five senses." This innate empiricism prevented him from being thrown off his course by the metaphysics all about him, and he boasts, in one of his lighter verses, of having achieved splendid results because he never lost his way "thinking about thought." We must not be led astray, therefore, into believing, because of the enormous range of his interests, that he possessed a variety of approaches toward his subjects. One approach—that of the interpretative imagination—underlies all Goethe's researches, from the theatre through the plastic and graphic arts, from the nature of the universe through the conduct of life, from religion and sociology through botany, mineralogy, and optics. Thomas Mann has spoken of the combination in Goethe of true naïveté with extraordinary intellectual power. Goethe's was the poet's naïveté, and this pleasing gift never dwindled.

Language is the insuperable barrier between Goethe and ourselves. Translations are not much help to the poetry, and Goethe's thought, at its purest and most forceful, is embedded in the poetry. "Goethe was particularly unfortunate in his English translators," D. J. Enright truthfully observes. "All along [his] natural, idiomatic German is debased into some or other kind of awful synthetic poesy. . . . The modern reader . . . after he has glanced at one or two of the *Faust* specimens [in English], may be led into abandoning Goethe on the ground that no really great poetry could ever look quite so dreadful in translation. But it can." C. F. MacIntyre's version of the first part of *Faust*, published in 1941, has helped dispel this unhappy tradition. One way of getting at *Faust* is to get it onto the stage. The ideal celebration this year would have been a full-dress production of *Faust,* in the exciting manner of Reinhardt's production of the Second Part in Salzburg in the early thirties. It would have put Goethe's poetry where it belongs—in the mouths of living and breathing characters.

The barrier of time is difficult to overcome. For Goethe is the epitome and one of the prime movers of a cultural period that was not only short-lived, in contrast to its importance, but, when it was over, was gone for good. It was the period between the charming yet rather sinister excesses of eighteenth-century German Rococo and, on the other hand, the "Biedermeier," a German version of English Early Victorian. It was the period of the informal "English" park, midway between the stiff, formal parterres of the past and the hideous, formal geranium and begonia beds of the future. It was the period of "bourgeois classicism" so well described by C. L. Laing when, writing of Beethoven, he says:

The sentimental irrationalism of the *Sturm und Drang* emptied into the quiet world of ideas. . . . The genius [of the times] recognized the validity of objective norms; boundless humanism gave way to a humanism which recognized its own limits. This moderation and equalization ripened into a classicism of which the German phase is the very symbol. Classicism beatified life and gave it lastingness by viewing it from the heights of the ideal. . . . Its art was devoted to the ideal of plastic beauty which it believed to be absolute; its principal object was man living in consort with nature, man beautiful in body and soul . . . man who became aware of his inner harmony, and who was the measure of all things. The result was an aesthetic world-picture, a Germandom reborn from the spirit of Hellas.

It was this idealism of an enlightened burgher class headed toward freedom that provided the climate for the time's "explosion of genius." Goethe, the young bourgeois from Frankfurt, all fire and temperament, was one of the constructors of this ideal and point of view. The gradual development of his feeling for classic depth, clarity, and equilibrium showed itself in his growing control over his life and impressed itself upon his surroundings. Far from being "a Prince's valet," he was the guide and teacher of his Weimar duke, and succeeded in making a humane man and ruler out of an irresponsible boy. We must look back at this period, of course, from across the Romanticist period that followed it (and that Goethe distrusted), and it is not easy to keep focus on the distant scene. That the period had its effect beyond the borders of Germany is proved by the reverence and admiration given it, during its brief existence, by the rest of Europe and even by America. It is the only cultural bridge between the eighteenth and the nineteenth centuries, at a time when France was exhausted by its fit of power and England had retreated from eighteenth-century "liberalism" into reactionary anti-Jacobinism and the small and dull frivolity of the Regency.

Goethe, except for Carlyle, made no great impression upon English thought or letters. English industrialism was a going concern long before Goethe's death. His point of view appealed more to Scotch moral idealism and American transcendentalism than to British hardheadedness. And soon, all over Europe and in America, Romanticist doubt, melancholy, and soul-searching began to negate the classic ideal. Goethe's age was at an end, and the poet for whom every living and evolving thing had importance, who was an enemy of the dry specimens of the museums, was turned over to the scholars and the commentators to be explained, ticketed, and mummified.

When we look for modern writers who have understood and profited from Goethe's poetry and ideas, we come upon an unexpectedly lively list. We find, to begin with, a young man who, visiting Rome in 1851, linked Goethe, quite naturally, with Dante, Shakespeare, and Michelangelo. This was Gustave Flaubert. We find continual references to Goethe in Flaubert's *Correspondance*. He defends Goethe against detractors, and everywhere tenders him admiration and praise, and one Goethian maxim helps him to run his life: *"Qu'est-ce que ton devoir? L'exigence de chaque jour."* The influence of Goethe upon Flaubert was a creative one as well; the first *St. Antoine* derives directly from *Faust II*, and the first *L'Education Sentimentale* from *Wilhelm Meister*. In our own time, we find Gide, in his *Journals*, constantly referring to Goethe. He reads the poetry with delight and attempts to translate it. He notes that "nothing in life so calms me as the contemplation of this great figure," and that "the greatest influence to which I have *submitted* is that of Goethe." We find among modern critics, philosophers, and historians who have submitted themselves to Goethe's intelligence and intuition the names of Santayana, G. Lowes Dickinson, Valéry, Toynbee, Albert Schweitzer, and, of course, Mann.

A Study of Goethe, by Barker Fairley, published in 1947, is the best modern critical work in English and should be consulted by anyone truly concerned with the poet's achievement.

To those who, although permanently baffled by German, can read French, a new and complete translation of *Faust,* published in 1947, can be recommended. It includes the Gérard de Nerval version of *Faust I,* together with *Faust II,* translated, with absorbing comments, by Alexandre Arnoux and R. Biemel. For those who can cope with German, a neat and well-printed pocket edition of *Faust,* in two volumes, has recently been published in New York.

The best introduction to Goethe's lyric poetry for the non-German reader is through music. Forgetting all the attempts of Romantic composers to deal with Goethe's work—from the sweetenings of Gounod, Tchaikovsky, Thomas, Massenet, and others, to the horrification of Berlioz—he can turn to three songwriters, two of whom were Goethe's contemporaries and one of whom is a modern. Beethoven's songs and incidental music for *Egmont,* and Schubert's songs written to Goethe's lyrics, bring us close to the poet's own music. The most extraordinary evocation of Goethe's power and poetic range, however, comes to us through the fifty-one songs written to his lyrics by Hugo Wolf. "Music as such," a learned critic says of Wolf's settings, "was never an aim to him, only a means to enhance the poem." Anyone who has listened to the wild longing of the Wolf-Goethe "Kennst Du das Land?" or to the noble and transcendent beauty of their "Prometheus" and "Ganymed" has experienced the only world it is important to share with any great poet—the world of his intense emotion and his piercing vision.

1 9 4 9

§ *Post-War British Poets*

A fair sampling of British poetry written just before, during, and since the war has been printed in the United States. What has been kept, by various editorial oversights, from these shores is a detailed survey of the currents of British thought and feeling that might indicate in what direction the newest generation of British poets is headed. Kenneth Rexroth, in his informative introduction to *The New British Poets: An Anthology,* now supplies this detail in quantity. He not only discourses upon the work of a variety of poets but traces the links between these men and women and their British and, when such links exist, European backgrounds. We find that a real shift has been made from the prewar school of wit and semi-realism, led by Auden, toward a new "Romanticism"; that certain "little mags" now promulgate "a new and dynamic variety of religious anarchism"; and that the most vigorous poetic talents are either Welsh, Scotch, Northern Irish, or sequestered in remote districts of England—Norman Nicholson, in

Cumberland, for example. Rexroth describes the decentralization from London as one that "seems to be true always of decaying capitals; generation by generation, the major Roman poets come farther and farther away from Rome."

Rexroth admits that the tenets of this Romanticism are hard to define. A non-Marxian revolt against "a depersonalized and collapsing society" is deeply involved. The recent "Apocalyptic" movement, headed by Henry Treece, was, he says, brief and uninteresting, but because of it Welsh literary influence became more pronounced. Dylan Thomas, according to Rexroth, exhibits in his poetry an intensity that derives from the ancient "savage Welsh Nonconformity." Thomas has, as a matter of fact, supplied to modern English verse—rather belatedly, it is true—the sort of visionary violence that Rimbaud brought to French poetry and that Hart Crane, in a lesser degree, introduced to American verse. He is certainly an eloquent outsider. Whether or not his poetry points toward "a cultural *coup d'état*," or is just highly enough charged to be overrated by his contemporaries, remains to be seen.

The "Romantics" are busily engaged in constructing a moral-philosophic system to back up their works. The accent is on "religious personalism and political anarchism," and the ancestors of the movement are many, unexpected, and oddly matched. The names of Eric Gill, Herbert Read, and D. H. Lawrence are arrayed side by side with those of the Orthodox Russian Berdyaev, the Alsatian Albert Schweitzer, and the Jewish philosopher Martin Buber. Henry Miller and Carl Jung also share in what is described as not merely an aesthetic but a world view—"the rejection of mechanistic civilization, sterile scientism, and top-heavy rationalism, the quest for a true integrality of the person." Lorca and Rilke inject other un-British strains.

After Rexroth's enthusiastic build-up, the poets in the collection, arranged in undramatic alphabetical order, seem fairly washed-out and feeble. The outstanding talents we already know: W. R. Rodgers, Dylan Thomas, Norman Nicholson, Laurie Lee, Henry Reed, Hugh MacDiarmid, and Lawrence Durrell, as well as the ex-Surrealists George Barker and David Gascoyne, and the older and reoriented Stephen Spender. A group of women poets, rather warmly normal in tone and subject, are highly derivative in style. But it is a pleasure to come upon the rough sincerity of Sorley Maclean, one of Rexroth's young Scots. Maclean's brief poem "Knightsbridge of Libya," translated from his own Gaelic, carries on the firm masculinity of the Synge tradition:

Though I am today against the breast of battle,
        not here my burden and extremity; not Rommel's
        guns and tanks, but that my darling should be
        crooked and a liar.

1 9 4 9

§ *The Auroras of Autumn*

Wallace Stevens is the American poet who has based his work most firmly upon certain effects of nineteenth-century Symbolist poetry. The title of his latest volume, *The Auroras of Autumn,* indicates that his powers of language have not declined; here is one of those end-lessly provocative, "inevitable" phrases that seem to have existed forever in some rubied darkness of the hu-man imagination—that imagination with whose author-ity and importance Stevens has been continually occu-pied in his later period. This preoccupation was once implicit in what he wrote; his images performed their work by direct impact. Stevens' later explicit, logical, and rather word-spinning defense of the role of the im-agination has weakened or destroyed a good deal of his original "magic." The whole texture and coloration of his later verse is more austere; his subjects are less ec-centric; even his titles have quieted down. What has always been true of him is now more apparent: that no one can describe the simplicities of the natural world with more direct skill. It is a natural world strangely empty of human beings, however; Stevens' men and women are bloodless symbols. And there is something theatrical in much of his writing; his emotions seem to be transfixed, rather than released and projected, by his extraordinary verbal improvisations. Now that he is so widely imitated, it is important to remember that his method is a special one; that modern poetry has developed transparent, overflowing, and spontaneous qualities that Stevens ignores. It is also useful to remember (as Apollinaire knew) that since the imagination is part of life, it must have its moments of awkwardness and naïveté, and must seek out forms in which it may move and breathe easily, in order that it may escape both strain and artificiality.

1 9 5 0

§ *The Skirting of Passion*

The publication of the last posthumous collection of Virginia Woolf's critical and biographical essays brings to a close that phase of her career which began ten years after her novelist phase. Her first novel was published in 1915; her first book of prose sketches came out in 1921; and *The Common Reader,* her first book of essays, was published in 1925. The present volume, *The Captain's Death Bed,* contains material from all periods; and its variety reminds us that Mrs. Woolf spent part of her time as a working journalist; that during the years she was endeavoring to expand, through various experiments, the English novel form, she was also quite capable of writing to order book reviews, pamphlets, and lectures.

One could just barely prophesy a critical future for the author of the earliest piece of critical writing here included: an "interior monologue" called "Reading," written in 1919. The stream-of-consciousness style was not Mrs. Woolf's invention; both Dorothy Richardson (since 1915) and Joyce (since 1916) had worked out the method fully; and by 1919 the earlier chapters of *Ulysses* were in print. Also in the background were E. M. Forster and Lytton Strachey. "Reading" is centered in an old library, in an old house, on an old estate; it is romantically conceived and romantically projected; quaint and highly colored side glimpses of history, nature, and this-and-that keep breaking into the stream of meditation, and there is no literary analysis as such. But it is possible to detect in this piece very nearly all the elements of Mrs. Woolf's later critical manner. It is quite clear that she is not blindly following anyone as a literary guide; in fact, she often seems to be dramatizing her material according to the methods of painting rather than those of literature; and we remember how closely she had followed, through the career of her painter sister, Vanessa Bell, and the enthusiasm of her friend, Roger Fry, the art of the Post-Impressionists, from the time of their first London exhibition in 1910. Like these painters, she chooses her angle with care, she colors with brilliance, and she establishes a pattern with shrewdness. And in a few years she has acquired tremendous competence; the review of Cobden-Sanderson's *Journals,* written in 1926 and here included, goes like the wind. For now she can control her speed as well as her lighting and her design. Everything is particularized; and the sheer pleasure given to the writer by the act of writing is apparent at every point.

"She liked writing with an intensity which few writers have attained," Forster says of Mrs. Woolf in his memorial essay; but she was at her best when she managed in some way to write at one remove from life. Even in her novels she was forced to get at life, for all her implicit insistence to the contrary, in some oblique or indirect fashion: through some perspective of time or some distortion of space. But when her material was the recorded facts of history and literature, she was able to function with a good deal of freedom; always in the past, it is true. She could not deal with her contemporaries; when she mentions them at all her remarks are either ordinary or catty: *Ulysses* is "obscene"; *Prufrock* is "obscure"; *Lady Chatterley's Lover* comes in for ridicule in *Orlando,* and both Lawrence and Forster (Forster, from whom she learned so much) have "failed," according to her, in their early books. It was often her feminist-reformist side that blocked her view; and her critical insight went down before her frequent indulgence in that "poetization" of fact which consists of "making things out more interesting than they really are—the imposition of the writer's personality for which there is no exact critical term," an indulgence against which Fry had warned her.

Once she had perfected her critical approach, however, she began to manufacture the most consistently acceptable version of "impressionist criticism" to be found in her time. It is of the highest interest to the student of this period to examine how she clung to the classical virtues of lucidity and balance; in spite of all her surface "originality," she never let go of the ancient classical rhetorical devices. And she never became the indolent "prose-charmer"—breaths of the vernacular float in from time to time, and the effects of these gusts are always finely judged. Writing thus by rule and by ear, Mrs. Woolf never allowed herself to become awkward, rough, truly baffling, or bizarre, as many of her more original contemporaries dared to be. She never makes a fool of herself in any manner of which she is conscious and can avoid. Before the unknowable, the ungraspable, her competence failed; but even here she was partial mistress of the situation: she stopped the investigation at the exact moment that it got out of hand. Time and again we come upon the little flourish of style as she avoids the abyss.

It is this skirting of evil, this inability to penetrate into the heights and depths that finally makes her critical work rather irritating. She claimed all the virtues and insights of the intuitive mind; but with true mystics, as with true poets, evil is never by-passed; a struggle is in order. One must talk back to God or Devil, so that the terror and horror of the facts can thereafter be absorbed into some acceptance of their mystery. With Mrs. Woolf the intellect continually intervenes. Her flights toward some "heightened state of being" are always coming up short against the sudden opacity of her spiritual nihil-ism: the underlying pessimism of the "enlightened" woman. Several of her female contemporaries who made no claim to any inordinate equipment of "brains" ac-complished these flights quite easily; one has only to think of Isak Dinesen, of Colette, of the early Elizabeth Bowen—even of Katherine Mansfield and of Dorothy Richardson—to see that Mrs. Woolf is frequently intel-lectually pretentious and always emotionally immature.

On the other hand, how remarkable it is that this "lady" who, to quote Forster again, "had not much sympathy," had enough to write the sympathetic and penetrating "Memoirs of a Working Woman's Guild" (1930)—the essay which is the high point of the present book, if not of her critical work as a whole, wherein we can watch Mrs. Woolf transcending her prejudices even as she states them. How remarkable it is that this woman novelist who was incapable of creating the shimmer and tension of emotional relationships between men and women, except rather synthetically and in fragments, could see straight into the heart of Turgenev's success with the delineation of such relationships. Her intelligence and taste set her firmly against intellectual sham, which she could instantly detect. And if she sometimes yielded to the demand which she herself had created in a body of readers, for her special "little sensation"—her small but brilliant effect obtained by focusing on a man, woman, or career at a striking but not representative moment ("The Captain's Death Bed" here is a perfect example of this)—she was also able to appreciate, humbly and sincerely, the qualities of men and women who had made contact with that fact, process, and mystery which she never completely yielded to or understood, but which she speaks of again and again in the simple words: "life itself."

1 9 5 0

§ *From Chaucer to Yeats*

The study of English literature as a respectable branch of learning is comparatively new. It came into being in a faltering fashion, making its appearance at Oxford as late as 1893, after having been put into practice at the new University of London and in Scotland. Once accepted, the new subject had to fight free from one hampering method after another. First it had to escape from the dry procedures of German philology, then from an equally arid habit among English professors of erecting barriers between "literary periods" and of implacably tracking down influences and sources. This methodology was abandoned, under Professors Saintsbury and Raleigh, only to be succeeded by teaching habits that substituted charm for insight, so that the central qualities of English poetry and prose were more or less obscured by masses of anecdotes and chitchat about the lives, domestic problems, wives, friends, and dogs and cats of this author and that. During the twenties of this century, the emphasis shifted to the texts themselves—a

shift all to the good, except that such direct analysis
soon became extreme. In the case of verse, the poem
was removed so far from any contact or contamination
(even from the poet who had written it) that it became a
sort of laboratory specimen, and its dissection, in some
scholarly quarters at least, was pursued with the relentless fervor usually allotted to a delicate, purely manual
operation, like the boning of a shad.

The critical and scholarly need that has gradually become pressing and obvious, as psychology, anthropology,
and a freshly ventilated sense of history have begun to
crowd in upon the study of literature from every side, is
one of relation and comparison. Although the subject
of comparative literature has grown in importance, the
relationship between literatures of different cultures and
languages, between literature and the changes of history
and opinion, of morals and manners, and between literature and its sister arts does not show up in many com-
mentaries or textbooks. *Poets of the English Language*
in five volumes, edited by W. H. Auden and Norman
Holmes Pearson, is a pioneer effort to place poetry in
the midst of history and life, and to connect it to other
arts with which it shares a common creative source. The
two editors, both scholars and teachers and one of them
a major poet, are uniquely fitted for a task that involves revaluation as well as valuation. The selections
range from the Middle Ages through modern times, but
the editors have wisely sidestepped controversy by not
touching upon the work of living contemporaries. The
first volume, "Langland to Spenser," brings English
poetry through Middle English (which, as the editors
remark, was close to being the language of a tribe) to
the beginning of the "Shakespearean poetic temper,"
when English became the language of a nation. Volume

II, "Marlowe to Marvell," deals with the poetic situation throughout the English Renaissance into the Baroque era; Volume III traces the story through a century of tremendous upheaval and change, from Milton to Goldsmith; Volume IV, "Blake to Poe," covers the early and great Romantics; and Volume V, "Tennyson to Yeats," copes with the Victorians and their successors, down to the year 1914. The introductions to the volumes describe, often with great originality, not only the central emotional, intellectual, and power drives of succeeding eras but take into account the more subtle climates of opinion, feeling, and taste that pervaded this or that period. These prefaces, moreover, emphasize the fact that while literature is produced by human beings, it is also touched by the mystery of the Muse—frequently breaking into new life and form just as history has, as it were, stopped happening; or at a moment when a culture seems so exhausted that nothing in the circumstances hints at the possibility of a renewal of imaginative life.

The editors' important achievement of relating poetry in English to European, British, and American history at large, over six centuries, has been accomplished with a minimum of machinery. Each volume opens with a calendar, one side of which lists poetry, work by work, while a neighboring column establishes the general background, event by event. This calendar, although it often bears out certain Spenglerian hypotheses, lacks any Spenglerian concealed pressures. To study its exposition of coincidences, time lags, and unexpected linkages is a delightful occupation. Here is French Impressionist painting showing up in the same year (1863) as Taine's "determinist" history of English literature and a year after Meredith's *Modern Love*. Here is Frazer's *The*

Golden Bough, published in 1890, along with the first series of Emily Dickinson's *Poems.* Nobel invents dynamite in 1867, the year of *Peer Gynt* and Mark Twain's *The Jumping Frog*; and Freud's *Die Traumdeutung* announces a new century, in 1900, contemporaneously with *Sister Carrie* and Stedman's *An American Anthology.* The tragic year 1914 has Joyce's *Dubliners,* Stein's *Tender Buttons* and Frost's *North of Boston* to its credit.

As many long works as possible are given in their entirety—*Antony and Cleopatra* and *Samson Agonistes,* for example. And the editors have not turned away from poems bristling with difficulty, such as Hopkins' "The Wreck of the Deutschland." The unexpected and the neglected (for instance, the hymns of the Methodist Revival, and the light and nonsense verse with which the Victorians worked off some of their unconscious conflicts) appear beside the "standard" pieces of the English poetic repertoire, while the poetry of two great "mad" poets, John Clare and Christopher Smart, brilliantly set off the works of their more reasonable contemporaries. Neglected Americans—Thoreau, Melville, and Longfellow as a translator—are given their just due. E. Talbot Donaldson has been called in to write a note on Middle English, and Auden contributes a short survey of English prosody that is certainly as valuable to the lover of poetry in English as a knowledge of musical form is to an amateur of music. *Poets of the English Language* is a peculiarly modern achievement. It could have been produced only in our time, and it is a work for which we should be grateful and of which we should be proud.

1 9 5 1

§ *The Later Dylan Thomas*

Dylan Thomas' attraction for contemporary readers, and particularly for the younger generation, is partly based on poetic procedures that are more traditional than one might at first suppose, and these procedures are becoming more marked as time goes on. He has moved beyond his earlier Surrealist phase, so he now not only makes more sense but is able to project a variety of emotions, including tenderness and pity, instead of keeping up the steady stream of rhetoric that often resembled the rantings of a Welsh revivalist rather than the song of a Welsh bard. Another part of his appeal, it is true, still lies in his positive emotional orientation. In a period when emotional blankness and inertia pervade poetry in general, Thomas' power to feel joy and express exuberance sets him apart and makes his work interesting and valuable.

Thomas' bardic side is strongly evident in his new collection of six poems, *In Country Sleep*. In spite of his off rhymes and his devious syntax, and his habit of paradoxical epithet ("The mustardseed sun"), a hold-over from Surrealism, the techniques of ancient balladry shine through. For he is clever with full rhyme as he is with assonance; he is a master of effective alliteration, and he can manipulate refrain to underline and clinch his meaning or to produce that incantatory quality on which all balladry thrives. He is as close to living nature, moreover, as any Romantic. He names bird, fish, animal, plant, and flower, and he has a sharp eye for the weather and times of day. A living world of Celtic myth sur-rounds him. He contrasts, in the book's title poem, a world of fairy tale and pagan folklore with a world of Christian ritual and belief. But he is not content with mere contrast. He contrives a connection between the two realms because he is aware of the buried instinctive life they share. His shift into liturgical diction in the poem's second part is in itself a brilliant feat, but he also manages a more subtle shift in key, modulating from the minor of fear and terror into the major of calm and peace. Joy in life as mystery runs through both.

Thomas breaks another modern poetic block in his direct celebration of sexual themes. The poem "In the White Giant's Thigh" derives its title from one of those immense prehistoric designs cut through the turf on the chalk hills of England and Wales. Lying at night in one of these haunted places, the poet hymns sexual feel-ing on a primitive level and in the most extravagant terms, working in echoes of ancient vegetative myth. The same sexual extravagance turns up in "Lament," but here the ballad structure and the theme (an old man's concupiscence) are reminiscent of Yeats in his last period. Yet Thomas has his own material, and has learned to use it with maximum effect, and thus much modern poetry, written mechanically according to rule

of fashion, sounds weak, cold, and insipid beside his. He
has moved toward the heart of his original inheritance
and by so doing has been forced to incorporate into his
work the formal techniques of the folk ballad—techniques that suit his thought and feeling and his clear
perception of nature better than any looser form possibly could.

1 9 5 2

§ *The Fable and the Song*

Miss Marianne Moore's eight years' labor of translating into English *The Fables of La Fontaine* would have gone for nothing if she had succeeded only in giving a fair replica of the French poet's form without being able to catch that most subtle factor in any poet's work— his underlying tone. In general, success in this sort of re-production depends primarily upon success in recog-nizing hidden intention as well as open character, and this recognition must be based on a certain sympathy between the translator and his subject. It is clear that any likenesses between two poets, one a modern Amer-ican and the other a seventeenth-century Frenchman who spent much of his life either close to or within the court of Louis XIV (the twelve books of the *Fables* first appeared between 1668 and 1694), must exist on the deep levels of poetic temperament or on the high levels of technical brilliance. There will be critics who will deny to Miss Moore any success with La Fontaine's limpid and seemingly effortless music, but no one can deny that she shares with the great French fabulist an idiosyncratic view of man and nature, a delicate irony and humor, and on the technical side, stylistic gifts at once elegant and inexhaustibly fertile. Both poets, moreover, share the desire to break bonds and to express themselves in their own fashion, for it must be remembered that La Fontaine was as much an original in his own day as Miss Moore is in hers.

Miss Moore mentions in her preface the governing principles of style she has adhered to—"the natural order of words, subjects, predicate, object; the active voice where possible; a ban on dead words, rhymes synonymous with gusto." These are almost invariably the rules of the best modern poetic procedure, and Miss Moore has been faithful to them. It is with her style that she has captured her subject, but not with her style alone. Her humor resembles La Fontaine's humor in the closest way; both are laconic, insidious, and "dry," and on the ground of intelligence, wit, and taste she and her forerunner meet again. These likenesses overshadow the superficial divergences between the two—the fact that La Fontaine's moral sense is more materialist and pragmatic than Miss Moore's and that while Miss Moore in her own work observes animals in detail as part of nature, La Fontaine uses them as symbols illustrating the foibles of mankind. But time after time the small, condensed phrase, the releasing epithet that encloses entire a turn of the Frenchman's thought has risen to Miss Moore's mind, and suddenly, in a flash, we get the La Fontainean quality complete. As for music, there is more of it in these versions than would at first appear. The exact transfer of the music of the *Fables* from French into any language, by anyone, is an impossible feat. But there is no doubt that Miss Moore has opened to us the heart and mind of one of the most humane and perceptive poets of all time, a poet who presaged some of mankind's most courageous efforts toward self-understanding, which were to develop in the centuries succeeding his own. Because of Miss Moore's gifts of serious yet witty precision, we now have La Fontaine in a modern English idiom, and we may well apply ourselves to the lessons he has to teach.

Léonie Adams, in her new volume, *Poems: A Selection,* has chosen poems from her first two books, long and ununderstandably out of print, and added to them a group of more recent lyrics. Miss Adams, like Miss Moore, has affiliations with poetry of high periods of the past; in her case the tie between Jacobean drama and seventeenth-century English lyricism is close. She has moments of cousinship with Webster and Tourneur, with Vaughan and Traherne, and her later poetry is so charged with meaning that it sometimes slips out of syntax, in the manner of the later Mallarmé. She expresses a few major themes, of which the entrapment of the spirit in the flesh and the shadow cast by eternity upon time are two. She interprets nature more than man; her emotions are meshed into the turn of earthly seasons, but the light of the universal constantly sheds across her landscapes a strange and phantasmal gleam. The large and crucial divisions of time as we know it are her constant subjects. In "Winter Solstice" and "Light at Equinox" she brings to their evocation extraordinary powers of description. An essential gravity and nobility of thought and feeling run through her work without a break; she is everywhere committed to the difficult task of outwitting conscious powers in order that subconscious ones may operate as pervasively as possible. The reader is made aware that Miss Adams' "difficulty" depends not upon any surface play with words but upon the tension and complication of her initial poetic impulse. Poems such as "Companions of the Morass," "For Harvest," "Grapes Making," and "The Runner with the Lots" spring from and are indications of a poetic endowment as deep as it is rare.

1 9 5 4

§ *The Minor Shudder*

When Goethe stated that the shudder expressed mankind's best side, he was thinking not of the Gothic atmosphere fashionable in his day so much as of the general feeling of awe at the mysteries of the universe, to which the most hardened materialist is not entirely immune. In modern poetry, this larger emotion is rare indeed; the whole emotional set of the period is against it. The minor Gothic shudder, on the other hand, appears with fair regularity. The Surrealists revived it while exploiting the dark marvels of the subconscious, and traces of Surrealist influence continue to crop up in modern verse, although the movement, on the whole, is exhausted. Four poets who have published recent volumes illustrate the methods—precarious at best and open to failure more than to success—by which the modern imagination tries to project feelings of mystery and awe.

One method involves a putting on of masks, or *personae*, through which the poet speaks. This seems a simple procedure; Browning was good at it, as well as Pound and Yeats. It is, nonetheless, a difficult feat; as Yeats quickly discovered, "there must be a living face behind the mask." The poet, that is, must take infinite care not to stiffen into an effigy of the character he assumes; he must remain integrated, alive, and himself behind his disguises. And if he holds to this method, he will soon be forced to provide landscapes for his figures, thereby involving himself with growing problems, both imaginative and structural.

Horace Gregory, from the beginning of his career, has occupied himself with building up such an allegorical world. He derives his scene from the most diverse sources: from the reality of the furnished room and the corner bar-and-grill, to the artifice of settings drawn from art, literature, or myth. He has peopled his backgrounds with a crowd of characters, ancient and modern, real and imagined. His later work, as it appears in *Selected Poems,* has taken a slightly different turn; his backgrounds tend to be real enough while his characters become more and more ghostly and decorative—passive *figurants* rather than actors. Gregory, too, is now fascinated not only by ghosts but by other kinds of magic. In his later poems, some final, transcendent, hair-raising event seems imminent. That it never occurs is not because of his lack either of ingenuity or of expressive range, for he has both. What is lacking is an ultimate daring that would crack the surface of his too carefully manipulated world, wherein the mask has come to disguise the face only too well.

Randall Jarrell, in his new volume, *The Seven-League Crutches,* is another poet who is obsessed with problems of reality and non-reality. Much of his recent work is wrapped in gauze—in the dreams and fantasies of childhood, in literary allusiveness, or in the distorting light of the legend or the fairy tale. His "adaptations" of poems by Rilke and Corbière are more vivid than his original writing; he catches the tone of both men and is particularly successful in bringing over into English Corbière's roughness, deliberate dislocation of meaning, and alternate coarseness and tenderness. But when Jarrell attempts these effects on his own, his suspension of ideas, quirks of language, and tenuous dramatic sense show signs of artificial inducement. There is something not so much eerie as bloodless in Jarrell's world, inhabited almost exclusively, as it is, with beings too young to have known life or too baffled to act in it. These creatures revolve in a limbo of pain and fear. It is difficult to animate such shadows or to attach any dramatic substance to them.

Richard Eberhart, on the other hand, is a poet who can turn the cube of reality (in William James' phrase) so that another facet comes into view. At his best, he does this with the mystic's ease. His *Selected Poems* finally brings his gifts into focus. Eberhart, possessing the innocent unself-consciousness of one to whom the spirit is a reality, in earlier volumes displayed the faults of his virtues in tendencies toward diffuseness of language and dilution of idea. The poems in this collection are concentrated, both in mood and form, and the total effect is remarkable. "The Groundhog" and "The Fury of the Aerial Bombardment," already justly famous in the annals of modern verse, are by no means solitary successes. Eberhart continues to be original because his vision is constantly self-refreshing, and he needs no masks to enhance either his meaning or his impact.

If Theodore Roethke's poetry in *Praise to the End!* seems at first glance more consciously produced than Eberhart's, it is soon evident that the two poets share an unforced power of imaginative penetration into the obscure, the hidden, and the inarticulate, and that they are both capable of that larger awe of which Goethe spoke. Roethke has added several long poems to passages from *The Lost Son,* published a few years ago, and these additions accent his original theme—the journey from the child's primordial subconscious world, through the regions of adult terror, guilt, and despair, toward a final release into the freedom of conscious being. Roethke's description of this progress attaches itself to recognizable myth and legend hardly at all; his rendition of a sub- or pre-conscious world is filled with coiling and uncoiling, nudging and creeping images that often can be expressed only with the aid of nonsense and gibberish. But it is witty nonsense and effective gibberish, since the poet's control over this difficult material is always formal; he knows exactly when to increase and when to decrease pressure, and he comes to a stop just before the point of monotony is reached. Behind Roethke's method exists the example of Joyce, but Roethke has invented a symbolism, in his searching out of these terrors, marginal to our consciousness, that is quite his own.

1 9 5 2

§ *Young Poets: 1944–1954*

1

After more than a quarter century of "experiment," a new formal English poetic style seems finally to have emerged. What Browning, Swinburne, Tennyson, and Matthew Arnold would think of it is anybody's guess, even though all these formidable Victorians contribute to its present form. The contributions of Eliot and Pound derive from various neglected English poetic sources, as well as many non-English ones (French Symbolism and translations from the Gaelic and Chinese). The insistence made by the English poets of the '30's upon satire and the sharpness of ordinary speech are factors, but not to an overwhelming degree. This style is now a supple instrument. It has lost its early stiffness, inherited from the Imagists, and it is no longer heavily weighted with the learned tags dear to bright young people, or encumbered with certain affected theatrics carried over from the late '90's.

It is a formal style, and therefore difficult to apprehend at first glance. Critics have spluttered and fumed over its "obscurity" and Marxists have labelled it with their limited and old-fashioned reproach "ivory tower." Whether this style, having tentatively formed, is capable of endurance and growth, it is too early to say. What it needs at the moment is practitioners and an attentive, disinterested audience. The folk line and the line of bourgeois literature can be counted on to keep flourishing; it is formal poetry that now needs critics and friends.

Two new books by American poets highly skilled in this new formal technique, who have highly complex mental and spiritual equipment to express by means of it, have recently appeared. Robert Penn Warren, a native of Kentucky, a Rhodes scholar, and a member of the Nashville "Fugitive" group, which, in the '20's, applied itself to a Southern renaissance of literature, philosophy, and classical learning, brings together work that dates from his student days on in *Selected Poems, 1923-1943*. His book is divided into two sections, in which the later poems come first. It is not easy, therefore, at once to trace the line of his growth, but the line is there, and, because it follows to some extent the emerging formal style, it is interesting to begin with his early poems and read backward toward his later ones. The "Fugitive" group was concerning itself with "regional" material long before the "regional" became a fashion. Mr. Warren's early treatment of his Kentucky background coincides with the "literary" stiffness which afflicted poetry at the time. Many of the poems show clear outlines of influence. Three very fine ones—"Pacific Gazer," "Calendar," and "The Garden"—are such close approximations of originals that the first two might be included in the canon of Hardy and the last in the canon of Marvell. But little by little the influences fuse. Mr. Warren ends by being able to write with great freedom. He can combine a clever approximation of "folk" with running comment in the manner of the late Eliot ("The Ballad of Billie Potts"). Consider "Mexico Is a Foreign Country: Five Studies in Naturalism" as proof of how Mr. Warren can at the moment absorb all sorts of material with the readiness of maturity. Language is beautifully handled throughout, and the poet has a point of view and the courage of his convictions. The two poems "Original Sin" and "Crime" show his complex perceptions and the modern poetic style working brilliantly together on subjects which perceptive modern poets keep coming back to: obscure psychological guilt and corruption, sadism, obsession—dissimulated under the fixed pattern of modern life and everyday conformity.

Robert Fitzgerald is some years younger than Warren. He is a graduate of Harvard, a classical scholar, and a translator, with a collaborator, of plays by Sophocles and Euripides. His expression, by the evidence of the poems in *A Wreath for the Sea,* is natively nimbler than Warren's. His observation is delicate but precise. He has a lyric gift which might easily have been diverted to petty uses. But the drawing back from tough reality, characteristic of the "aesthetic" period of modern poetry, has been overcome. Baudelaire's lesson on how the modern world can be incorporated into verse has been relearned. Fitzgerald's grasp of classic resonance and balance brings him out always on the side of simplicity; he is incapable of either rhetoric or bombast. His effects are sometimes rather muffled, but soon the expected translucence returns, and we are back in that humane region where the gravity of learning and the seriousness of art function, never out of touch with life.

It is in writers such as these that a style which avoids

the confusions of Surrealism and the bigotries of polem-
ics, which has no place for the accepted idea in the
slick rhythm, for the academic-maudlin, for the fake
man-in-the-street-tough, for the high-minded, simple-
minded conventions, begins to come into its own.

1 9 4 4

2

It is a hopeful sign when judges unanimously and with
enthusiasm make an award to a young, fresh book of
verse instead of to an old, stale one. Last year, the three
judges of the Houghton Mifflin Poetry Prize Fellowship
did just that in the case of Elizabeth Bishop's *North and
South*. Miss Bishop's poems are not in the least showy.
They strike no attitudes and have not an ounce of
superfluous emotional weight, and they combine an
unforced ironic humor with a naturalist's accuracy of
observation, for Miss Bishop, although she frequently
writes fantasy, is firmly in touch with the real world and
takes a Thoreau-like interest in whatever catches her
attention. She can write descriptions of New England
and of Florida seascapes, of a mechanical toy, or of a
mysterious pile of old boxes. And she has unmistakably
her own point of view, in spite of her slight addiction
to the poetic methods of Marianne Moore. Like Miss
Moore, Miss Bishop, thoroughly canvassing all sides of
a central idea, will make a poem out of one extended
metaphor (as in "The Imaginary Iceberg"). Or she will
bring into imaginative relation with one central theme
a variety of subjects, making a poem out of a list of

things or out of attributes related to a title (as in "Flor-ida"). She often starts with a realistic subject, which, by the time she has unravelled all its concealed meaning, turns out to be the basis for a parable—the poem "Roost-ers," for example, contains all manner of references to war and warriors. Miss Bishop is a natural lyricist as well, but she does not use her lyrical side as often as she might. None of these thirty poems gives up its full mean-ing at once, so it is a pleasure to read them repeatedly. Miss Bishop has evidently put in eleven years on their composition; the first appeared in print in 1935. It is to be hoped that we shall get thirty more, equally varied, unexpected, and freshly designed, in rather less than another decade.

1 9 4 6

3

Religious conversion, in the case of two modern poets writing in English—T. S. Eliot and W. H. Auden—brought an atmosphere of peace and relief from tension into their work. But Robert Lowell, a young American who has forsaken his New England Calvinist tradition for the tenets of the Roman Catholic Church, exhibits no great joy and radiance in the forty-odd poems now published under the title *Lord Weary's Castle*. A tre-mendous struggle is still going on in Lowell's difficult and harsh writing, and nothing is resolved. These poems bring to mind the crucial seventeenth-century battle be-tween two kinds of religious faith, or, in fact, the battle between the human will and any sort of faith at all. They do not have the sweetness of the later English "metaphysical" writers; Lowell faces the facts of modern materialism more with the uncompromising tone and temper of the Jacobean dramatists, Webster and Tourneur, or of Donne, who (to quote Professor Grierson), "concluding that the world, physical and moral, was dissolving in corruptions which human reason could not cure, took refuge in the ark of the Church." (Lowell, it is clear, has not taken refuge anywhere.) He also bears some relationship to Herman Melville, the American with Puritan hell-fire in his bones. The more timid reader would do well to remember these forerunners, and the conditions that fostered them, when confronted with young Lowell's fierce indignation.

Lowell's technical competence is remarkable, and this book shows a definite advance over the rather stiff and crusty style of his first volume, *Land of Unlikeness,* published in 1944. This competence shows most clearly in his "imitations" and arrangements of the work of others, which he hesitates to call direct translations. "The Ghost" (after Sextus Propertius), "The Fens" (after Cobbett), and the poems derived from Valéry, Rimbaud, and Rilke reveal a new flexibility and directness. These poems might well be read first, since they show the poet's control of both matter and manner. The impact of the other poems in the book is often so shocking and overwhelming, because of the violent, tightly packed, and allusive style and the frequent efforts of nightmare horror, that his control may seem dubious. The extraordinary evocation of the sea's relentlessness and the terror of death at sea, in "The Quaker Graveyard in Nantucket" (an elegy to a drowned merchant seaman) is equalled in dreadfulness by the grisly emblems of "At the Indian Killer's Grave," a poem wherein successive layers of spiritual and social decomposition in the Massachusetts Bay Colony come to light through a descent into the King's Chapel Burying Ground in Boston. Lowell, again in the seventeenth-century way, continually dwells upon scenes of death and burial. He is at his best when he mingles factual detail with imaginative symbol; his facts are always closely observed, down to every last glass-tiered factory and every dingy suburban tree. To Lowell, man is clearly evil and a descendant of Cain, and Abel is the eternal forgotten victim, hustled away from sight and consciousness. And the modern world cannot reward its servants; no worthy pay is received by the good mason who built "Lord Wearie's Castle." (The old ballad from which the book's title is taken runs: "It's Lambkin was a mason good As ever built wi' stane: He built Lord Wearie's castle But payment gat he nane.") These are the themes that run through this grim collection. Lowell does not state them so much as present himself in the act of experiencing their weight. It is impossible to read his poems without sharing his desperation. Lowell may be the first of that postwar generation which will write in dead earnest, attempting to find a basis for a working faith, in spite of secretive Nature and in defiance of the frivolous concepts of a gross and complacent society. Or he may simply remain a solitary figure. Certainly his gifts are of a special kind.

1 9 4 6

4

What is now called the war generation continues to turn out poetry, and although some of its productions, taken singly, are rather inconsiderable, the over-all effect is interesting. This new and crucial age group is again appearing in numbers; we now have a larger basis for comparing these poets with their elders, and with each other.

The youngest, Richard Wilbur, is twenty-six. His publishers have felt impelled to use the words "romantic" and "emotional" in describing his volume of verse, *The Beautiful Changes,* and they are quite right; in the best senses of these words, it is both. Wilbur is still quite plainly entangled with the technical equipment of his favorite poetic forerunners, specifically Marianne Moore, Eliot, Rilke, and Hopkins, from whose work he has pretty well absorbed certain lessons. He has had the wit, however, to point up these influences from time to time with the invisible quotation marks of near-parody. Wilbur surpasses the majority of his contemporaries in range of imagination and depth of feeling. He has a remarkable variety of interest and mood, and he can contemplate his subjects without nervousness, explore them with care, and then let them drop at the exact moment that the organization of a poem is complete. This ease of pace, this seemingly effortless advance to a resolute conclusion, is rare at his age; the young usually yield to tempting inflation and elaboration. Wilbur's gift of fitting the poetic pattern to the material involves all sorts of delicate adjustments of the outward senses to the inner ear. Fidelity to Nature (that old-fashioned virtue) underlies every word, and this fidelity is directed by intelligence and taste. Wilbur's is a talent so sure of its bases that using the despised word "the beautiful" (which he employs not as an adjective but as a noun in his title) does not harm it in the least. Let us watch Richard Wilbur. He is composed of valid ingredients.

Both William Jay Smith and John Ciardi deserve mention in this convocation of the young. Smith, in his recently published *Poems,* has a quick and cutting way of summing up his material, but it does not always come off. He is, however, able to write a true lyric often edged with effective satire. Ciardi's new work, *Other Skies,* covers his war experiences. He saw combat duty in his late twenties, as a B-29 gunner in the Pacific, for a long period. He brings out many overlooked sides of aerial warfare—its tremendous stylization, for example, and its inhuman scale. His elegies to dead friends are warm and direct, without omitting any detail of their deaths by fire or drowning. Ciardi also describes his postwar let-down—the rapid and ironic realization of the meaning-lessness of the entire nightmare experience.

1 9 4 7

5

Young poets at present are more interested in the tex-ture of their poems—that is, the effects they can produce with vowels and consonants, regardless of rhyme and rhythm—than in other technical matters. Very few trouble themselves with severe and complicated rhyme schemes or take any pleasure in ringing the changes on verse forms that have long proved successful. Having ruled out many possible shifts in emphasis, shape, and speed, they end up by writing a sort of squarish or rec-tangular poem that presents no challenge to the eye and little to the ear. Any young poet who breaks away from this formula, therefore, makes a special claim on our attention.

W. S. Merwin, whose first volume, *A Mask for Janus,* won last year's Yale Series of Younger Poets' Award, is twenty-five, a graduate of Princeton, and already a highly proficient poetic technician. He has gone back to certain French, Spanish, and English verse patterns not merely in order to repeat them but to freshen and revive those that still have charm and power. We remember how Theodore de Banville, during the French Second Empire, managed to revive the fifteenth-century rondel of Charles d'Orleans, making it a delightful carrier of the sentiment of his own time. Mr. Merwin, a far more contemplative and inner poet than Banville, has concentrated on rendering the weight and color of contemporary thought and feeling rather than on bringing to life items from the contemporary scene. He has, it is apparent, allowed each poem its freedom, within well-defined limits but without other restriction. So we get two sestinas, ballads (with and without a refrain and sometimes in more than one voice), a rondel and a "half-rondel" (original and very pleasant), a piece of blank verse, two long sets of quatrains, and an extremely skillful colloquy in six voices, with a refrain rhyming on two "o" sounds throughout. Not one of these poems shows the slightest sign of strain, and all point to a warm affection for the infinitely various possibilities of English rhyme and metre. This is a young man, obviously mad about writing the hard way, who has struck a balance between formal exigency and imaginative force that is rare at any time and almost nonexistent at the moment. The foreword by W. H. Auden emphasizes Merwin's instinctively dramatic use of mythical material—another aspect of his work that makes a promise for the future.

Peter Viereck's third volume, *The First Morning,* offers, in tone and intention, the sharpest kind of contrast to Merwin, in spite of the concern with traditional poetic prosody the two men share. It was partly Viereck's ingenuity in the use of conventional form that aroused so much interest in his first volume, *Terror and Decorum*, which won the Pulitzer Prize in 1949. His attack on the more arid and drooping kind of "modernism" has been frontal, and his admirers have cheered his championship of a new and rather reactionary poetic future wherein poetry, with Eliot and Pound finally vanquished in open combat, could once more "communicate" to a large and eager audience. Nothing much has come of Viereck's crusade. In this book, he still displays a strong belief in his own powers, both poetic and polemic, and he is still full of vigor and zest, but much of his originality seems to be stiffening into eccentricity. He overindulges in epigraphs, he pushes personification and allegory to boring extremes, and although he makes attempts to write in the American vernacular, he has no ear for it whatever. His vocabulary is not used with real sensitivity, and he is continually lapsing into shrillness. Viereck, in short, now appears to be a writer of verse that is fundamentally not serious, that verges not so much on modern "light verse" as on nineteenth-century *vers de sociètè*—something quite different from what he was originally taken for. He works almost entirely from the conscious—intellect and will—and for this reason is forced to manipulate many situations that the unconscious alone is capable of controlling. Tricks come more and more into evidence; Viereck's puns, parodies, and typographical eye-games carry us back to the more amusing side of Christian Morgenstern. Surely a new era of poetry is not announced by poets who lack a tragic sense or who are consistently rude to the elders from whom

they have learned much. A return to form has its haz-
ards as well as its rewards.

1 9 5 3

6

To become the spokesman for one's generation is a
difficult and often ultimately unrewarding role for a
poet to take on. Karl Shapiro, after the publication of
his first book in 1942, a year that found him, at the age
of twenty-nine, a soldier in the South Pacific, was as-
signed this position by many of his contemporaries and
elders. His recent *Poems, 1940-1953* is a remarkably full
chronicle of a troubled and tragic era. Shapiro grew up
surrounded by the problems and confusions, both spiritual and material, of a crucial period of transition in
America and the world at large. To the young writers of
the early '30's, the poetry of the British Auden-Spender-
Day Lewis group made a particular appeal. Shapiro
learned the possibilities of poetry based on concrete situations from which large conclusions could be drawn, and
a satiric sense showed up in his poetry from the first. He
revealed, moreover, a skill in form from the beginning.
The young American was therefore well prepared to
chronicle the disturbing features of his time and place,
including his experiences as a soldier. As a participant
and survivor, he not only put down in detail the facts of
a soldier's life but he mourned and celebrated, in elegies
distinguished for their rightness of tone, the death of
comrades-in-arms. War poems fade quickly, but two of
Shapiro's—"Troop Train" and "Elegy for a Dead Soldier"—will certainly long engage interest and admira-

tion. The poems in the present volume are not arranged chronologically, so lines of development and growth are difficult to trace. Shapiro has written several excellent poems since the war, but his latest work seems to have become rather embittered. A predilection for the nightmare concept appears in several later pieces; "The Phenomenon" and "In the Waxworks" have the quality of dark and entrapping dreams. Shapiro's best writing—so rational, so filled with a high sense of idealism—stands in direct contrast to these, and one can only hope that some freeing upward curve of the imagination will give him, in his maturity, access to new subjects to which his gifts may be fruitfully applied. Targets for the satirist surely exist at present, although in a more complacent decade it is difficult to find them, and courage is required to name and make them known.

1 9 5 4

7

Barbara Howes' second volume (her first appeared in a fine limited edition in 1948), *In the Cold Country*, announces the most accomplished woman poet of the youngest writing generation—one who has found her own voice, chosen her own material, and worked out her own form. Miss Howes is daring with language, but she is also accurate. Her originality stands in constant close reference to the material in hand, and although much of that material is fantastic or exotic, it is never so simply for its own sake. Her diction becomes more exact the more it is applied to certain dissolving effects in nature that attract her, and her poems are full of movement. She can unfold a landscape, or plunge through ordinary surfaces, as in her delightful poem "The Undersea Farmer." Her connoisseurship, always evident, is of an active kind that illuminates instead of merely skimming over this subject or that. In addition, she has strong, positive emotions that continually resolve into a major key. Here, watching a cultivated sense of tradition work through modern attitudes and techniques, we sense the possibility of a new reconciliation in modern verse, for so long filled with division and dissent.

1 9 5 4

§ Index

—